THE INNER CONSULTATION

DEDICATION

I offer this book to my trainer and partner
Peter Tomson
who by his example has taught me many things – not least, to
follow my nose

Also by Roger Neighbour:
*The Inner Apprentice: An Awareness-centred Approach to
Vocational Training for General Practice.* Petroc Press
ISBN 1–900603–05–5

THE INNER CONSULTATION

How to develop an effective and intuitive consulting style

ROGER NEIGHBOUR

MA, MB, BCHIR, DOBSTRCOG, FRCGP

General Practitioner, Abbots Langley, Hertfordshire
Trainer and Late Course Organiser
Watford Vocational Training Scheme

with cartoons by

PATRICK READE, BA, MB, BS

 PETROC PRESS

Petroc Press, an imprint of LibraPharm Limited

Distributors
Plymbridge Distributors Limited, Plymbridge House, Estover Road, Plymouth PL6 7PZ, UK

Published in the United Kingdom by
 LibraPharm Limited
Gemini House
162 Craven Road
NEWBURY
Berkshire
RG14 5NR

A catalogue record for this book is available from the British Library

ISBN 1 900603 67 5

Printed and bound in the United Kingdom by
MPG Books Limited, Victoria Square, Bodmin, Cornwall PL31 1EG

Contents

When at the first I took my pen in hand,
Thus for to write, I did not understand
That I at all should make a little book
In such a mode; nay I had undertook
To make another, which when almost done,
Before I was aware, I this begun.
And thus it was: I writing of the way
And race of saints in this our Gospel-day,
Fell suddenly into an allegory
About their journey, and the way to glory …

This book will make a traveller of thee,
If by its counsel thou wilt ruled be;
It will direct thee to the Holy Land,
If thou wilt its directions understand:
Yea, it will make the slothful active be,
The blind also delightful things to see.
Art thou for something rare, and profitable?
Would'st thou see a truth within a fable? …

This book is writ in such a dialect
As may the minds of listless men affect:
It seems a novelty, and yet contains
Nothing but sound and honest gospel-strains…

Would'st read thyself, and read thou know'st not what
And yet know whether thou art blest or not,
By reading the same lines? O come then hither,
And lay my book, thy head and heart together.

John Bunyan
The Author's Apology For His Book
'The Pilgrim's Progress'

Foreword to the Original Edition

There have been many changes in general practice in the last 15 years; few people, be they doctors, practice staff or patients, have been unaffected by them. The recent development of vocational training has brought considerable benefit to patient care by defining the content of general practice, by promoting its emergence as an academic discipline and by encouraging doctors to review critically what it is that they are trying to achieve through their work.

Undoubtedly the content and organization of general practice will continue to change. In future, more people now cared for in hospital will be looked after in their own homes by general practitioners and community-based nurses. Other changes will result from the increasing specialization in medicine as a whole, for this will mean that the general practitioner will have to take on the responsibilities of the general physician to a greater degree than hitherto.

The philosophy of practice is changing. Now, many practices are beginning to exploit the benefits of the registered list system which is a feature of the British National Health Service and which enables practices to adopt a more population-based approach to their work. More practices actively seek out the at-risk groups within their populations and offer them a range of preventive services; the application of computers in general practice helps in this.

Nevertheless, no matter how much general practice changes nothing will ever undermine the central role of the consultation. No matter how much the responsibilities of general practice increase, and irrespective of more efficient practice management, the consultation will always remain the basis for good quality patient care. General practitioners will always need to develop and maintain their consulting skills. The ability to find out and to understand why an individual patient has sought help and advice, and together to be able to agree the most appropriate way forward, is an enduring attribute of the general practitioner. For this reason, teaching young doctors consultation skills and how to understand people's behaviour, including their own, during a consultation, is an important part of vocational training for general practice. A range of teaching techniques directed towards this has been developed. Most of these are based on small group work – on doctors sitting in on each other's consultations, on the review of audio and video recordings of actual consultations and on the analysis of role play, using professional actors or doctors themselves playing their own patients.

The literature on this subject is increasing, with *Doctors Talking to Patients* by Pat Byrne and Barrie Long published in 1976 as an early and important work. Roger Neighbour's book is a major contribution in this area. It sets recent literature on the consultation in context and provides the basis for greater understanding of the content and interactions of the consultation, and the behaviour of its participants. There is much in this book to guide the clinician in any medical speciality and also perhaps those in other professions, such as lawyers and politicians, who are consulted by clients.

Roger Neighbour is a product of the outstandingly successful Watford Vocational Training Scheme and from 1979 to 1986 was one of its course organizers. A feature of that scheme has always been its approach to the consultation and the enthusiasm of those on it to improve their consulting skills. Undoubtedly this has been a reflection of the work and example of Peter Tomson, who established the Watford course.

Roger Neighbour's interest in the consultation extends over many years. In preparing this book he has read widely and has weaved into much of English literature, classical history and the work of Chinese philosophers and religious writers. He has drawn heavily on the teaching strategies pioneered by Milton Erickson (see Bibliography) and this has been the source for many of the innovations that the book contains.

A period of prolonged study leave enabled Roger Neighbour to travel to the United States and also to spend time testing his ideas with a wide range of people. His energy and enthusiasm for understanding the consultation and teaching about it are infectious and are transmitted undiminished through the pages of his book. A series of complex philosophies is presented with clarity and the running dialogue that he has employed with a trainee is an excellent device for bringing together various points and tying up loose ends.

The Inner Consultation provides a basis for the reader to understand what may be going on within each consultation and within him/herself – to learn from this; to obtain satisfaction from a greater understanding; to enjoy consulting and, perhaps most important of all, to improve skills in helping patients. It is a practical manual for change rather than a theoretical homily. As such, it provides the basis for us to continue learning about the consultation throughout our careers – from our days as medical students, through our time as trainees, and adding to our experiences as established principals.

General practice can easily become humdrum as the ritual of successive consultations monotonously plays itself out. Yet each one is a unique interaction between at least two people – sometimes more. As general practitioners we are fortunate that these occasions make up our daily lives – providing a framework for our work and, if we know how, countless opportunities for continued learning for the benefit of ourselves and of those who seek our service. *The Inner Consultation* helps us towards this and is to be greatly welcomed.

Bill Styles
Honorary Secretary of Council
Royal College of General Practitioners
Regional Advisor in General Practice
North-West Thames Region

Foreword to the Paperback Edition

Week by week, and year by year, the literature of general practice expands inexorably. Thousands of articles and hundreds of books together try to unravel the subtleties of this most fascinating of medical specialities. Precious few succeed, and even fewer become classics. But no one could doubt that Roger Neighbour's *The Inner Consultation* has become one of the very few contemporary medical classics.

But there is a problem with being considered a classic. How many people actually have read, rather than have just talked about, Marcel Proust, or *The Odyssey*, or *War and Peace*? The risk is that the classic book becomes reduced to a cipher – something that is enough to know exists, to drop in conversation, to quote in an examination. I have lost count of how many MRCGP examination candidates have quoted 'Neighbour', almost certainly having simply read a digested summary in a revision guide. Phrases like 'safety netting' and 'housekeeping' have become part of the language of general practice education. But the thing we forget about all classics is that they became that way because they are superb books.

This remarkable book focuses very clearly on both parties in the medical consultation. It is now well accepted that the consultation is the epicentre of general practice. Quality consulting makes us more effective, and makes our task both more interesting and more worthwhile. It would be wonderful if this new edition could also impart its message to doctors who work primarily in hospital. Both they, and their patients, would benefit greatly. Their consultations are important too.

I was deeply honoured to be asked to write this preface. I was deeply humbled when I re-read the book so that I could prepare these few words. I had forgotten quite what an astonishing book this is – how beautifully written, how wise and incisive and witty and fun it is. If you have never read this book, you are in for a treat. If you have lost or leant your old copy, and are buying a replacement, then read it again. It might be a classic, but it deserves not to be treated as one. Don't just respect it – use it!

April, 1999

David Haslam, MB, CHB, D(OBST)RCOG, DFFP
General Practitioner
Ramsey
Huntingdon

Chairman
Examination Board and Assessment Network
Royal College of General Practitioners

Honorary Reader in Primary Health Care
de Montfort University
Leicester

Acknowledgements

I owe more than I know how to say to the Trainers and Trainees of the Watford Vocational Training Scheme, who over the last seven years have kept me supplied with curiosity and enthusiasm, scepticism and friendship. If this book has any merit, they are its true source.

I love Patrick Reade's cartoons – thank you, Patrick.

I'm grateful to Jeffrey Zeig of Phoenix, Arizona, and to Stephen and Carol Lankton of Pensacola, Florida, for introducing me in print and in person to the work of the late Milton Erickson (and for living in such lovely places).

I'm grateful too to Timothy Gallwey, whose books on the Inner Games of tennis and golf started in me a line of thought that initially seemed unrelated to the business of consulting, but turned out to be central to it. He gave me very practical help with identifying the Inner Consultation distractors.

I am fortunate to have been granted a period of extended study leave to research and write this book. I received valuable support in this from Dr Bill Styles, Regional Adviser in General Practice, and from Drs John Lister and Elizabeth Shore, successive Regional Deans of the British Postgraduate Medical Federation, North West Thames Region.

Schering Pharmaceuticals and The Royal College of General Practitioners generously awarded me a RCGP Schering Scholarship that allowed me to travel in the USA, during which time the ideas in this book crystallized.

Finally, writing this book has yet again confirmed for me what extraordinarily tolerant, generous and kind partners I have: thank you, Peter, Michael, Maureen, Peter and Ian.

Guarantee

I guarantee that reading this book will enable you to consult more skilfully, more intuitively, and more efficiently.

Isn't memory a funny thing? Have you ever had the experience of one moment being seemingly intent on some task in hand, and the next finding your thoughts carried miles away by a train of memories and associations? And, intriguingly, don't you sometimes in hindsight find a relevance in the daydream that you couldn't have predicted?

Around the time I began this book, I was looking in a bookshop for something to read on a journey. Unexpectedly I found myself leafing through an edition of Homer's *Iliad* – the story of Helen of Troy and the Wooden Horse. Seeing that text, reading the evocative names of Paris and Agamemnon, evoked long-submerged associations of my old Greek teacher, now dead; of the faces of classmates I can't now put names to; of the contrast between the effort of learning the Greek language and my "love at first visit" for the khaki and languorous land of its origin.

Twenty-two centuries ago (just to refresh your memory!), Helen, daughter of Zeus, wife of Menelaus King of Sparta, eloped with Paris, Prince of Troy. Agamemnon, brother of Menelaus, pursued her and laid siege to Troy for ten unavailing years. Then one of the Spartan commanders, Odysseus, conceived his famous plan. The Trojans looked out one morning to find the Spartans seemingly gone, leaving behind them only a gigantic wooden horse. You can imagine the arguments about what they should do with it. Was it, as some Trojans thought, a propitiatory gift in defeat to the goddess Athena? Or was it a trick? Curiosity prevailed, and the horse was dragged into the city. That night, under cover of darkness, Spartan troops slipped from their hiding place within the horse and opened the city gates from the inside. Troy fell.

How do you decide to buy a particular book? And having bought it, how do you get the most out of it? Choice can often be an unconscious compromise between need, risk, trust and commitment. This book sets out to improve doctors' performance of their central professional skill – consulting with patients. Some people would consider this to be too arrogant a goal, and would put it back on the shelf without more ado. For even browsing through this book implies that you might be willing to contemplate allowing some changes in your professional style.

As you know, practising medicine skilfully can be exhilarating. But to become a little more skilful does mean extending your repertoire of professional behaviour and trying things the results of which you can initially only imagine. The price of exhilaration is risk. To live safely with risk you need a degree of trust and commitment. If you decide to buy this book, you are making a commitment to some degree of change and taking a certain amount of risk, even if only financial: you might regret spending the money. For the moment, I can only ask you to take on trust my claim that reading this book will benefit your skills, your intuition and your efficiency (and therefore indirectly your patients).

If your read this book passively, as if it were a novel, you will nevertheless benefit from the associative links its structure is designed to bring about.

But the book also lends itself to being read 'interactively', by which I mean at a thoughtful pace, pausing from time to time to compare what I write about with your own interests, experience and patients, and trying out the various 'thought experiments' and training exercises I'll be suggesting. The next chapter, 'Overview', goes into more detail.

As I stood in the bookshop I found myself recalling another book from my schooldays. One of the set books I read for O-level was called *The Wooden Horse* – Eric Williams' Second World War story set in Stalag-Luft III, a German concentration camp. Prisoners of war in the camp built a wooden vaulting horse and positioned it near the perimeter fence. While their friends used it for physical exercise, a small group of would-be escapers hidden within the horse dug a hundred and twenty foot underground tunnel to freedom. So the wooden horse becomes an image not just of risk but of fitness and liberation.

Possibly now or at some time in the future you may be involved in teaching other doctors, perhaps less experienced than you are. It will be nice, when they ask you for help in their own professional development, for you to have some thoughts not only about *what* to teach them but also *how*. So, as they say, "what have you got to lose?"

– only the security of continuing to work in general practice untroubled by any suggestion that you might possibly be able to do it better!

Now read on.

Overview

What is now proved was once only imagin'd
William Blake, *The Marriage of Heaven and Hell*, 1790–93

In a Greek restaurant, if you find it hard to choose from an unfamiliar menu, you can settle for 'mezes' – a small portion of everything. This has several advantages. It is a meal in itself, it gives you a taste for dishes you might otherwise not have tried, and it helps you decide what you want the next time you go there.

This chapter (which I'd like you to read at one sitting) summarizes the rest of the book, and suggests how you use it to obtain the best return on your time investment in reading it. I think it's easier to learn new material if you're given a preview of what's in store and some inkling of how it will be presented and taught. The poet Rilke thought so too, when, in *Letters to a Young Poet*, he wrote

> The future enters into us, in order to transform itself in us, long before it happens.

Air travel is a common experience for many people nowadays, but even so you have to be pretty blasé not to be moved by the opportunity of looking down in detached comfort as well-known landmarks take on a new perspective and merge into less familiar terrain. Even the white-knuckled passengers who can't believe the wings are going to stay on find that when they land, and anxiety gives way to relief, the everyday world has taken on a new vibrancy.

I don't know whether by nature you are more of an optimist or a pessimist in the field of medical education. They both have their versions of Parkinson's Law ("Work expands to fill the time available for its completion"). The pessimist's version might be something like

> Problems redefine themselves to swamp the resources available for their solution.

The optimist, proud of still maintaining some neurological plasticity, would affirm

Achievement expands to fill the opportunities made genuinely available.

Let me see if I can tempt you.

———————

The Inner Consultation is organized in 3 sections:

> A. **Goal-setting**
> B. **Skill-building**
> and C. **Getting it together**

This structure, which recurs in different contexts like a 'leit-motif' throughout the book, embodies the three key stages in mastering a complex behavioural skill, whether it be consulting with a patient, or playing a musical instrument, or shooting at a target.

'Goal-setting' refers to fixing in mind at the start a clear idea of the end point, the outcome, the result you are wanting to achieve. The desired outcome needs to be visualized or imagined in as much specific sensory and behavioural detail as possible, and acts as the equivalent of focusing on the bull's-eye, or hearing the piece you're practising played by an expert.

'Skill-building' is the process of anticipatory training in the repertoire of component skills you require to achieve the outcome. These resources are instilled in advance of being invoked, so that they are in place when needed. This stage is like preparing and loading a rifle, or practising scales and exercises on an instrument.

'Getting it together' is akin to pressing the trigger, or walking onto the concert platform to perform. Well-intentioned and well-rehearsed, all (!) that is needed is for you to rely on the adequacy of your preparation and give yourself over to the inspiration of the moment, trusting your intuitive and unconscious processes to function appropriately and automatically. This is surprisingly difficult to do – a nagging voice inside your head keeps trying to interfere – but some simple techniques can make it easier.

Here, chapter by chapter, is a more detailed synopsis.

GOAL-SETTING

A1 "Problem? What problem?" aims to convince you, if you need convincing, that there is such a thing as being skilled at consulting. Consulting skills are different from, and supplementary to, the traditional skills in diagnosing and treating that you were taught at medical school. Not everyone would agree at first that consulting skills can be learned.

A2 "How have you been taught previously?" reviews the usual methods of medical education, and finds it not too surprising that even the latest techniques of consultation teaching have their shortcomings.

A3 "Models of the consultation" looks at some of the ways in which the consultation has been studied and analysed in order to make consulting skills easier for trainees to acquire.

A4 "On having two heads". Unfortunately, the effect of modelling and analysing too enthusiastically is often to confuse the trainee, who finds it difficult to attend to the patient while at the same time trying to remember all the theories of what he ought to be doing. It's like having two heads – one in charge, and another whispering instructions, advice and criticism in your ear like a back-seat driver. This 'inner dialogue' can become intrusive and unhelpful. The two heads are christened the 'ORGANIZER' and the 'RESPONDER'.

A5 "Keeping it simple" is the first step in reducing the complexities of the consultation to manageable proportions. The key concepts of some important models of the consultation can be condensed into a simple metaphor of 'the consultation as a journey'. The consultation becomes no longer a check-list of things to do and points to cover, but rather a short series of places to get to, one after the other, and in your own way.

A6 "Five 'en route' checkpoints" are sufficient staging posts along the way of each consultation. Each is a sub-goal in its own right, each ideally needing to be reached before moving on to the next. The 5 checkpoints are:

> Checkpoint 1 – 'Connecting'
> Checkpoint 2 – 'Summarizing'
> Checkpoint 3 – 'Handing over'
> Checkpoint 4 – 'Safety-netting'
> Checkpoint 5 – 'Housekeeping'

During the course of making for these checkpoints, you will find yourself accomplishing, almost in passing, the various tasks and objectives that other models of the consultation describe. Section B – 'Skill-building' describes each of the five checkpoints, equips you with the necessary 'mini-skills' to reach them, and helps you determine when you've arrived and are ready to move on.

SKILL-BUILDING

B1 "How people learn". This section begins with a reappraisal of the processes involved in human learning. In teaching, the emphasis in the past has been almost exclusively on cultivating the analytic and intellectual faculties broadly associated in neurophysiological terms with the 'dominant' (usually the left) cerebral hemisphere. Yet increasingly we are becoming aware of how much the 'non-dominant' (usually the right) hemisphere contributes to perception, under-standing, intuition and learning. The right hemisphere learns in different ways from the left, but both hemispheres need to be involved in the learning of a complex behavioural skill such as consulting. This book combines left and right hemisphere teaching techniques in order to develop skills at both the conscious and unconscious levels.

The remaining chapters in Section B consider each of the 5 checkpoints in turn. You need to know what the checkpoints are, to have some techniques for getting to them, and also to know how you can tell when you've arrived.

B2 "Connecting" is the first checkpoint to make for in the consultation. This means systematically establishing rapport with the patient, getting on the same wavelength and achieving empathy. Checkpoint 1 is reached when you can answer "yes" to the Key Question, "Have we got rapport?"

The chapter also includes material, carefully sequenced and structured to involve both left and right hemispheres, which will draw out from you your intrinsic abilities to relate to other people and help you enhance them in the professional setting. These 'rapport-building skills' provide your means of transport to the Connecting checkpoint.

B3 Checkpoint 2 – "Summarizing" is the point at which the patient's reasons for attending, his hopes, feelings, concerns and expectations, have been well enough explored and acknowledged for the consultation to move on. To do this, you need to develop skill in listening and 'eliciting'. The Key Question for the doctor here is, "Could I demonstrate to the patient that I've sufficiently understood why he's come?"

B4 This book is not primarily about the more obviously scientific aspects of medicine. Nevertheless, to reassure you that we have not lost sight of clinical relevance, this chapter is entitled "Interlude – the clinical process in general practice". In general practice we rely on a process of hypothesis-testing when assessing problems. And, even if we don't always make a formal diagnosis, we must always make a management plan.

B5 The consultation reaches a point, after all your medical skills have been deployed in assessing and diagnosing the presenting problems, and after you have explained, negotiated and agreed a management plan, that the patient has got as much as possible out of his encounter with you and becomes ready to take his leave. This point is Checkpoint 3 – "Handing over", the moment when the patient is fully back in charge of his or her subsequent behaviour. The Key Question requiring a "yes" answer at this stage is, "Has the patient accepted the management plan we have agreed?"

The range of communication skills needed to reach the 'Handover' checkpoint is considerable. I have grouped them under 3 headings – 'negotiating', 'influencing', and a variety of ways of giving information in an acceptable way that I call 'gift-wrapping'.

B6 General practice has been called "the art of managing uncertainty". The doctor needs to make a habit of predicting what could happen to the patient and his problem, both if things go as well as he hopes and also if things take an unexpected turn. Before the patient leaves the room, the doctor needs the security of knowing that he has prepared (or could prepare if the need arose) contingency plans to deal with an untoward clinical development, or some departure from the intended management plan. The stage of running through a selection of "what if ...?" possibilities, which may or may not be explicitly discussed with the patient, I call Checkpoint 4 – "Safety-netting". The Key Question to answer at Checkpoint 4 is, "Have I anticipated all likely outcomes?"

B7 The first 4 checkpoints have involved both doctor and patient. Checkpoint 5 – "Housekeeping" deals solely with the doctor's own internal experience. General practice is notorious for the stresses it imposes on the doctor's powers of concentration and equanimity. We owe it to ourselves, our staff, our families and our other patients to try to clear ourselves as far as possible of any accumulated emotional responses to the patients we have already seen and of too many preconceptions about the patients we are yet to see. Part of professional competence is the ability to offer each successive patient a caring and compassionate state of mind uncontaminated with our personal preoccupations. Clearing the mind to a state of readiness is Checkpoint 5, which I call "Housekeeping". The Key Housekeeping Question is, "Am I in good condition for the next patient?" This chapter suggests a variety of methods for 'taking care of yourself'.

GETTING IT TOGETHER

C1   People can increase their skills in two ways. One is 'improving by trying', and the other is 'improving by allowing'. With complex skills like consulting, improving by allowing is more effective, though the concept may be unfamiliar. In order to learn, you have to overcome the fear of forgetting. In order for this to occur, and the sensation of having two heads to subside, you have to know how to achieve 'nowness' – a heightened awareness of events in the here-and-now.

By this stage, you have a clear idea of where you are going, and will have a sense of 'potential on the verge of action'. Much of the learning acquired earlier in the book will have occurred below full conscious awareness, in your non-dominant cerebral hemisphere.

C2   "The inner consultation" goes into detail about how to direct your attention to the right things in the here-and-now, so that the distracting internal dialogue subsides. Then the way is clear for your conscious and unconscious resources to combine in intuitive listening, effective speaking, and reliable thinking. Gradually you will find that any awkwardness of these various training techniques dies down. The learning process becomes internalized, and you find yourself functioning effortlessly at a level of attainment higher than before, as if on auto-pilot. Behaviour that might earlier have seemed contrived or elaborate becomes imperceptibly delegated to levels of your nervous system's architecture below self-conscious awareness. The paradox of 'the self observing the self' evaporates.

C3   From here on you will increasingly find that the consultation can become, without exploiting the patient, a medium for your own personal growth and self-fulfilment. "Zen and the art of the consultation" offers, as an optional extra, points of departure from *The Inner Consultation* into some of the areas of self-transcendent experience to be found when dwelling in the immediate present. As the spontaneously competent and intuitive self grows, the assertiveness of that self diminishes, and compassion develops.

Appendix 1   Throughout the book, various training exercises are proposed as the occasion demands. This appendix puts together a programme for you to develop 'Inner Consultation' skills in a systematic manner.

HOW TO USE THIS BOOK

> To expect a man to retain everything he has ever read is like expecting him to carry about in his body everything he has ever eaten.
>
> Schopenhauer

Pitstops

At intervals in the text you will come across this:

PITSTOP

(possibly followed by some instructions)

Pitstops are points at which I would suggest you pause in your reading for a while. Attention span is limited; you need to do the visual equivalent of chewing and swallowing in order to avoid indigestion. You may also want to attend to your own physiological needs for rest, fluid balance and blood glucose. Pitstops provide the opportunities for you to put the book down and pick it up again with minimum disturbance to your concentration.

I also have an ulterior motive in providing pitstops. Besides nourishing the intellectual faculties of your left hemisphere, I'm attempting simultaneously to involve your right hemisphere as an equal partner in learning. As I've already implied, and as will become gradually clearer, the right and left hemispheres learn in different ways and communicate in different languages. The left hemisphere is good at learning facts and concepts; it speaks and understands straightforward logical prose. On the other hand the right hemisphere, whose activities tend to occur at or below the threshold of consciousness, prefers to be addressed indirectly, in analogies, metaphors, aphorisms, humour, imagery, fiction, poetry and art. Its responses come in the form of feelings, attitudes, memories, flights of imagination, the ingrained routines of behaviour, and associations of ideas. The right hemisphere's role in our task is to offer these unconscious resources for inclusion in the overall learning process in addition to the more analytic understanding which is the left hemisphere's contribution.

My task in trying to help you improve your consulting skill is made easier by the knowledge that you already have all the components of attitude, understanding and behaviour that you need. They may at the moment be partly unconscious or linked to contexts other than your professional one. As you read, I shall be helping you to create a sequence of thoughts and associations that will evoke and retrieve your unconscious learning resources so that they become available to you in the consulting room. My difficulty is that although we shall need to use examples from your own personal experience in the mosaic we shall jointly design, I of course don't know exactly what these are. Please use the pitstops to reflect on the preceding section and make connections and comparisons with cases and situations of your own. Your right hemisphere sometimes needs time to catch up – be patient with it!

If for any reason you stop reading in mid-chapter, please go back either to the beginning of the chapter when you resume, or to the pitstop immediately before where you left off.

Exercises

A really intelligent man feels what other men only know.

Montesqieu

A cannibal chief once captured a missionary lady, who, in exchange for life, offered him her two most cherished possessions, a recipe book and a sex manual.

"What are those?", asked the cannibal.

"This one is about making delicious cakes", replied the lady, "and this one is about making babies."

Solemnly the cannibal tore a page from each book and intently chewed first one, then the other. Finally he pronounced, "They both taste the same to me."

I mentioned above my hope that as you read you will interact with me and match my examples with your own. From time to time I shall ask you to carry this a stage or two further by outlining some simple training exercises. Some of these are 'thought experiments' which can be done without even putting the book down. They can be done with your eyes open or closed, although 'visualizations' are probably best done with eyes closed after reading the instructions. Others are pencil and paper exercises; if you want to use the spaces available in the text (which is the best way), and are embarrassed that someone may see, use an eraser before passing the book on to someone else.

Other exercises are a little more complex, designed to give you maximum reinforcement of your developing skills. They need to be done in the real world, either during everyday life or at work. Don't do these until you feel really ready.

After you've finished the main text, you will find in Appendix 1 a graduated programme of training in 'Inner Consultation' skills. How much of this you feel inclined to try depends on how much curiosity I've aroused in you and what you perceive to be the 'reward/risk ratio'. Good luck. I have a genuine wish to hear your comments – my correspondence address is given elsewhere.

I hope you won't feel too awkward at not resisting your natural eagerness to try the various exercises for yourself. The learning of skills, as opposed to knowledge, relies sooner or later on doing rather than intending. The taste of a cake is literally indescribable, though it can be conveyed as a set of instructions for recreating the taste called a recipe. A musical score is a set of instructions which, if followed by the musician, reproduces a version of the composer's original experience.

As Heinz von Foerster put it – "If you desire to see, learn how to act."

And what's more

> Chi Wen Tzu always thought three times before taking action. Twice would have been quite enough.
>
> Confucius

Early in this chapter, I wondered whether you were pessimistically or optimistically inclined. Have you decided?

There were two brothers, one a hopeless pessimist, the other an incurable optimist. On Christmas morning they awoke, eager to see what Santa Claus had brought them. The pessimist found a sack full of shiny new toys at the foot of his bed.

"Oh no," he wailed, "they'll all break, and the batteries will run out, and I've got two of those already."

The optimist found his room full of horse manure. With a whoop of glee, he threw himself into the manure with a shovel and great abandon.

"What on earth are you doing in all that?" asked his brother.

"With all this horse manure, there's got to be a pony in here somewhere!"

Section A
Goal–setting

"Problem? What problem?"

A1
Problem? What problem?

This chapter is about subtlety – the extra quality that goes to make a general practice consultation skilful instead of merely adequate, the thing people mean when they talk about "the art of general practice". Although a GP should never be less than clinically competent, he or she can also be so much more. In this chapter, I want to show you three things.

First, I want to satisfy you that you can recognize subtlety when you see it.

Secondly, I want to show you that what looks like subtlety of style from afar is in fact quite precise and specific when you look more closely.

Thirdly, I want to leave you with a sense of the possibility that you can take hold of subtlety and make it your own.

When I was a trainee in the early 1970s, my trainer was fond of quoting this paradoxical insight from R.D. Laing's book, *Knots*[1]*. Please read it (and all the other poems and aphorisms in this book) a little slower than usual, and allow yourself a few moments to reflect at the end.

There is something I don't know
that I am supposed to know.
I don't know *what* it is I don't know,
and yet I am supposed to know,
and I feel I look stupid
if I seem both not to know it
and not to know *what* it is I don't know.
Therefore I pretend I know it.
This is nerve-racking
since I don't know what I must pretend to know.
Therefore I pretend to know everything.

* References indicated in square brackets are to entries in the annotated bibliography, Appendix 2.

I feel you know what I am supposed to know
but you can't tell me what it is
because you don't know that I don't know what it is.

You may know what I don't know, but not
that I don't know it,
and I can't tell you. So you will have to tell me everything.

I was once in a discussion group talking about 'problem patients' with a group of trainee GPs. The trainees (who included my own trainee, Chris) were at different stages of their careers, some still working in hospital specialities, others in general practice. The cases they presented had been chosen for the usual reasons when doctors talk shop – partly because they were interesting, and partly because they seemed to show the presenting doctor in a pretty good light!

One trainee, whom I'll call George, described an attractive young lady, Miss Redlitz, who had come to see him suffering from sinusitis. He had taken a careful history, undressed her to the waist, and conscientiously examined her respiratory system, including a surprisingly thorough palpation and auscultation of her chest. He had prescribed an antibiotic and told her to return in a week. She had indeed returned, but had asked to see one of the partners instead of George again. George felt put out about this, and commented that patients just didn't seem to understand the importance of continuity of care and sticking to one doctor.

There was a nervous silence as the rest of the group wondered whether and how to challenge George's insistence that his management had been impeccable. It seemed evident to most people that important things had gone on during the consultation of which he has been less than fully aware. Eventually someone – possibly feeling, like Oscar Wilde's Gwendolen, that 'On an occasion of this kind it becomes more than a duty to speak one's mind. It becomes a pleasure,' – spoke up.

"Do you think, George, she might, perhaps, you know, have read something into the way you examined her?"

It didn't go down well. George was indignant; if the traditional methods of history and examination were good enough for generations of doctors and patients, they were good enough for him and Miss Redlitz. Yes, she was pretty. What of it? He had enough self-control to keep that side of himself out of the surgery, thank you very much. He hadn't nearly been a gynaecologist for nothing!

We moved on to another trainee's case. Peter recounted the latest in a series of weekly consultations he was having with Mrs M'Lone, a middle-aged lady who had been unexpectedly widowed. Peter had recently been on a counselling course using Transactional Analysis

[2]. For two or three sessions he had tried to play the role of Nurturing Parent to the sad and frightened Child he saw in Mrs M'Lone. In an earlier discussion the trainee group had suggested that his style of therapy, though helpfully meant, might have seemed a little contrived. Last week he had tried to put the formal jargon of Transactional Analysis out of his mind, and instead had just chatted to her in everyday language. This week she had come to say she felt a lot better, and gave him a pot of home-made jam to say 'thank you'.

"Well done", said the group. "You used to say that counselling wasn't a GPs business, but you wouldn't have been so helpful to Mrs M'Lone three months ago."

"And what I've just told you proves it", Peter maintained. "I went on this counselling course, and when I try to put it into practice you say I sound contrived. Yet when I forget about techniques and ego-states and so forth, and just act naturally, everyone says I've done a good job."

"So you seem to have changed", said someone. "Isn't that a good thing?"

Peter was almost wailing with frustration.

"But I don't know *how!*"

A TUTORIAL

At our next tutorial, Chris and I found ourselves still thinking about that case discussion group. "What did you make of George and Peter?" I asked.

Chris: They both seemed to be saying the same thing in different ways – they were all right as they are. George thought it was enough to make a diagnosis and prescribe the right treatment, and there was no point agonizing over the way he'd handled the consultation or how the girl might have interpreted what he'd done. But Peter worried me more. He really wasn't sure whether it was because of or in spite of his counselling training that he'd been able to help Mrs M'Lone.

Me: What do you think?

Chris: I'd like to think he'd learned something from the course, but I'm not sure. I know there are plenty of good doctors who are very understanding with patients, or who seem to get straight to the heart of their problems, but do you think that type of skill can be taught to someone who hasn't already got it?

Me: "The library is full of books that assume it can – Balint, Byrne and Long, *The Future General Practitioner* . . . [3,4,5]

Chris: I'm not sure that proves anything. I agree that if you take someone who's very good at consulting and ask them how it's done, they'll come up with a description or a model or a theory that analyses what they've been doing – in hindsight. But I don't think the process works in reverse. Just reading other people's ideas of what I ought to be doing doesn't make me actually think and feel and react like them.

Me: You're right. Books are good ways of passing on information at a conscious intellectual level, but unfortunately it's often a matter of chance whether new ideas get far enough beneath the surface to change our behaviour at the unconscious automatic level. We'll come on later to why that is, and what we can do about it. But you know from your own experience that it is possible for new ideas to become incorporated into the way you work. Remember what an effort it was the first few times you clerked a patient as a medical student? But now you can do it almost without thinking. Maybe you can learn to be good at consulting, too.

Chris: Okay, teach me.

Me: I'll try. The first thing I want you to do is have a think for a moment, then tell me about a consultation of your own that you feel proud of – one that if you were to see it on video, you would say, 'That was really skilful.'

Chris: Right ... I remember recently seeing Sonia Doughty. She's about 16½, and she said she wanted something for her acne. Her skin wasn't very bad, but something made me ask whether it was worse around period time. She said it was, and asked if there was anything I could do about her irregular periods. I explained that sometimes people went on the pill for that reason. She said no, she didn't mean that, but I thought at the time she was just sounding me out. So I gave her some cream for her face and asked her to come back the following week. She brought her boyfriend with her the next time, and you can imagine the rest. I felt pleased that she was able to trust me like that.

EXERCISE

Read these instructions over, then carry out this 'thought experiment'.

Please do now what I asked Chris to do. Cast back in your mind for one of your own consultations where you felt you displayed whatever you mean by skilled consulting. Remember the patient's name, what he or she looked like, how the room was arranged, the positions and body postures of yourself and the patient. Run through 'in your mind's ear' as much as you can remember of what was said. Picture the patient's facial expressions. Was there any particular moment where things clicked? Try and recapture something of the feeling you had during that successful consultation, and take some pleasure in knowing you are able to work that well.

Do this with your eyes closed, so that the memory can become as vivid as possible.

PITSTOP

Write down the name of the patient in the last exercise.

. . . . . .

If you didn't manage to do the exercise, please try again. It takes less than 2 minutes. Remember what Confucius said about Chi Wen Tzu?

Let's think some more about how you tell a good consultation from a bad one. A general criterion seems to be the doctor's ability to pay attention to clues and events in the periphery of his vision; to hear and respond to the conversational nuances in the patient's speech and in his own; to be sensitive to the meanings underlying the behaviour patterns of the patients who come his way.

This awareness that there is more in a situation than just the obvious mechanics is far from being the prerogative of doctors. Writers, artists and poets are usually better at it. As an example let me quote the beginning of a poem by Henry Reed, a poet of the Second World War, called *Naming of Parts*. While being instructed in the components of his rifle, a new recruit's attention begins to wander.

> Today we have naming of parts. Yesterday
> We had daily cleaning. And to-morrow morning,
> We shall have what to do after firing. But to-day,
> To-day we have naming of parts. Japonica
> Glistens like coral in all of the neighbouring gardens
>   And today we have naming of parts.

CASE ILLUSTRATIONS

Here are five clinical situations, each handled in two ways.

A child with tonsillitis

Mrs Wriggler brings Jeremy, aged 3, to the doctor because she thinks he may have his tonsillitis back again. Jeremy sits on his mother's lap.

Dr A gets out of his chair, picks up a tongue depressor, stands over Jeremy and tells him, "I'm not going to hurt you. Show me your throat." Despite persuasion and a little force, Jeremy's teeth remain clamped shut. "Lie him on the couch, then, while I examine his abdomen," says Dr A grimly.

While Mrs Wriggler tells Dr B about Jeremy's symptoms, Dr B goes and kneels beside him, playing casually with the child's fingers as he talks. "What nice teeth you've got, Jeremy", says Dr B. "Have you got teeth at the back as well? Is that the biggest mouth you can make?" Spreading his arms wide he continues, "Now come and sit on my knee while I make sure your tummy's all right."

"There's a lump in my throat, Doctor"

Mrs Timid sometimes, but not always, feels it's an effort to swallow her saliva. Food doesn't actually stick, although she's afraid it might. She feels well in herself, has not lost any weight, and she has no other gastro-intestinal symptoms.

Dr A carries out a physical examination, which is entirely normal. "Nothing to worry about here," he says, "just some tension in the throat muscles, which we call globus. Best thing to do is try and put it our of your mind."

As Dr A escorts her to the door, Mrs Timid turns and asks, "Can't I have an X-ray?"

Before examining Mrs Timid, Dr B says, "So this feeling of a lump comes and goes, and it doesn't actually interfere with swallowing your food, but nevertheless it's been worrying you." Mrs Timid nods. Dr B continues. "I expect you've been thinking about this for a while, and I dare say you had some thoughts yourself about what it could be. I was wondering what had gone through your mind."

"Well actually, Doctor," says Mrs Timid, "what made me come was I saw that programme on the television about throat cancer ..."

A new diabetic

Mrs Hogg, a widow aged 64, has just been found to be suffering from maturity-onset non-insulin dependent diabetes. She will need weight reduction, an oral hypoglycaemic drug, and regular surveillance.

"Right," says Dr A. "I've explained to you all about your pancreas, and your blood sugar. Now I'll go over the dose of tablets, and tell you about our repeat prescription system. You're going to need to come for regular check-ups – ask the receptionist to book you in to the next clinic, and tell her you'll need a blood test a few days beforehand. I'll be making you an appointment to see the dietician, but in the meantime here are some leaflets about carbohydrate and fibre intake."

From one of Mrs Hogg's glazed eyes a tear begins to trickle.

"Right," says Dr B. "The main thing is to get you feeling well again. You're going to need to come and see me again soon so that I can keep a check on how things are going, and today I'm going to start you on some tablets. Now while I write out the prescription, you be thinking of the questions you want to ask me."

A tale of two blood tests

Two blood samples are waiting in the Haematology laboratory for a glandular fever (infectious mononucleosis) screening test. Both are from young men of 18 who will be doing examinations in a few weeks.

Gary went to see Dr A with what looked like bacterial tonsillitis. He was given penicillin, but returned 24 hours later saying his throat was no better. "Of course not," said Dr A, "you haven't given the antibiotic long enough to work." The following day Gary returned feeling worse if anything. Dr A sent a throat swab for bacteriological investigation. Three days later, feeling now quite ill, developing a faint rash, and accompanied this time by his father, Gary returns and sees another doctor. Dr C provisionally diagnoses glandular fever and arranges a blood test.

"Now at last we're getting somewhere," says Gary to his father as they leave. "I'm not seeing Dr A again."

Barry went to see Dr B with what looked like bacterial tonsillitis. "If I'm right, this penicillin should begin to take effect within 48 hours," said Dr B. "In case I'm wrong, though, and it's a virus infection or possibly glandular fever, come and see me in a few days if you're not feeling better."

"I've got this rash now," says Barry, four days later.

"We'd better check for glandular fever after all, then," says Dr B. "I'ld like to do a blood test and take a throat swab."

"Pretty impressive," says Barry to his father when he gets home. "Dr B was on to that right from the start."

On and on and on

It's the last appointment on Friday evening. Mr and Mrs Battle are seeing their doctor for a session of what is supposed to be marital therapy. As usual, the doctor finds it hard to interrupt Mrs Battle, who is in full flight complaining about her husband. Everything she says is a put-down. She doesn't like his habits, his family or his wage-packet. He doesn't talk right, or think right, and now he can't even make love right. Right?

Dr A grits his teeth and tries to keep looking helpful. What about my own wife, he thinks. We're supposed to be going out this evening, and now I'm going to be late, and the traffic will be impossible. He wonders why his receptionist hasn't the sense to interrupt him and pretend there's an urgent call for him to attend to. At last the phone rings.

"Sorry, Doctor," says the receptionist, "but there's an extra patient to see and the others have all gone home. Will you see him after you've seen the Battles?"

"No I damn well won't," he snaps. He slams the phone down and turns back to the Battles. "Do go on."

Dr B grits his teeth and decides it's too much of a strain to pretend he wants to hear any more.

"Do you know what you make me feel like doing?", he asks Mrs Battle.

"What?", she says.

"This!", he says, and raises two fingers in the traditional gesture of defiance.

There is an awkward pause, then Mrs Battle turns to her husband.

"Do you ever feel like that?", she asks him, her voice considerably gentler than before.

"Just sometimes, dear", he replies, with a hint of tenderness.

"You never said. Why didn't you say? You should have said." Mrs Battle begins to weep. Her husband puts a comforting arm around her.

"There, there, love. Let's get home."

PITSTOP

Here now is *Naming of Parts* in full[6].

Today we have naming of parts. Yesterday
We had daily cleaning. And to-morrow morning,
We shall have what to do after firing. But to-day,
To-day we have naming of parts. Japonica

Glistens like coral in all of the neighbouring gardens
  And today we have naming of parts.

This is the lower sling swivel. And this
Is the upper sling swivel, whose use you will see
When you are given your slings. And this is the piling swivel,
Which in your case you have not got. The branches
Hold in the gardens their silent, eloquent gestures,
  Which in our case we have not got.

This is the safety-catch, which is always released
With an easy flick of the thumb. And please do not let me
See anyone using his finger. You can do it quite easy
If you have any strength in your thumb. The blossoms
Are fragile and motionless, never letting anyone see
  Any of them using their finger.

And this you can see is the bolt. The purpose of this
Is to open the breech, as you see. We can slide it
Rapidly backwards and forwards; we call this
Easing the spring. And rapidly backwards and forwards
The early bees are assaulting and fumbling the flowers:
  They call it easing the Spring.

They call it easing the Spring; it is perfectly easy
If you have any strength in your thumb: like the bolt,
And the breech, and the cocking-piece, and the point of balance,
Which in our case we have not got; and the almond-blossom
Silent in all of the gardens and the bees going backwards and forwards,
  For today we have naming of parts.

THE TUTORIAL RESUMED

Chris: When you said you would teach me how to consult better, I
        was expecting you to give me some sort of advice, or a list of
        points to cover in the consultation. I'm a bit puzzled.

Me: If I were to give you a list of do's and don'ts at this stage
        (even if I knew what to put on the list) I think I know what
        would happen: you would start to criticize. You might
        criticize yourself for not doing everything you were told. You
        might criticize me or my list for being too complicated.
        Finally you might start to criticize the patients for not
        making things easy for you. Those kinds of criticism tend to
        make it harder to learn, not easier. For the moment it's
        enough for you to be able to tell the difference between
        better and worse consultations, and to be able to imagine
        yourself in the better ones.

Chris: What happens next?

Me: I want to show you how what we're doing fits in with what you've already heard about the consultation. I also want you to become aware of *how* you're learning *while* you're learning, so that you can become better able to teach your own patients and students. In Marshall McLuhan's phrase, 'The Medium is the Message'. Here's another of R.D. Laing's *Knots* to close on.

If I don't know I don't know
                               I think I know
If I don't know I know
                               I think I don't know

A2
How have you been taught previously?

The impression I hope you've gained from the previous chapter is that there are indeed such things as consultation skills, even though so far they have not been explicitly defined. But since you can recognize them when you see them, it's possible for you to learn them.

The next step is to take a critical look at the various educational methods so far available to teach clinical skills in general, and consultation skills in particular. There are some shortcomings in the existing methods, and part of the difficulty trainees sometimes have in learning consultation skills is the result of limitations inherent in the teaching methods currently in use. If you're not happy about *how* you're learning, you don't find the subject matter easy to absorb. This book offers you a simpler and more practical 'tool-kit' of consultation skills, and also attempts to teach them to you in a more thorough-going way.

THE TUTORIAL CONTINUES

Me: If I'm going to introduce you to a fresh way of learning consultation skills, I'm afraid first of all I need to give you a slight sense of dissatisfaction with the old ways. Otherwise there wouldn't be much incentive for you to try a new approach. While I was thinking about how to put this over, I remembered a little verse I saw somewhere, which went:

> The centipede was happy, quite,
> Until a toad in fun
> Said, "Pray, which leg goes after which?"
> This worked his mind to such a pitch
> He lay distracted in a ditch
> Considering how to run.

Chris: Thanks for the warning!

Me: Nevertheless, at risk of leaving you quivering in a ditch like the centipede, I'm going to go over some of the theories about teaching in general, and skills training in particular. It might reassure you that there is some method in the teaching you've had in the past, and perhaps give you an interest in moving beyond it. But even as I say that, I'm aware that a lot of the medical education you've received has been a bit 'ad hoc'. Traditional teaching methods like lectures and ward-rounds tend to be used "because we've always done it that way", rather than because they're necessarily the best way to get a particular lesson across. Let's recall a few familiar settings where learning is supposed to take place ...

The informal chat over coffee

"I saw young Jimmy with a stomach ache. Turned out to be his tonsils again."

(In other words, "I might as well tell you, and maybe you'll remember.")

The lecture

"Today we'll go through the causes of postmenopausal bleeding, a favourite exam question. Copy this down ..."

(In other words, "I'm telling you, and you'd better remember!")

Sitting with Nellie

"Good morning, students, I'm the Professor's House Surgeon. This is how to do a venepuncture. Now take 50 ml each off the ten new admissions."

("I've told you, now get on with it.")

The ward round

"Typical case of von Jabberwock's disease. Come along now. Anybody? Nobody?..."

("Even if I tell you, I bet you won't remember.")

Sitting-in

"Sit over there and watch me closely while I inject this shoulder joint. Because you'll be doing the next one."

("Try and remember what I've as good as told you.")

The reading list

"Rather than waste our tutorial time going over topics that have already been written about..."

("You may not remember, but you can't say I didn't tell you.")

The harangue

"How often do I have to tell you the innervation of latissimus dorsi? Now, for what I hope is the last time! ..."

("If you can't remember what I've told you, there must be something wrong with you.")

The tutorial

"I thought we'ld talk about hypertension. First of all, what do you mean by 'high blood pressure'?"

("I'll tell you if you'll tell me. You start.")

EXERCISE

Think of examples of these forms of learning in your own experience. Try and put names, places and topics to the examples. Maybe you can think of other types of occasion which it was assumed you would learn from. What were the unspoken messages and assumptions underlying them?

In recent years medical teachers have become much more thoughtful about their teaching methods. Most undergraduate curricula, and some postgraduate courses, are based to some extent on the Educational Paradigm of OBJECTIVES, STRATEGIES and ASSESSMENT (Figure A2.1). The Educational Paradigm is an educationist's simplified model of how to teach people, just as HISTORY, EXAMINATION and SPECIAL TESTS is a doctor's simplified model of how to diagnose people.

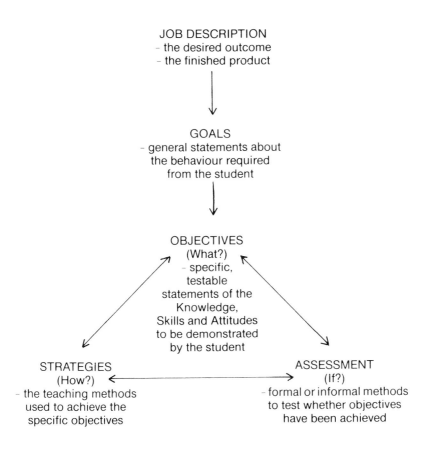

Figure A2.1 The Educational Paradigm

In figure A2.1, the top 3 headings – job description, goals and objectives – are about *what* should be taught. The bottom 3 – objectives, strategies and assessment – are about *how* things should be taught. Stripped of jargon, all this model tells a teacher is: "Get clear in your mind, in great detail, everything the students needs to know. Decide what teaching methods are best for particular topics. Then go ahead and do some teaching. Afterwards, check up to see whether the student has in fact learned what you wanted him to. If he has, move on to the next topic. If he hasn't, try again, perhaps in a different way."

This sounds like, and is, common sense. In fact, however, much orthodox medical education neglects to choose clear and relevant objectives; it often fails to use assessment methods of a type and at a time most likely to be helpful to the student; and it can be slow to reconsider its teaching methods in the light of how students perform. Take the examples of the teaching situations described earlier: each makes certain assumptions, and each ignores some important variables. Each is a form of the usual "instructive" style of teaching, where the aim is to transmit factual knowledge or simple skills from a teacher who has the knowledge to a pupil who does not. Ideally, the transmitted knowledge is intended to arrive in the pupil complete, uncontaminated and undegraded, and immediately begin its task of improving the pupil's performance. It is assumed for practical purposes that telling leads to remembering, and remembering leads to altering. Little thought appears to have been given to how knowledge is best presented for maximum retention, or how theoretical knowledge leads in turn to practical usefulness.

The examples were also short on assessment methods. In some, such as the chat, the harangue and the ward round, there might be no way of telling what had been learned unless a similar occasion were to arise in future. In others – the lecture, the reading list or sitting-in – the threat of assessment (perhaps in the form of exams) might seem too remote, too unlikely or too daunting to be helpful.

It has become a truism to speak of Knowledge, Skills and Attitudes in one breath as an inseparable triad, the three areas where the aspiring GP should seek improvement. The Educational Paradigm is at its most helpful in the realm of Knowledge teaching, where the material to be learned can be broken down into manageable 'chunks' which are easy to define and relatively easy to assess.

At the other extreme, the teaching of Attitudes is an altogether more difficult topic, not least because of the wide spectrum of opinion about what constitutes a desirable attitude. While most teachers of general practice feel relatively comfortable making constructive comments about their trainees' knowledge base, they feel themselves entering quicksand if they seek to modify personal values and personality traits. Most trainees end up with attitudes rather like their trainers' anyway! [1] Only when a trainee's attitude becomes glaringly inappropriate is he likely to meet much in the way of constructive confrontation, and even then it will probably come from an embarrassed trainer whose educational theory has flown out of the window.

The area of Skills training, on the other hand, is one where general practice has marked out its own distinct territory and gradually built up an enviable tradition of theory and technique. Under the heading "Skills" we might include, for example:

counselling and psychotherapy of various types (individual, marital, sexual, family);
practice management;
non-verbal communication;
practical procedures, like manipulation or joint injection;
hypnosis;
alternative or complementary medicine.

Most teachers of general practice, I think however, would agree that the skill they would most like their trainees to acquire is that of effective consulting – consulting with empathy, style, elegance, humanity, versatility, and a sense of genuine caring. When it comes to teaching consultation skills, general practice is already way ahead of other professions (such as legal and financial) and other branches of our own. I believe it is the energy and thought that has been given to studying and teaching the consultation process which have transformed general practice from Cinderella to First Lady at the Medical Ball.

Although different authors describe and analyse the consultation in apparently diverse ways, there has until now been considerable agreement upon the best methods by which to use their observations for training purposes. Compared with methods of teaching purely factual knowledge, the learning of skills introduces two additional requirements:

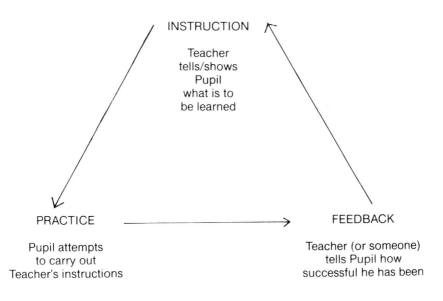

Figure A2.2   Simple model of skills training

(i) Practical experience – the trainee has to try for himself to carry out the skill he has been shown or told about; and

(ii) Feedback – someone (the trainee or the trainer or some third party) has to tell the trainee to what extent he has been successful, so that he knows whether or not to do it differently the next time.

Figure A2.2 summarizes the process of skills training at its most basic. It is very like the Educational Paradigm, with INSTRUCTION representing OBJECTIVES, PRACTICE representing STRATEGIES, and FEEDBACK representing ASSESSMENT.

Superficially attractive, this simple model can in practice all too easily degenerate into something like this:

Instruction   A trainer tells a trainee, "It's a good idea to find out what the patient believes is wrong before you go on to suggest treatment. We call this 'eliciting'. If you don't elicit the patients' ideas, concerns and expectations, you may find they don't accept what you say at a later stage. Please try this during your next surgery."

Practice   The trainee asks his next patient, "What do you think's the matter with you?" The patient replies, "You're the doctor – you tell me!" The next patient only wants a certificate because he has a broken leg, so the question seems pointless. When he asks the third patient, a man with irritable bowel syndrome, "What do you expect me to do about it?", the patient takes offence.

Feedback   When a discouraged trainee reports back, the trainer says, "Perhaps you weren't doing it right. Try again." The trainee agrees, secretly wondering whether it's worth the effort.

It is easy to recognize that something is wrong in this example; it is harder to tell exactly what. One important factor is that in postgraduate education the relationship between trainer and trainee is a co-operative one, unlike the teacher–pupil relationship at school where power and responsibility are vested almost exclusively in the teachers. Vocational training takes place between consenting adults who generally come to develop equal regard for each other. Trainer and trainee prefer to arrive at their teaching agenda by consensus, not by diktat. In the example, the trainer's instructions were not sufficiently clear and precise; the trainee had to work out his own way of trying to implement them; and the trainer's feedback comments were unconstructive and non-specific. The trainee didn't learn what the trainer meant to teach, and what he did learn wasn't what was intended.

A more refined model of skills training, taking account of this critique, is shown in Figure A2.3. It represents a more participatory style of teaching, and is culled from the ideas of John Heron [2].

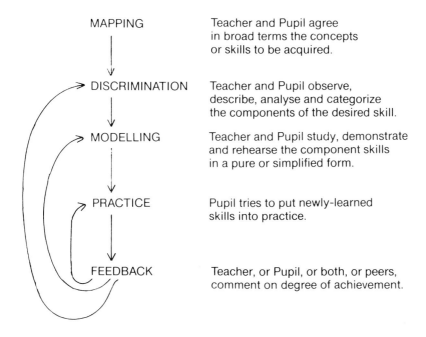

MAPPING — Teacher and Pupil agree in broad terms the concepts or skills to be acquired.

DISCRIMINATION — Teacher and Pupil observe, describe, analyse and categorize the components of the desired skill.

MODELLING — Teacher and Pupil study, demonstrate and rehearse the component skills in a pure or simplified form.

PRACTICE — Pupil tries to put newly-learned skills into practice.

FEEDBACK — Teacher, or Pupil, or both, or peers, comment on degree of achievement.

Figure A2.3   Model of participatory skills training, after Heron[2]

The essential differences between this and the former model are:

(i) The degree to which the trainee is involved in recognizing the relevance and extent of what he is invited to learn; and

(ii) The addition of a 'rehearsal' stage, where the trainee practises new behaviours in a model or idealized form before the new skills are attempted in real life.

Continuing the previous example, a teaching sequence based on this model might go like this:

Mapping   Trainer and trainee are discussing why it is that patients don't always take their medication as prescribed. Factors they think might be important include: the severity of the patient's symptoms; side-effects of treatment; the patient's degree of trust in the doctor; the quality of the doctor's explanation; and the patient's under-standing of how treatment will affect the outcome.

Discrimination Trainer and trainee concentrate on ways of finding out the patient's view of the problem. They decide they need to consider the patient's IDEAS, CONCERNS, EXPECTATIONS and FEELINGS. They agree that, ideally, each of these four aspects should be elicited in the consultation.

Modelling	*Trainer:*	How could you ask the patient to find out what her expectations of the consultation were?
	Trainee:	I could say, 'What do you expect me to do about your problem?'
	Trainer:	I think that might come across as a bit abrupt or uncaring. See if you can put it a bit more subtly.
	Trainee:	How about, 'I was wondering whether you had any particular thoughts as to how I could best help you.'?
	Trainer:	I think that sounds better.
	Trainee:	I'll try that, then.

Practice The trainee makes a video recording of his next surgery, during which he tries out various forms of words which he thinks might be appropriate to the particular patient.

Feedback Trainer and trainee review the video tape, at first looking only at the trainee's attempts to elicit the patient's views. They adhere to the usual guidelines or ground rules, i.e. the trainee comments before the trainer, and they both acknowledge what was done well before constructively criticizing specific points. Together they decide whether the trainee is ready to move on to learn something else, or needs to practise this skill a bit more.

One of the most comprehensive approaches to the teaching and learning of consultation skills is found in a recent book by Pendleton *et al.*[3]. They use a refinement of the Heron model, summarized in Figure A2.4

PITSTOP

Take a short break to clear your head: go for a walk, or have a cup of tea!

MORE FROM THE TUTORIAL

Me: Chris, I'ld like to know what you make of these various theories about how to teach the consultation. And because I

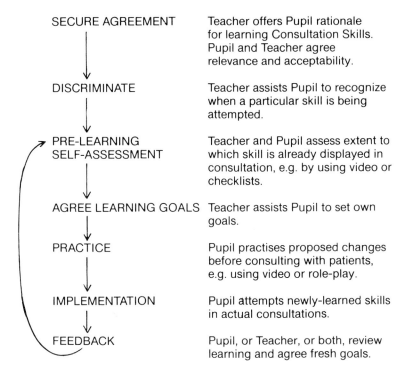

Figure A2.4 Systematic model of consultation skills training, after Pendleton *et al.*[3]

know that's a big question, I'd like you to imagine yourself divided into two parts, and answer for each part in turn. We could call the two parts your intellect and your intuition. I'm wondering first what your head thinks, and secondly what your gut-feeling is.

Chris: To my head it sounds fine. It makes sense to think in terms of breaking down a complex activity like consulting into its component bits, polishing up each bit, then putting them back together. And the descriptions of the training process, especially the last one, seem to have taken into account all the factors I should have thought were important.

Me: And what about your gut-reaction? Or, if you prefer, what does your heart tell you?

Chris: That's a bit more complicated. I know the theory makes sense, and therefore I ought to feel enthusiastic about the training programme that stems from it, but there's a 'but'. It's hard to put into words. Whenever I've tried in the past to practise a consultation skill, for instance trying to be more 'patient-centred', I've found that I got confused by trying to remember too many instructions at once. Sooner or later I got fed-up with trying and just reverted to my old ways of doing things. And to be honest I don't know if either of us – I or the patient – was any worse off.

Me: I had a patient once, a young chap, who was 'heavily into motor-bikes'. He used to go off on bike trials, and he had all the gear, and knew all the technical jargon. Then he had a very nasty accident, with compound fractures of his legs, and he couldn't walk for months, let alone ride. While he was recovering, he spent the time stripping his bike down. He had the engine apart, and cleaned it and greased it, and tinkered with it, and put it back together. Then he did it all again. And again. When his legs at last recovered, he took the bike out on the road, but it just didn't feel right. It didn't respond the way it used to, and in lots of ways it felt unfamiliar. He thought of dismantling and re-assembling it one last time, but by then of course he was impatient to be fully mobile. So he sold the bike and bought a car.

Chris: That fits. Too much technical know-how resulted in disenchantment.

Me: Notwithstanding, I'd like to do one last bit of tinkering before we forget about educational theory for the time being. It might help us to understand where some of the sense of misgiving stems from. Let's think about some of the assumptions that underlie the usual skills teaching process. I've summarized them in Figure A2.5. Some of these assumptions you might accept; others you might feel like taking issue with ...

CONCEPTS
(1) are organized into
THEORETICAL MODELS,
(2) from which are derived
COMPONENT SKILLS,
(3) which, once SEEN AND DESCRIBED
(and possibly DEMONSTRATED)
(4) can be CONSCIOUSLY PRACTISED.
(5) Practice, with a bit of luck, leads to
IMPROVEMENT,
(6) which somehow or other becomes
INTERNALIZED AND INCORPORATED
into the doctor's
REPERTOIRE OF CONSULTING SKILLS,
(7) which, if he can use them appropriately, add up to
COMPETENT CONSULTING.

Figure A2.5 The assumptions underlying traditional skills training methods

The first assumption, (1) in Figure A2.5, is that skills training starts with some feat of mental architecture (model-making) on the part of an expert observer or teacher. The material to be taught needs first to be analysed and organized into a set of concepts which can then be presented to the learner. The teacher, in deriving his conceptual model, proceeds from the particular to the general. The learning process, on the other hand, is thought to be best encouraged by working back from the general to the particular. In theory, children should be taught topology and materials science before learning to tie their shoelaces!

The second assumption (2) is that complex behaviour can be broken down into 'chunks' of manageable size. That's true, but is it true that all you have to do to reconstitute the original skill is put all the chunks back together again? Is the whole neither more nor less than the sum of its parts?

(3) In presenting examples of the component chunks, the teacher draws primarily on his own resources to provide models for the pupil. It's assumed that "telling and showing" will equip the pupil with a sufficient grasp of what is expected for him to be able to produce his own first version of a new skill "good enough to try". In reality, of course, a good teacher uses the pupil's own experience and examples to build on.

(4) It is possible (and probably desirable) for a trainee to carry on a consultation while at the same time trying consciously to carry out a newly-acquired piece of behaviour. In fact, as you know, this can often lead to the sensation, described in a later chapter, of 'having two heads', which is a mixed blessing.

(5) The proverbs are true – "practice makes perfect", and "if at first you don't succeed, try, try, and try again." The main thing required from the trainee is persistence.

(6) If he keeps trying, the trainee finds that he becomes less and less self-conscious about using his new skills. He doesn't have to keep reminding himself about them. This is not because they have lapsed, but because they have become assimilated below the level at which he is consciously aware of using them. This indeed is the case. But it's further assumed that there's not a lot anyone – teacher or pupil – can do to facilitate this process of internalization. It's an automatic process we don't have any control over.

(7) Training equips the doctor with a repertoire or palette of consulting skills which have either become automatic or can easily be retrieved if the occasion demands it. All he has to do now is use them – play the part, mix the desired combination of ingredients. Hey presto – competence!

Me: ... so you can see, I share your sense of unease. Although the teaching processes we've been considering can be extremely useful, I think there are two important additions which will make the learning process both easier and more profound.

The first is this: every doctor – in fact every human being – already has in his or her repertoire all the resources and components and ingredients for skilful consulting. It may well be that the context you've been using them in wasn't a medical one. But then it becomes a question not of learning new skills, but rather recognizing new occasions to use old ones, and that's an easier task. For example, you spoke earlier of getting 'mental overload' when you were trying to be more patient-centred. I'll bet you don't have that problem when you talk quite spontaneously to a small child, and use the right level of language quite automatically. Couples going out on a date don't have to try very hard to remain 'other-person-centred' – it just happens. So skills training is really only about retrieving resources from one context and re-associating them into the setting of the consultation.

The second important point is this: it *is* possible to facilitate unconscious learning. The internalizing of complicated behaviour sequences and the process of their becoming automatic *can* be speeded up and made more efficient. It needs a wider range of techniques than the rather intellectual concepts we've been discussing if the conscious and the unconscious minds, the left and right cerebral hemispheres, are to learn simultaneously, but it can be done. Indeed here again, you've been doing this all your life in other contexts; for instance, when you learned to walk, or to get on with the other members of your family, or to get your own way in an argument. How did you develop a sense of humour? I'm sure you didn't ever go to 'Joke Practice' – "Today we start with the easy jokes; next week, the mother-in-law."

How about this for a second verse to the 'centipede' poem?

Sadly he thought, "The toad was right –
I *can't* think how to run."
"I'm trapped down here for good," he cried.
But then, as in despair he sighed,
He felt his feet themselves decide
The way back to the sun

A3
Models of the consultation

The previous chapter was a review of *how* medical skills are taught, generally by the cycle of Analysis, Practice and Feedback. I concluded that, while this process was fine for many purposes, I would want to make two caveats: first, that the contribution of the learner's pre-existing resources might be underestimated; and secondly, that the learner's powers of unconscious learning can be actively assisted and not just left to chance.

This chapter reviews some current ideas about *what* consultation skills are. To do this, we have to think about 'models'. The phrase 'model of the consultation' has crept imperceptibly but ubiquitously into books, articles, papers and presentations about general practice, usually as a means of conferring academic respectability on the author's distillation of his clinical experience. (One ever-popular 'model' is the hobby-horse!) So this chapter tries to answer some important questions, such as:

- Why all this talk of models?
- What's the point of making models of the consultation, or of anything else in medicine, for that matter?
- What types of model are there?
- What use is a model when you've made it?

And, as I'm sure it won't surprise you to learn that I'm shortly going to present my own model of consulting, the conclusion I shall hope to bring you to is that model-making is an essential step in mastering consultation skills. Essential, that is, *as long as* the model is simple, and you can actually do something with it.

You may or may not have realized that models are all about us. That ambiguous phrase – 'all about us' – is true in both senses. Models are all around us, and also all to do with us. Like most things in adult life, they have their equivalents and origins in childhood. We've all played with models as children – teddy bears, dolls, toy cars, games, puzzles – all miniature or simplified versions of some part of the complicated world of the adults who seemed to know everything. Play is a model of living, nature's way of learning in safety. To a baby, a cuddly toy is a model of where 'self' ends and 'non-self' begins. When as older children we played mothers and fathers, or doctors and nurses, we were all the time putting together our own models of human relationships.

The really universal modelling kit, more widely distributed even than Lego, is language. The function of the human brain is to simplify the turmoil of experience to the point of predictability. Language is one of the brain's tools for bringing the world under control. In speech and verbal thought we create a set of symbols which stand for, and which can be manipulated as if they were, events in what by general agreement we call 'real life'. Language has an additional advantage. Real events run in real time and have real consequences. In speech and thought, the time context of mental events can shift instantaneously between past, present and future, and possible outcomes can be considered from the safety of the imagination. For right-handed people and most left-handers, verbal language, logic and conceptual thought are predominantly the business of the left cerebral hemisphere. In the language of the right hemisphere, images, feelings and memories form the equivalent of parts of speech, and the unconscious rules of emotional life provide the syntax.

So when we speak about 'models' of some complex experience, we are in the realm of metaphor, of analogy, of maps and representations, of 'pars pro toto' – the part standing for the whole.

If you fly above the surface of the earth, you look down and see the world as it really is. You see mountains and rivers, towns and roads. But you don't see frontiers, or county boundaries, or lines of latitude, or isobars, or the Iron Curtain. You couldn't tell the areas that were democracies, or English-speaking, or members of NATO. All these invisible things are concepts whose only reality is their usefulness. They help people to understand, predict and control what happens to them.

And so we draw maps. Maps are models of the real world. On a map we recognize some features of the real world, but the mapmaker superimposes a representation of whatever concepts or properties of the real world he particularly wants to bring to our attention. Maps allow us to cut down our exploring time and learn from the experience of other people. They are short-cuts to security.

A map is one example of a model, a model of all the possible journeys you could make. But other models turn up everywhere, sometimes in forms we don't immediately recognize as models. For example:

- A recipe is a model of a sequence of things to do if you want a cake;
- A photograph is a model of an instant in time;
- Shakespeare's 'Othello' is a model of the consequences of pathological jealousy;
- The law of gravity is a model of why apples sometimes fall on your head;
- Logic is a model of how to settle an argument;
- The scientific method is a model of how to predict the behaviour of the natural world;
- Heisenberg's Uncertainty Principle is a model of why you can't always predict the behaviour of the natural world.

Notice that no matter how concrete or abstract the model appears – recipe book or quantum theory – the model ultimately represents some real events in the real world which we experience through our sense organs – a cake, a sunny beach, a reading on an ammeter, or what you say to your wife if you think she's been unfaithful. Sensory experience is the only reality we can ever directly know. One of our basic human needs is to understand what is happening to us. Models make sense of sensation.

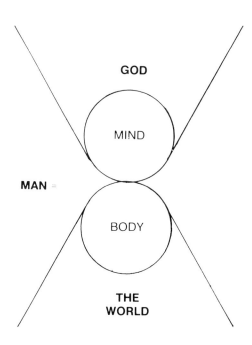

Figure A3.1 Cartesian model of man

MODELS IN MEDICINE

Medicine is an enormous model-shop in which to browse, occupying as it does the common ground between mankind's physical, mental and spiritual experiences. One of the evergreen models in the West, underpinning centuries of scientific and religious debate, is the 'dualistic' model of Man associated with the name of the 17th century French philosopher René Descartes. (It's interesting to note in passing that his name in translation is 'René of the maps'. What's in a name?)

Cartesian dualism holds that the body is nothing more than a mechanism, obeying physical laws, while the mind is of altogether different stuff, God-given and not susceptible to physical explanation.

Another medical model, from medieval physiology, held that bodily and mental constitutions were determined by the interplay of four 'cordial humours'; the choleric (bilious and angry), the sanguine (full-blooded and optimistic), the phlegmatic (wet and withdrawn), and the melancholic (ruled by black bile and prone to looking on the black side). Before dismissing this model as out of date, consider the current speculation about the role of suppressed anger and grief in the aetiology of cancer and auto-immune disease; the division of personalities into the adrenaline-addicted Type A and the laid-back Type B, and the higher cardiovascular morbidity among Type A's; the location of the 'gall'-bladder, source of black bile, in the 'hypochondriac' region of the abdomen. Plus ça change!

Another model of key importance to medical and philosophical thought this century has been the psychoanalytical model of the mind originating with Freud and endlessly revamped by generations of psychiatrists of different schools. The mind is conceived as tripartite, with ego, superego and id, and awareness divisible into conscious, pre-conscious and unconscious.

But in medicine the most pervasive model of all is so entrenched that it has become known as 'The Medical Model'. The Medical Model, rooted in science and wielded with professional authority, is the one most thoroughly taught to medical students. They find it attractive because it stretches their intellects (which tend to be well-developed anyway) and spares them much involvement of their feelings (of which they are much less sure).

Strictly applied, the medical model consists of a series of assumptions or axioms.

(1) A state of normal health exists (though is rarely encountered) which can be defined in terms of bodily structure and function compatible with comfort and survival. The normal state is studied in the disciplines of anatomy, physiology and biochemistry.

(2) Disease processes exist, defined in terms of departures from normal structure and function which are incompatible with comfort or survival. Disease is studied in the discipline of pathology.

(3) A patient's complaint of illness or symptoms is evidence of some malfunction. The malfunction can be rationally investigated and identified by the process of diagnosis.

(4) Accurate diagnosis allows the selection of appropriate corrective measures from the doctor's repertoire of therapeutic skills, which might be surgical or technological or pharmacological.

(5) Successful therapy restores diseased processes to, or in the direction of, normal, thus curing or improving the patient's illness.

While respecting the important contribution the medical model has made to the understanding and relief of suffering, we must at the same time acknowledge that its shortcomings and misplaced emphasis have resulted in a great many errors of omission and commission. Examples of the apparent disregard for the patient as a person make easy ammunition for those who accuse doctors of professional arrogance. The same feeling governs people who nostalgically oversimplify medicine into the 'art' of general practice contrasted with the 'high-tech' science associated with hospitals. Some penetrating and provocative critiques of the medical model are to be found in the writings of Ivan Illich and Ian Kennedy [1,2].

MODELS OF ILLNESS

In the medical model, 'illness' is seen as a subjective experience complained of by the sufferer (who is thereby defined as a patient) and indicating to the doctor that a disease process is at work. We could call this the 'pathological' model of illness. But there are many other models of 'illness', each with something useful to say: for example,

– a 'magic' model. Illness is the result of possession by evil or spirit forces. Flourishing in the voodoo culture of Haiti, the magic model is still alive in the mind of the Hounslow mother who says of her sullen teenager, "I wish you'd talk to her, doctor. I can't think what's got into her lately." I also wonder how our frequent talk of "virus infections" comes across to someone who has never seen an electron micrograph!

– a 'moral' model. Illness is retribution for deviant behaviour, Nature 'serving the patient right'. "There, what did I tell you?", says the parent of a ten-year-old with a cold. "Perhaps that'll teach you to do as you're told and wear your coat."

– a 'political' model. Illness is a signal of surrender or defiance to an oppressing society. Does, for instance, unemployment 'cause' peptic ulceration; or should workers with low back pain be referred to a Trades Union to negotiate improved conditions?

– a 'behavioural' model. Illness can be manipulative behaviour designed to produce a desired response from other people. How many patients remove themselves from clinics and waiting lists once compensation claims have been settled?

– a 'psychoanalytical' model. Illness is the ego's attempt to defend itself against unresolved unconscious conflicts. Before you dismiss this as untestable, ask yourself why cancer is more likely to arise within 18 months of a bereavement. There's an opportunity for research – 'The Immunology of the Death Wish'.

– a 'cognitive dissonance' model. Illness is the result of inescapable discrepancies between the patient's idealized self-image and reality. Anorexia nervosa is one example that comes to mind [3].

– a 'systems theory' model. Illness is a regulating factor modifying or stabilizing a family's interpersonal processes. A six-year-old developed asthma when her parents' marriage broke down and divorce looked likely. Because she became so ill, however, they 'had' to stay together.

– an 'antipsychiatric' model. Illness is the booby prize for the loser in a family's internal power struggle. A mother brought her son up from the day he was born with constant reminders that "although I wouldn't swop you for a daughter, you'll only grow up a no-good like your father." As a child he had undiagnosed abdominal pains; in adult life he became schizophrenic.

– a 'radical' model. Illness is an invented label attached by a monopolistic medical profession in order to catch, subjugate and exploit its clients. Ask Ivan Illich [1] about this one – he in turn would ask you to explain different rates for tonsillectomy and hysterectomy under different health care systems, or to justify your treatment of mild hypertension or hypercholesterolaemia.

– a 'sociological' model. 'Illness' is what you call homosexuality, or delinquency, or school refusal if you want doctors to deal with it. If you want lawyers to deal with them, you call them 'anti-social behaviour'.

– a 'humanistic' model. Illness is a sign of frustrated human potential and an opportunity for personal growth. A middle-aged executive begins to suffer chest pains but has a normal exercise ECG. This either means he should have coronary angiograms or that he should review his diet, his occupation, and his way of life. The extreme slogan of this model would be "Death is Nature's way of making you slow down."

Four doctors on holiday went out to shoot duck – a physician, a surgeon, a pathologist and a GP. When the first flight of duck flew over, the physician took aim, but then lowered his gun without firing.

"Why didn't you shoot?", asked the others.

"Because I hadn't excluded the possibility that they might be parrots," he replied.

Next it was the GPs turn, but he too failed to fire as the birds went over.

"Why ever not?", they asked.

"Because I thought I'd better get a second opinion that they were indeed duck," he said.

When the third flight went over, the surgeon let fly with both barrels. Fifteen birds fell from the sky. He turned to the pathologist and said,

"Have a look at those for me, old man, and tell me if one of them's a duck."

PITSTOP

CASE HISTORY

Harriet, a relatively inexperienced trainee, learned a lot from an old man, Ben, a widower. Ben would come two or three times a week during Harriet's first two months in general practice, always late for his appointment, always presenting vague or unlikely symptoms, and never admitting he ever felt better. She was never able to diagnose a definite medical condition, and all her good suggestions for cheering himself up fell on deaf ears. Harriet felt her normal friendliness gradually turning to irritation. Harriet discussed Ben with her trainer.

"How does he make you feel?", asked the trainer.

"As if I want to run away, as if he's overwhelming me with problems, as if I can never give him enough," said Harriet.

"Think about those three 'as if' feelings," said her trainer, "and ask yourself where they come from. Are they your feelings, or Ben's? I think they could be Ben's, because you didn't have them until he brought them into the room. Maybe *he* feels like running away, maybe *he* feels overwhelmed, maybe he feels *he* doesn't have enough strength to carry on."

The next time she saw Ben, Harriet cut short his usual recital of problems. "Look", she said, "I was thinking, the way your life is, you might be feeling lonely, and overwhelmed by everything you have to do, and I expect you wonder sometimes whether you can manage to keep going."

Ben's eyes misted. He reached for a handkerchief, blew his nose, and said, "I still miss her so, Molly, that was my wife." For the next ten minutes he told Harriet of their life together, her unexpected death two years earlier, how she had been his strength, how he had never expected to have to cope without her, and how he still grieved. Harriet felt a tightness in her own throat as he talked, and found herself looking forward to seeing him again. "Next week when you come," she told him, "just come and tell me how you've been managing. I expect Molly would have been proud of you."

MODELS OF THE CONSULTATION

Until recently the notion that the process of consulting merited any special attention would have been widely discounted. In the 'medical model' described earlier, the consultation serves merely as the setting within which the doctor gets on with the job of diagnosing and treating. In the out-patient department at St Elsewhere's you can still see this philosophy in action. But when the penny began to drop that patients don't function purely as machines, they have feelings too, (and what's more, so do doctors), serious attention began to be paid to what was going on behind and beneath the purely clinical business of the consultation. One of the first attempts at understanding the consultation process was the 'role model'.

The 'role model'

Roles are 'shorthand outlines' of the ways people are expected to behave in different social settings, and each individual acts out many roles according to the circumstances of the moment. One man may combine the roles of husband, father, son, lover, boss, friend, shopkeeper, ratepayer, darts team captain and blackmail victim, each of which will structure his relationship with different people on different occasions. In each role he will accept various rules, contracts and expectations, and will in turn impose expectations on other people – wife, children, mother, mistress, customers – whose roles in each setting are complementary to his own.

The role theory of patient–doctor relationships starts by describing the expectations each has of the roles of 'doctor' and 'patient', and looks at the rules and contracts (stated and implied) governing their interaction.

Traditionally, when a patient enters the 'sick role', he temporarily hands over partial or complete responsibility for his well-being to the doctor. He accepts some restriction of his capacity to make free choices about his health, and grants the doctor some degree of power of attorney to make decisions for him. He is expected to acknowledge his own vulnerability and the doctor's authority. Adopting the sick role may allow him to opt out of some of his other roles, such as breadwinner, and legitimates his behaving in a more regressed and dependent way, such as staying in bed and having special meals served. However, the sick role also places an obligation on the patient to seek recovery, and failure to comply with this leads to social disapproval and withdrawal of privileges.

Every society assigns to certain individuals the responsibility for relieving the physical and spiritual pain endemic in the human condition. In this sense society itself is 'iatrogenic' – it creates doctors. The role of doctor (and also priest) is endowed with power, authority and respect, both in recognition of his anticipated skill and dedication and also in preparation for the Atlantean burden of suffering he is required to shoulder. In exchange for this esteem the doctor is expected to give a ration of his exclusive skill and attention to whatever problem the patient presents, and to pursue singlemindedly the patient's best interests.

The 'oracle and suppliant' flavour of a traditional medical consultation is reinforced by the trappings or 'role signals' that attend it. The consultation usually takes place on the doctor's home territory (or if on the patient's, only after he has humbled himself with a show of helplessness). Access to the doctor requires the patient to state his needs in a way acceptable to the doctor as a 'ticket of admission' or 'password', usually in the form of symptoms. There may be 'access rituals' like appointment systems and waiting lists, or attendant spirits such as receptionists and nurses to be propitiated. The patient may be asked to make gifts of his own body fluids to secure the attention of the doctor. The doctor is symbolically robed in white coat or expensive suit, enthroned behind a desk in an upholstered chair, giving away nothing of his private thoughts and feelings. The patient by contrast is actually or symbolically naked, sitting (since nobody kneels these days!) on a hard chair, with every part of his body and psyche potentially accessible to the doctor's scrutiny. The doctor's utterances, like those of the Pythoness at the Delphic oracle, may be few, ambiguous, or couched in language difficult for the patient to interpret.

'Doctor-centred' or 'patient-centred' consultations

During the 1970s and 1980s there began to be felt a sense of discomfort with the medical model and the traditional doctor/patient roles. The voice of the consumer is heard in our land; the mood of the time is reflected in words like 'holistic' and 'deprofessionalization'. Many doctors welcomed, and some indeed led, the move away from autocratic stereotypes. Most doctors have now clambered down, with varying degrees of eagerness, from their traditional pedestal. Against this background it is not surprising that many analyses of the consultation have been in terms of 'doctor or patient centredness' – the extent to which the consultation's agenda, process, and outcome are determined by the doctor or by the patient.

These same categories – doctor-centred or patient-centred – can be applied to models of the consultation. Doctor-centred models describe the doctor's aims or behaviour; patient-centred models focus on the patient's aims or behaviour.

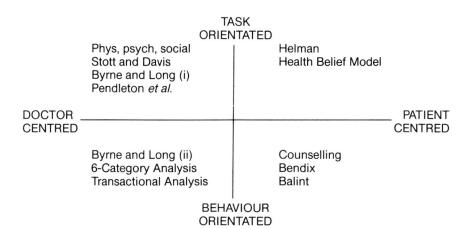

Figure A3.2 Classification of consultation models

'Task'- or 'behaviour'-orientated models

A second axis of classification for consultation models is the degree to which they focus on the tasks to be achieved as opposed to the behavioural methods used in the consultation. Another way of describing the same thing is to distinguish 'content' from 'process'.

In Figure A3.2, I've taken a selection, by no means exhaustive, of current models, and positioned them in relation to the two axes of 'doctor- or patient-centred' and 'task- or behaviour-orientated'. I'm then going to offer a brief summary of each model. The purpose of this is not to overwhelm you with erudition (though it may, and that doesn't matter). I want rather to bring you to a point of 'stimulus overload' so that you might the more gratefully consider the diagnosis and treatment plan offered in subsequent chapters of this book.

Task-orientated models

In these task-orientated models, the consultation is viewed as an amalgam of separate and definable tasks, a checklist of points to be covered. The 'hand holding the check-list' can be either the doctor's or the patient's; the first four of the six models are doctor-centred. Note that in all these models, the methods to be used in achieving the various goals are not specified, being left to the doctor's ingenuity or previous experience.

'Physical, psychological and social' terms

This well-known triad derives from the job definition of a GP formulated by a working party of The Royal College of General Practitioners as the starting point for their seminal study of the educational framework of Vocational Training, *The Future General Practitioner – Learning and Teaching* [4]. In their words:

> The general practitioner is a doctor who provides personal, primary and continuing medical care to individuals and families. He may attend his patients in their homes, in his consulting-room or sometimes in hospital. He accepts the responsibility for making an initial decision on every problem his patient may present to him, consulting with specialists when he thinks it appropriate to do so... His diagnoses will be composed in physical, psychological and social terms. He will intervene educationally, preventively and therapeutically to promote his patient's health.

The effect of this very simple model is to extend the doctor's thinking process beyond consideration of the purely organic, and to include the patient's emotional, family, social and environmental circumstances in his diagnosis. If the doctor's awareness of these factors is heightened, he is more likely to include them in his management.

Stott and Davis

In a very thoughtful paper called *The exceptional potential in each primary care consultation*, Stott and Davis [5] describe four areas which could be systematically explored each time a patient consults (see Figure A3.3).

A	**B**
Management of presenting problems	Modification of help-seeking behaviours
C	**D**
Management of continuing problems	Opportunistic health promotion

Figure A3.3 The potential in each primary care consultation (Stott and Davis, 1979)

Besides dealing with the presenting problem (A), the doctor could:

(B) modify the patient's help-seeking behaviour, e.g. by educating the patient about the natural history and self-medication of minor illness, or suggesting how better to use the practice's appointment system;

(C) review any of the patient's known long-term problems, by for instance checking the blood pressure, or asking about drinking habits or the state of marital relations;

and (D) take the opportunity to undertake health promotion measures such as vaccination, cervical screening or smoking advice.

Byrne and Long (i)

In 1976 Patrick Byrne and Barrie Long published *Doctors Talking to Patients – A study of the verbal behaviour of general practitioners consulting in their surgeries* [6]. They analysed more than 2000 tape recordings of consultations made by over 100 doctors, and derived a classification of the sequence of events in the consultation which has underpinned the studies of most subsequent researchers. Byrne and Long describe six 'phases' forming a logical structure to the consultation. (They admit "the logical form ... rarely appears in practice and should be seen as an ideal.") The six phases are:

Phase I   The doctor establishes a relationship with the patient.
Phase II   The doctor either attempts to discover or actually discovers the reason for the patient's attendance.
Phase III The doctor conducts a verbal or physical examination or both.
Phase IV The doctor, or the doctor and the patient, or the patient (in that order of probability) consider the condition.
Phase V   The doctor, and occasionally the patient, detail further treatment or further investigation.
Phase VI The consultation is terminated usually by the doctor.

The usefulness of this simple model became apparent when Byrne and Long went on to look in more detail at those 'dysfunctional' consultations where something evidently went wrong and confusion or bad feeling ensued. Consultations are particularly likely to go wrong if there are shortcomings in Phase II or Phase IV, or both. If the patient's reasons for attending (Phase II) are incompletely grasped, the doctor either finds himself in a consultational cul-de-sac, or is faced with remarks like "by the way, doctor", or "while I'm here", or "and another thing", all gambits which in accordance with the law of diminishing returns usually reduce the doctor's concentration and goodwill. If the doctor is not seen to be giving adequate consideration to the full range of ramifications of the patient's problem (Phase IV), the patient will feel misunderstood, with obvious dangers of dissatisfaction and poor compliance.

Pendleton et al.

The book by Pendleton, Schofield, Tate and Havelock (*The Consultation – An Approach to Learning and Teaching*) has already been referred to (Chapter A2, reference [3], Figure A2.4), when we were looking at versions of the skills training process. These authors also detail "seven tasks which, taken together, form comprehensive and coherent aims for any consultation ... The first five tasks are separate statements of what the doctor needs to achieve, while the final two tasks deal with the use of time and resources, and the creation of an effective doctor–patient relationship ... (The tasks) can be achieved using many different approaches and skills, (and are) set out in a logical sequence, but this is not necessarily the order they will be tackled in each consultation"[7]. The 'tasks' are listed as:

(1) To define the reason for the patient's attendance, including:
    (i)   the nature and history of the problems;
    (ii)   their aetiology;
    (iii) the patient's ideas, concerns and expectations;
    (iv) the effects of the problems.

(2) To consider other problems:
    (i)   continuing problems;
    (ii)   at-risk factors.

(3) With the patient, to choose an appropriate action for each problem.

(4) To achieve a shared understanding of the problems with the patient.

(5) To involve the patient in the management and encourage him to accept appropriate responsibility.

(6) To use time and resources appropriately:
    (i)   in the consultation;
    (ii)   in the long term.

(7) To establish or maintain a relationship with the patient which helps to achieve the other tasks.

Helman's 'folk model' and the Health Belief model, while still task-orientated, view the consultation predominantly through the patient's eyes.

Helman's 'folk model'

Cecil Helman is a medical anthropologist, with constantly enlightening insights into the cultural factors in health and illness. He suggests [8] that a patient with a problem comes to a doctor seeking answers to six questions:

(1) What has happened?
(2) Why has it happened?

(3) Why to me?

(4) Why now?

(5) What would happen if nothing were done about it?

(6) What should I do about it or whom should I consult for further help?

Health Belief Model

Patients' decisions to accept or reject medical advice are affected by many factors, not all of them within the easy control of the doctor. The beliefs and motivations the patient brings into the consultation significantly govern the understandings and intentions he takes away from it. Becker and Maiman [9] synthesized a number of patient beliefs and attitudes into a 'health belief model'. Their model includes elements such as

– The individual's general interest in health matters, which might correlate with personality, social class, ethnic group;

– How vulnerable the patient feels himself to be to a particular disease, and how severe a threat the disease is believed to pose;

– The individual's estimate of the benefits of treatment weighed against the costs, risks or inconvenience of treatment;

– Factors that prompt the individual to take action, such as the development of alarming symptoms, advice from family or friends, or items in the mass media.

From the doctor's point of view, a useful 'aide-memoire' to eliciting considerations like these is:

IDEAS
CONCERNS
and EXPECTATIONS.

Behaviour-orientated models

The remaining models look less at the tasks to be achieved in the consultation, but rather at the range of behaviours that are called for within it. The more patient-centred ones deal with styles of doctor behaviour which draw out the patient's own problem-solving capacity with minimum intrusion of the doctor's agenda. The more doctor-centred models are concerned with extending the doctor's personal repertoire of consulting behaviours, which he can use to further the patient's interests as he sees them.

Byrne and Long (ii)

Byrne and Long's description of the six 'phases' of the consultation has already been mentioned. Their study also analysed the range of verbal behaviours that doctors used when talking to their patients. They described a spectrum ranging from a heavily doctor-dominated consultation, with any contribution from the patient as good as excluded, to a virtual monologue by the patient untrammelled by any input from the doctor. Between these extremes they described a gradation of styles from closed information-gathering to non-directive counselling, depending on whether the doctor was more interested in developing his own line of thought or the patient's. A selection of these component verbal behaviours is displayed in Figure A3.4.

Byrne and Long used this model to derive profiles of doctors' consulting styles according to the frequency with which they used the various types of behaviour. Depressingly, they "discovered that the doctors in our study appeared to have achieved set routines of interviewing patients, and that few of them demonstrated the capacity for variations of normal style and performance to meet the needs of those patients whose problems did not fit into an organic disease pattern."

Fortunately, this pessimistic view of the immutability of professional style has not been shared by later bearers of the educational torch. The lesson to be drawn from Byrne and Long's study is not that doctors can't change, but rather that they need more to help them change than merely looking at themselves in a mirror.

Six Category Intervention Analysis

In the mid-1970s the humanistic psychologist John Heron [10] developed a simple but comprehensive model of the array of interventions a doctor (counsellor or therapist) could use with a patient (client). Within an overall setting of concern for the patient's best interests, the doctor's interventions fall into one of six categories. The categories are:

(1) **Prescriptive** – giving advice or instructions, being critical or directive;

(2) **Informative** – imparting new knowledge, instructing or interpreting;

(3) **Confronting** – challenging a restrictive attitude or behaviour, giving direct feedback within a caring context;

	Use of patient's knowledge and experience			*Use of doctor's special skill and knowledge*	
Patient-centred					*Doctor-centred*
"Absent doctor"	Silence Listening Reflecting	Clarifying and Interpreting	Analysing and Probing	Gathering information	"Absent patient"
Boredom	Using silence	Offering observation	Direct question	Direct question	Rejecting pt's offers
Indifference	Seeking pt's ideas	Summarizing to open up	Correlational question	Closed question	Rejecting pt's ideas
Not Listening	Using pt's ideas	Repeating for confirmation	Placing events in sequence	Correlational question	Evading pt's question
Being "miles away"	Encouraging	Seeking pt's ideas	Suggesting	Self-answering question	Drowning pt's words
Confused noise	Indicating understanding	Placing events in sequence	Offering feeling	Suggesting	Justifying self
	Clarifying	Challenging	Exploring	Placing events in sequence	Confused noise
	Reflecting	Open-ended question	Open-ended question	Repeating for confirmation	
	Offering observation	Concealed question	Repeating for confirmation	Reassuring	
				Justifying self	
				Chastising	
				Summarizing to close off	

pt = patient

Figure A3.4 Classification of doctors' verbal behaviours, after Byrne and Long

(4) **Cathartic** — seeking to release emotion in the form of weeping, laughter, trembling or anger;

(5) **Catalytic** – encouraging the patient to discover and explore his own latent thoughts and feelings;

(6) **Supportive** – offering comfort and approval, affirming the patient's intrinsic value.

Each category has a clear function within the total consultation. In training seminars the categories can be practised separately, then gradually integrated into sequences of greater complexity.

Transactional Analysis (TA)

Many doctors will be familiar with Eric Berne's model of the human psyche [11] as consisting of three 'ego-states' – Parent, Adult and Child. At any given moment each of us is in a state of mind when we think, feel, behave, react and have attitudes as if we were either a critical or caring Parent, a logical Adult, or a spontaneous or dependent Child. Many general practice consultations are conducted between a Parental doctor and a Child-like patient. This transaction is not always in the best interests of either party, and a familiarity with TA introduces a welcome flexibility into the doctor's repertoire which can break out of the repetitious cycles of behaviour ('games') into which some consultations can degenerate.

Counselling

The extreme of patient-centred behaviour is represented by a formal counselling model, in which a number of GP's have been trained. The essence of this approach is to allow the patient to explore in his own way and at his own pace the origins, implications and solutions to his problem. This requires of the doctor the ability to keep his own opinions and suggestions to himself, and instead to use techniques such as reflecting, interpreting and the judicious use of silence in order to bring the patient to an insight which is his own and nobody else's.

Bendix

In a pithy and eminently practical book called *The Anxious Patient* [12] a Dutch psychotherapist Torben Bendix has succeeded in distilling the essential ingredients of counselling into seven 'rules of thumb'. For anyone with the inclination but not the confidence to embark on non-directive counselling, this book is the equivalent of a 'Teach Yourself' manual.

Balint

Michael Balint was a Hungarian psychoanalyst who in the 1950's led a series of case-discussion seminars with general practitioners at the Tavistock Clinic, London. The experience of this group formed the basis of one of the most important of all contributions to general practice literature. *The Doctor, His Patient and the Illness* [13]. Balint's influence shaped the professional development of a generation of GP's. His pioneering study explored the importance of the doctor–patient relationship, the use of transference and counter-transference in diagnosis and treatment, and the pharmacology of the drug 'doctor'.

CASE HISTORY (CONTINUED)

A fortnight after Harriet had her closer encounter with Ben, another doctor in the practice was called urgently to see him during the night. He had acute abdominal pain and vomiting. He was admitted to hospital immediately, diagnosed as having large bowel obstruction, and later that night had a laparotomy. A carcinoma of descending colon was resected. After a stormy postoperative course he came home with a defunctioning colostomy.

Harriet knew she ought to go and see him at home, but felt guilty that she had not diagnosed his condition earlier instead of 'wasting time', as she put it, talking about his bereavement. With some trepidation she knocked at his door.

Ben, far from being critical, was of course delighted to see her. Cutting short her awkward explanations and apologies, he told her, "Anyone could have sent me into hospital. But you were the one who helped me settle Molly to her rest, and very few doctors could have done that."

"Do you remember," Ben continued, "telling me you thought I was lonely, and overwhelmed, and not sure whether I could carry on? I think it's your turn to feel like that now."

Harriet felt so completely understood that she burst into tears, and so completely relieved that she laughed at the same time. She had lost track of who had what feeling and why; there remained only a sense of communion. When she got back to the surgery so she told her trainer what had happened. He didn't seem surprised.

That afternoon Harriet found a parcel on her desk. Inside was a copy of Balint's book, a present from her trainer, inscribed "When the Pupil is ready, the Master appears". That day Harriet grew up.

PITSTOP

> For hundreds of pages the closely-reasoned arguments unroll, axioms and theorems interlock. And what remains with us in the end? A general sense that the world can be expressed in closely-reasoned arguments, in interlocking axioms and theorems.
>
> Michael Frayn, 1974

> Hard is the Journey,
> Hard is the Journey,
> So many turnings,
> And now where am I?
>
> Li Po, c. 750 AD

Conclusions

Let's step back from all this theorizing and see if we can tell the wood from the trees. It's apparent that creating models is an attempt to get clear in one's mind what to do in the consultation and how to do it. The trouble is, as someone said, when you've got two doctors you've got four opinions. The abundance of models is either confusion or richness, depending on how you look at it.

What are we to do with our models? How are we to use them? As Mark Twain said, "When you've got a hammer in your hand, an awful lot of things look like nails." The answer is so simple every child can see it.

Having models of things is a normal feature of children's play. It is normal for a child to sharpen his or her imagination on 'let's pretend' versions of the real world. Consulting isn't child's play, but we can learn as if it was. We can learn what to do with the range of models offered to us by thinking about what a baby does with all the cuddly toys its doting relatives and friends press upon it as soon as it is born. Before long the baby becomes attached to one particular item – let's say a teddy-bear – in preference to all the others. (And it's not usually the most expensive or intricate teddy that the baby falls for.) For a time the child won't let it out of his sight, and feels lost without it . Gradually, however, the child matures, and the teddy from which he was once inseparable is only cuddled occasionally, in moments of stress, before being finally forgotten.

In the normal development of every baby a transition has to be made, between at first perceiving the entire world as an extended part of the child's own body and the later realization that there are events and objects separate from the self that have to be related to. Newborn babies appear to have only a very hazy perception of the world beyond their own bodies, and seem to experience no boundary between themselves and their environment. Within a few weeks or months, however, an inkling develops that the world divides itself into 'me' and 'not me'. The major task of infancy (and some would say of life itself) is the exploration of the 'self–other relationship'.

According to the psychoanalyst D.W. Winnicott [14], an early step in this exploration is often the use by the child of a 'transitional object' – some special item that is not part of the infant's body and yet at the same time is not fully realized as belonging to the outer world. Commonly the transitional object, the child's first 'not me' possession, is a teddy or a woollen blanket. It is so special and significant for the child that it functions in many ways as if it were a part of himself, yet things happen to it that don't happen to its owner. It gets grubby, and mislaid, and grown-ups talk differently to it. In this way the baby is eased into encountering the properties of the world beyond his skin. The special object inhabits a kind of intermediate space between the individual and the environment, between inner psychic reality and the public world we all share.

The relationships between child, world and transitional object are complex and paradoxical. They take place in an area which is neither wholly objective nor entirely subjective. In Winnicott's words, this intermediate area is "a resting-place for the individual engaged in the perpetual human task of keeping inner and outer reality separate yet interrelated." The transitional object – teddy, blanket – is a part of the real world, created by adults and presented to the child. Yet if it is the world that makes the object, it is the child who makes it special. The child endows it with properties which an outsider could not have predicted. And so the teddy bear belongs simultaneously to two realities – an objective one where it is subject to the usual laws of the physical universe, and the child's subjective one where it becomes so larded with his own projections and significance that it forms an extension of his own personality. This paradox of being neither 'real' nor 'imaginary', but both at the same time, is never resolved. It is just accepted, tolerated and for the time being, lived with. By using the transitional object as a half-way stage, the child gradually becomes able to differentiate inner and outer realities. Ultimately, its purpose served, the 'real' teddy is forgotten and thrown away, while its effects on the child's thought and perception live on.

The analogy between transitional objects and consultation models is obvious. This chapter has reminded you that your pram is already loaded with models and toys and teddies of all descriptions. Maybe you have already experienced the paradox of wondering whether the models are 'real' or not, and felt the dilemma of not knowing whether and how to play with the model while you are consulting. The half-way stage can be very uncomfortable. This paradox forms the subject of the next chapter. We shall then go on to choose a nice teddy, play with it, learn with it, and finally grow out of it.

A4
On having two heads

There is a road from the eye to the heart that does not go through the intellect.

G.K. Chesterton

We are thinking beings, and we cannot exclude the intellect from participating in any of our functions.

William James

A TUTORIAL

Me: ... so that's the consultation buttoned up, then. All you have to do now is go away and practise, make some video recordings of yourself consulting, and correct whatever faults you see. Bear in mind the importance of making a diagnosis in physical, psychological and social terms; make sure you're clear about the patient's reasons for attending; deal with all his ideas, concerns and expectations; don't forget that what you and the patient mean by a problem might be two different things; remember the consultation is an opportunity for health education, screening and managing chronic disease; treat the patient as an equal partner in the decision-making, otherwise you might not get the right balance between being doctor-centred and patient-centred; so it's important to maintain an awareness of what's going on in the doctor–patient relationship. Let me know when you're happy about that, and we'll move on to another tutorial topic.

Chris: I have a problem.

Me: Tell me your problem.

Chris: It's not that I don't know what to do, it's that I don't do what I know.

Me: That sounds important. Say it again.

Chris: IT'S NOT THAT I DON'T KNOW WHAT TO DO, IT'S THAT I DON'T DO WHAT I KNOW.

Me: Go on.

Chris: When I see a good GP consulting, I think "That's really skilful," and I wonder "Is it just experience, or confidence, or flair, or knowing the patient for a long time; and is it something I could learn, or have I just got to be patient until I've enough experience too?" Then I find there are all these models and analyses and frameworks and training pro-grammes, and I can then see more precisely what it was that I admired in the good GPs performance, and I think "Okay, I'll try and do it that way." And when I sit down and read about these ideas, or we talk about them, it makes perfect sense and sounds not too hard.

But then I start my surgery, full of good intentions about, say, finding out the patient's own ideas of what's wrong, and one of two things happens. Either I'm so preoccupied with getting my preplanned questions in that I concentrate on them to the exclusion of everything else; or else I get so absorbed in dealing with the patient that I forget to do the one thing I'd intended. It's very discouraging.

Me: Shall I tell you why that happens?

Chris: Tell me.

Me: I'll tell you in a riddle, to start with. When you're consulting with a patient, how many consultations are you having?

Chris: One.

Me: No, two. And how many voices can you hear?

Chris: Two.

Me: No, three. And how many heads are in the room?

Chris: Two.

Me: No, four.

Chris: Explain.

Me: I'll start with the voices. You can hear the patient's voice, and your own 'out loud' voice. But there's also a silent voice in your head, the voice of your thoughts, whispering a commentary or instructions or questions in your mind's ear. It whispers things like "we're running late, get a move on," or "I'm bored," or "I don't know what to do next – how about getting a haemoglobin?". There's an extra voice with which you conduct an internal dialogue.

Chris: I see. What about the heads?

Me: It helps to think of the internal dialogue as being like having a second head on your shoulders, an invisible one that nevertheless whispers in your ear to the real head that talks out loud. The patient has a second head too, but you can't hear what that one's saying.

So there are really two consultations going on. There's the 'outer' one between you and the patient, the 'out loud' one that the patient knows about and a video recorder would pick up. And then there's the 'inner consultation' – the thoughts that go back and forth between you and your second head.

In mysticism this phenomenon is sometimes called 'the Self observing the Self', but there's nothing mystical about it. Everyone knows that there is an important part of our mind which hovers around the edge of awareness and which emerges in our thoughts, our fantasies and dreams, our ideas and intuition. People variously call this the 'preconscious', the 'subconscious' or the 'unconscious', and it has a sound base in neurology which we'll consider in due course. Our sense organs detect more information than we actually register; we perceive more than we actually attend to; we think more than we say; and we imagine more than we do. It's part of the way in which our intelligence explores possibilities in advance of reality. The same subliminal semi-automatic part of the mind also assesses and selects which aspects of all the potentially available experience will reach our full conscious attention. So think of the second head as being both an 'explorer', looking out into the world, inwards to the imagination and back into memory for useful information, and also as a 'censor', saying "do this, not that; go here, not there."

Chris: I understand the analogy of having two heads – it's a good description of the difficulty I was telling you about. But how will it help?

Me: It goes further than just an analogy. Of course, the image of having two heads is just that – an image. But the experience of having an internal train of thought quite separate from one's outward flow of speech and behaviour is perfectly real. It's inherent in the way (or rather, the ways) the brain works.

As to how it will help; if the comments from your second head become too insistent or complicated, then you get distracted from the outer consultation. Your concentration goes, and you grow frustrated because your internal dialogue doesn't match up with the turn of events in the real consultation. Having a successful outer consultation with the patient depends on having an inner consultation that contributes and works *for* you, rather than getting in the way and working *against* you. Both heads are trying to help; every part of your mind works to your advantage to the best of its ability. So we need to understand what each head is trying to achieve, so that we can let each get on with what it's good at and train it not to interfere in what it's not good at.

Let's take some examples of what I mean by 'comments from the second head'. I'll lay this out in two columns, 'outer consultation' on the left and 'inner consultation' on the right.

OUTER CONSULTATION	SECOND HEAD COMMENTS
It's half way through morning surgery. You buzz for the next patient.	
	I wonder how this will go. Try and look friendly. Maintain eye contact, smile, lean forward a bit.
"Hallo Mr Grizzly. Come in, sit down. What can I do for you?"	
	I don't like this man. I've never liked him, he's prickly. Even now I can feel my neck and hands and jaw getting tense. If he says I'm too young to be a doctor ...
"I'ld like a check-up please, doctor."	
	That means he's afraid of something but he wants me to guess what. Heart disease, maybe, or the big C.
You ask some questions, then examine him. There's nothing abnormal to find ...	

"What can I do for you, Mr Grizzly?"

54

I'm doing this rather well.
Perhaps he's not so bad after all.
Who does he remind me of? Maybe
that's why I don't like him. I
know, that dreadful anatomy lecturer
I once had.

... but he is a smoker.

He really ought to have a chest
X-ray, but he'll think I think he
thinks he's got lung cancer and
I'm just humouring him, so he
probably won't go; but it is just
possible, but I can't say in case
he thinks I think that's what he's
got, and then what will he think?

"Mr Grizzly, part of the
routine check-up is a chest X-ray. I'll just
fill this form in, and you send it to the
hospital."

He's not looking at me. Look at
me when I'm talking to you. He's
in a world of his own. I wonder
what he's thinking. Coo-eee!

"Got that then?"

Now, have I forgotten anything?
Height and weight, urine, blood
pressure, chest X-ray. It's not
worth doing a haemoglobin. I'll
do that when he comes back. If he
comes back. Or an ECG. Maybe an
ECG next.

"Come back and see me about a
week after you have your X-ray –"

– when with a bit of luck I'll be on
holiday.

He leaves.

Not bad. Try asking a few more
open-ended questions. He took
five minutes too long, though.
I'll need to hurry the next
patient along a bit. I could
murder a cup of coffee. Who's
next? Oh no, Mrs Linger. She
always takes a long time, blast her ...

EXERCISE

In your mind, run through a few patients you have seen recently. See whether you can recall some of your own internal dialogue. It's not really enough for you just to think 'Oh yes, I expect I have thoughts like that.' It's worth getting a piece of paper and jotting some of them down.

Two heads are better than one (?)

I had a young cousin once who was given a plastic assembly kit for his birthday. He looked at the picture on the outside of the box and saw that it was a model of a super-looking fighter plane. But when he opened the box, and saw all the fiddly little pieces and the complicated instructions, he got a bit anxious. He wasn't sure whether he should try and make the model on his own, or ask one of his friends to do it with him, or ask a grown-up for help. Part of him wanted to do it all by himself, but another part didn't want it to end up a mess. Eventually he asked his Dad what he should do.

"Two heads are better than one, son," said his father. "I'll watch over your shoulder while you do it."

My cousin set to work. But the glue went everywhere, and the cockpit didn't fit, and he dropped one of the wheels onto the carpet and couldn't find it. Before long, his father was fuming with frustration at the mess his son was making.

"Here, let me," he said crossly. And he took over. He found the missing wheel, and trimmed the surplus glue from the joints, and got the cockpit to fit. But the lad had got bored and had gone out to play football with his friends. When he came indoors again, he found his father holding the finished plane and pretending to fly it round the room, going "Brrrm brrrrrrm". He thought his Dad looked silly.

Naming the two heads

British social protocol dictates that people who have not been introduced may not begin to get to know each other. So I want to give names to the two heads. I want to call them the **Organizer** and the **Responder**.

Your two heads take it in turns to be in charge. Sometimes the Organizer is the one on your shoulders doing the talking, with the Responder invisibly whispering in your ear; and at other times the Organizer takes a back seat while the Responder takes the lead. They alternate. Although, in order to draw a clear distinction between the different functions of the two heads, I shall polarize my description almost to the point of caricature, in fact the two heads are merely extreme positions of a mental pendulum that swings smoothly to both sides, or different faces of one coin. I want now to describe the qualities of each head; then go on to show how in real life they work together in partnership; and how the metaphor of two heads is in accord with contemporary neurological thought.

The Organizer

The Organizer is the intellectual part of your brain, the part that most of your formal education has been aimed at. During the consultation it analyses what is going on in a logical way. It plans and calculates and anticipates, trying to stay one jump ahead all the time. It likes to be in control, and all the time is waiting for a chance to take over. It is the part of your mind that sets goals, both for you and the patient; it is the part that 'wants' certain things to happen. The Organizer's preferred mode of thought is analytical, logical and verbal. It takes a 'white collar' managerial role in the conduct of the consultation.

The Organizer and the Responder

The Responder

The Responder is an altogether more spontaneous and naïve part of you. Where the Organizer is intellectual, the Responder is intuitive. It notices everything uncritically. Like Janus, it faces in two directions. It pays attention outwardly via your sense organs to what the patient is communicating verbally and especially non-verbally; and it also registers the stream of internal messages arising within you, the doctor, keeping track of your own feelings and emotions and sensations. All the time the Responder is wondering what to do with the mass of information it can't help noticing. The Responder is perfectly happy to be carried along by the experience of the present moment. Its preferred mode of thought is pattern recognition, imagery, and the association of ideas. Whereas the Organizer thinks by a process of logical deduction, the Responder perceives in a 'Gestalt' way, filling in the gaps of perception and reacting to the patterns it infers. Where the Organizer is managerial, the Responder is a blue-collar artisan.

I'll go through the 'Second Head Comments' from the extract of 'Inner Consultation' given earlier, this time indicating with (O) and (R) which head is whispering the internal dialogue. On the right is some further explanation.

INNER CONSULTATION	COMMENTS
(R) I wonder how this will go.	
	The Responder notices a little anxiety, some slight 'fear of the unknown'.
(O) Try and look friendly.	
	The Organizer tells you what to do about the tension the Responder has noticed ...
(O) Maintain eye contact, smile, lean forward a bit.	
	... and, remembering some of the things you learned about non-verbal communication, specifies precisely how to "try and look friendly".
(R) I don't like this man. I've never liked him, he's prickly.	
	The Responder remembers previous encounters with Mr Grizzly, and associates them with a bad feeling ...
(R) Even now I can feel my neck and hands and jaw getting tense.	
	... and confirms to you that the same bad feeling is starting this time too.
(R) If he says I'm too young to be a doctor ...	

The Responder senses a chance to
display a currently-sensitive
attitude, and, whatever the
patient says, is poised to feel
patronized.
> Tension + Negative Attitude
> = equals Potential Trouble

When it hears the patient's
request for a check-up, an opening
gambit full of double messages,
the Organizer is quick to jump in
and defuse the situation.

(O) That means he's afraid of
something but he wants me to
guess what. Heart disease,
maybe, or the big C.

The Organizer advises "don't get
cross, get competent," and makes some
suggestions.

(R) I'm doing this rather well.
Perhaps he's not so bad after
all. Who does he remind me of?
Maybe that's why I don't like him.

You're feeling better. The Responder
pats you on the back and shifts to an
attitude of curiosity . . .

(R) I know, that dreadful
anatomy lecturer I once had.

. . . and, having made a connection
between this patient and a previous
acquaintance, feels satisfied.

(O) He really ought to have a
chest X-ray, but he'll think I think
he thinks he's got lung cancer and I'm
just humouring him, so he probably won't
go; but it is just possible, but I can't
say in case he thinks I think that's what
he's got, and then what will he think?

Thinking ahead and planning your next
remarks to the patient, the Organizer
is getting itself in a muddle.

(R) He's not looking at me.
Look at me when I'm talking to
you. He's in a world of his own.
I wonder what he's thinking.

The Responder sees that your
speech (largely the Organizer's)
isn't having the anticipated effect
on the patient.

(R) Coo-eee!

The Responder interrupts what you
are saying, and probably
communicates its concern non-verbally
by having you try to get eye contact
with the patient.

(O) Now, have I forgotten anything? Height and weight, urine, blood pressure, chest X-ray. It's not worth doing a haemoglobin. I'll do that when he comes back. If he comes back. Or an ECG. Maybe an ECG next –

The Organizer is thinking ahead, making a clinical management plan. But the Responder still isn't sure it likes this patient.

(R) – when with a bit of luck I'll be on holiday.

(O) Not bad. Try asking a few more open-ended questions. He took five minutes too long, though. I'll need to hurry the next patient along a bit.

The Organizer is quick to take credit, make a few criticisms, and issue instructions for the next consultation.

(R) I could murder a cup of coffee.

"Excuse me, but I've got a suggestion too," the Responder chimes in, with a certain insistence.

And as in your head the Organizer and the Responder begin to argue about whose ideas should take precedence, what chance does the next patient, Mrs Linger, stand of receiving your undivided attention?

Sometimes it is the Organizer who is in charge of what you are saying and doing and takes over your 'real head', the one the patient can see and hear; when this is the case the 'second head' that only you can hear is the Responder. At other times you are intent on giving your attention to what the patient says and does; on these occasions your real head becomes the Responder, and it is the Organizer that sits invisibly beside it. The inner voice that you hear alternates rapidly, moment by moment. It is as if the Organizer and the Responder were at opposite ends of a seesaw. First the Organizer may find itself in charge, down on your shoulders and on active duty, as if it carried the greater weight, while the lighter Responder floats poised and invisible, audible only to you. Then the balance of attention shifts, and the Organizer temporarily is lifted aside in favour of the Responder.

When you're perceiving sensory cues and reacting spontaneously to them, you're being a Responder.

When you're consciously making plans, and thinking carefully about how you're going to carry them out, you're being an Organizer.

If you want to be at your most intuitive, noticing the full range of sensory information that could be useful to you and reacting appropriately to it, you need to be in the Responder mode.

If you want to be at your most logical and analytical, thinking and acting systematically, you need to be in the Organizer mode.

The internal dialogue that we discussed at the start of this chapter – the 'Inner Consultation' – consists of the comments whispered in the background by whichever head is not currently in charge.

It may help to have an idea of what is happening neurologically as you oscillate between the two 'attention sets' that I have called Organizer and Responder. A gross oversimplification (but one nevertheless worth making) is to identify the Organizer mode with neural predominance of the dominant cerebral hemisphere, and the Responder mode with a functional emphasis on the non-dominant hemisphere and limbic system.

Attention, arousal, physiological homeostasis, emotion, mood, and the initial uncritical processing of sensory information are primarily the province of the brain-stem, mid-brain and limbic system. These structures function as the brain's 'auto-pilot'. In our evolutionarily more recent cerebral hemispheres there is an important division of function between left and right sides. In right-handed people and most left-handers, language is located in the left (dominant) hemisphere. The left hemisphere's way of thinking and processing information seems innately to be logical, systematic, analytical, taking things in order, verbal – in a word, Organizing. By contrast, the right hemisphere processes information non-verbally, passively, intuitively, dealing with things as a whole, using images, memories and the association of ideas. It is, in a word, Responsive. Communication pathways between the hemispheres (via the corpus callosum) and between limbic system and neo-cortex are relatively poorly established compared with the free flow of association within each hemisphere. The alternative modes of awareness that I have called Organizer and Responder represent two different positions of stable equilibrium that can be reached by our heterogeneous neural organization. An analogy would be the 'On' and 'Off' positions into which a switch can equally easily be pushed.

A brief review of the neurological evidence, and of other descriptions of the duality of the human psyche, is given in reference [1].

Press your eyeballs, and lo and behold; two moons!

Sengai

PITSTOP

THE TUTORIAL RESUMES

Me: Do you remember my cousin I was telling you about, with his plastic aeroplane?

Chris: And the father who took over and interfered, and spoiled the kid's fun? I think you were trying to put a message over about the two heads. Why?

Me: I'ld like to tell you the rest of the story.

That day ended, as the lad's mother predicted, with tears before bedtime. The finished model looked very nice, but, she asked herself, was it worth it if she ended up with a grumpy husband and an upset child? Then she had an idea for which I've ever since admired her.

The next Saturday she went to the toy shop and brought home two identical model plane kits. She gave one each to her husband and son, and said, "We're going to have a model-making competition. The prize is, I'll make the winner his favourite tea." (Wise woman, she knew they both adored sausages and baked beans!)

She sent the boy off to his bedroom with one kit, and her husband to his workshop with the other. But before they went, she gave them this single instruction.

"The only rule is, when you've each completed your model, and you show them to me, I don't want to be able to tell which of you made which. They must both look the same."

Think about it.

Chris: I guess your cousin tried a bit harder to do it neatly, and probably found he'd picked up a few hints from his Dad on the previous occasion. And his father would have had to compromise on his idea of perfection and try to match the best standard he thought his son would be capable of.

Me: And since they both wanted the same prize, nobody lost out.

Chris: That's clever. I don't suppose you told me just for interest, either.

Me: True. Two heads are better than one *just as long as* they are each working towards the same goal, and each respects the strengths and weaknesses of the other.

Chris: How does that apply to the Organizer and the Responder? I agree the internal dialogue can be distracting, but can that be

62

altered so that the two heads work in co-operation?

Me: If you want to consult to the best of your ability, we have to find ways of allowing both Organizer and Responder to make equal contributions. We do this by programming the Organizer (your left hemisphere) with goals it can easily understand and can plan how to achieve. And we equip the Responder (right hemisphere) with the component skills and resources necessary to carry out your intentions. Some of these already exist in your memory and experience; others need to be specially installed. If this sounds complicated, don't be alarmed. Your ability to learn consciously is very great, and your powers of unconscious learning are even greater.

In the remaining two chapters of Part A, I'm going to describe a simple way of moving smoothly through a consultation, via five 'checkpoints', which your Organizer will be able to handle perfectly confidently. And in Part B, I'll be reinforcing the necessary skills and resources so that they will be in place when your Responder needs them. In Part C, I'll show you how, by directing your attention in the right way, you can make sure that Organizer and Responder each do what they're best at, and only that.

———————

EXERCISE

It will help very greatly to establish the idea of the two heads if you
spend a few moments with a pencil writing in a selection of your own
captions to this cartoon. What might the second head be whispering?
Which head is the Organizer and which the Responder? Think of
several examples until you're happy you can tell the two heads apart.

A5
Keeping it simple – the consultation as a journey

A very brainy professor who wanted to know all about Zen visited a master, who poured tea for his guest, but kept pouring until the visitor cried, "Stop, stop! The cup is full and brimming over!" "Indeed", said the master, "like yourself."

To probe a hole we first use a straight stick to see how far it takes us. To probe the visible world we use the assumption that things are simple until they prove to be otherwise.

E.H. Gombrich

In this chapter and the next, I shall tell you a way of thinking about the consultation which is powerful enough to give you a sense of purpose and direction, but at the same time simple enough to be unobtrusive. I shall present it simultaneously in two forms – 1, in language that the analytical Organizer in your left hemisphere can readily learn, and 2, in a metaphor which the Responder can intuitively recognize with your right hemisphere.

In chapter A3, 'Models of the Consultation', we drew a distinction between 'task-orientated' models and 'behaviour-orientated' models. The task-orientated models listed various tasks or goals a doctor should try to fulfil, while the behaviour-orientated ones dealt with differences in doctors' styles and methods.

The difficulty with models that tell you *what* to do is that they are often vague about *how* to do it, or how to decide the priorities and order of doing things. Conversely, when you are concentrating on *how* to speak and behave towards a patient, it's easy to lose track of *what* you are trying to achieve. We need a simple model to draw together 'How?' and 'What?' in a balanced way.

A METAPHOR

Let's suppose you receive out of the blue a letter from your old American pen-pal, now planning a honeymoon trip to Europe. The newly-weds want to spend five days in Great Britain, and they ask you to help them get the most out of that short time. You'll probably want to suggest that they see some of the favourite tourist highlights, and combine their sight-seeing with a broad experience of the British way of life. Before you reply, you draw up lists.

The first list is a list of places they ought to 'do'. Most American tourists like Stratford-on-Avon. And the Scottish highlands are worth seeing. London, of course; and it would be nice if they spent a day with you, just relaxing and chatting. Where else? Perhaps Cambridge.

Your pen-pal used to be keen on cars and plane-spotting. So you make a second list of assorted methods of transport to add some variety. They might like to try driving on the left, so they could hire a car for part of the trip. Trains provide a good view of scenery and some interesting glimpses of the British character. Since time is limited they'll probably need to fly part of the way, but then again you don't really feel you've been to a place unless you tour it on foot.

What would happen if when they arrived you just gave your friends the first list – Stratford, Scotland, London, home, Cambridge – and nothing more?

"Where shall we go first," they ask, "and how do we get there?"

"Oh, it doesn't really matter where you start," you answer. "Do one place first, then ask a policeman how to get to the next."

Alternatively what would happen if you just gave them a piece of paper bearing nothing but your second list – car, train, plane, walk?

"But where shall we make for?", they would ask.

And it wouldn't be very helpful if you merely replied "Britain's full of lovely places. Stop somewhere and buy a guide book."

In reality you would probably draw up an itinerary for your American friends, combining both lists. Depending on where you live, it might go as follows:

"Take a train to London, and ask at the station about sight-seeing tours. Next day go by train to Cambridge and stroll round the colleges. Hire a car and drive to Stratford on the third day, then take a plane from Birmingham to Glasgow, where you can book a coach tour. Finally fly back to my nearest airport, and I'll meet you, and we can spend some time quietly together before you move on."

And to help further, you might present them with an envelope containing a copy of the Highway Code, rail and air timetables, some maps, and the names of car hire companies.

A plan like that would help your friends see everything you intended, in a logical and efficient order, and at the same time provide them with a variety of travel options. Your overall plan would be sufficiently detailed for them to have a good time if they stuck rigidly to it, but it would also be flexible enough for them to make some unplanned detours if they felt inclined.

––––––––––––

Can we draw up an itinerary for the consultation in a similar way? I believe we can.

An American psychiatrist, the late Milton Erickson [1], whose ideas have substantially shaped this book, said,

> In therapy, success is a journey, not a destination.

I'ld like to rephrase this as:

In general practice, the consultation is a journey, not a destination.

It's very important to keep a sense of movement and change while you're consulting with a patient. Patients expect things to change as a result of seeing you – that's why they come. If patients don't feel things have progressed as a result of seeing you they will be worried and disappointed. If you also don't feel things are moving, you may become puzzled or frustrated, and develop a feeling of impotence. So the consultation is a process of transition – a journey – from one state of affairs to another. It is a gradual evolution of one set of symptoms, problems, thoughts and feelings into another.

This unfolding process never comes to an end. Each individual consultation finishes, of course, but actually at some arbitrary or convenient holding-point in an overall course of events which continues indefinitely. There is always another occasion, another problem, another consultation. You can never expect to be able to say, "That's it – the problems are finally solved." If you expect your involvement with a patient to reach a destination, you will feel perpetually thwarted, and run the risk of developing professional 'burn-out' or stress-related illness. As the actress said to the bishop, "If you want everything buttoned up, we shall never get anywhere."

I expect you've experienced moments of feeling temporarily 'stuck' while working with a particular patient. It might have been because you were uncertain of a diagnosis, or wondering about possible management, or maybe it was because you felt you and the patient weren't communicating effectively. You probably found yourself wondering, "What haven't I done yet? What else can I do?"

These questions are the voice of your Organizer trying to help you re-establish control. But they are the wrong questions. The right questions, the questions to train your Organizer to ask if it needs to ask anything, are:

Where shall we make for next, and how shall we get there?

In the metaphor, you gave your American friends a series of landmarks, places to make for. Because you had better knowledge of the country than they did, you decided the best route for their journey, the route that in your judgement would most please them, and you were able to provide the general information you knew they would find useful along the way. But within the overall plan you left them to make the detailed arrangements, in the light of their own common sense and preferences.

In effect, you said to them, "These are the places to make for. Here's a travel information pack which will help. Off you go now, and have fun."

At the beginning of the 'Overview' chapter of this book, I described the three stages necessary in helping someone master a complex behavioural skill. I have given the same names to the three main sections of the book – GOAL-SETTING, SKILL-BUILDING, and GETTING IT TOGETHER.

These three stages mirror the way you acted as travel agent to your tourist friends:

"These are the places to make for."   (Goal-setting),
"Here's a travel information pack."   (Skill-building),
and "Off you go now, and have fun."   (Getting it together)

In the consultation, there are five places to make for. I call them 'CHECKPOINTS'. They are:

Checkpoint 1 – Connecting
Checkpoint 2 – Summarizing
Checkpoint 3 – Handing over
Checkpoint 4 – Safety netting
and Checkpoint 5 – Housekeeping

It's handy that there are five checkpoints, because you need to remember them. Five is a literally 'handy' number, because you've got five digits on a hand. Most children use their fingers when they're learning to count. Many adults, too, tick off their fingers when, for instance, they're making several points in a speech, or trying to recall items from a list they have learned for an exam. For convenience, we'll link the five checkpoints to the fingers and thumb of your left hand as follows:

Index finger – Connecting
Middle finger– Summarizing
Ring finger   – Handing over
Little finger – Safety netting
and Thumb   – Housekeeping

MEMORIZING EXERCISE

Now is as good a time as any for you to commit these checkpoints to memory. It's important that you involve as many sensory modalities as possible in the act of remembering, so do it this way. First of all, look at Figure A5.1

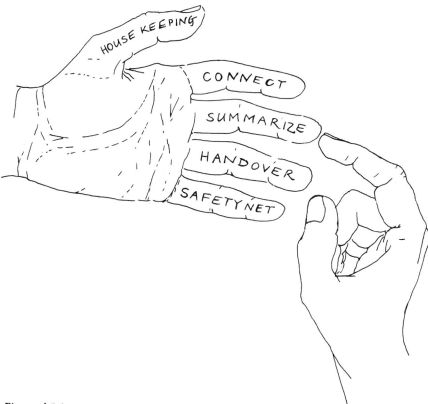

Figure A5.1

Now place your own left hand in the same position as the one in the drawing. In your mind's eye, picture the word CONNECT written on your left index finger. When you can 'see' it, say the word "connect" out loud a few times, and as you do, lightly tap the tip of the finger with the index finger of your other hand. In this way you combine the sense modalities of sight, sound and touch with the concept of 'connecting', and imprint them in a single mnemonic, your left index finger.

Use the same 'see, say, tap' sequence to imprint the word(s)

SUMMARIZE onto your left middle finger,
HAND OVER onto the ring finger,
SAFETY NET onto the little finger,
and HOUSEKEEPING onto your thumb.

Finally, say the sequence "connect, summarize, hand over, safety net, housekeeping" quietly to yourself a few times, looking at each digit in turn as you do, and giving it a tap or two with your right index finger-tip. Once or twice in the next half hour, reinforce this learning by ticking off the checkpoints on your left hand's fingers, until you're satisfied that the mnemonic is in place.

And so, to summarize: think of the consultation as a journey with five checkpoints to be visited along the way. Taken in order, these checkpoints mark out a route which will accomplish the tasks that are important in the consultation. The next chapter describes each checkpoint a little more fully, and Section B (Skill-building) provides you with the equivalent of a travel information pack to help you on the journey.

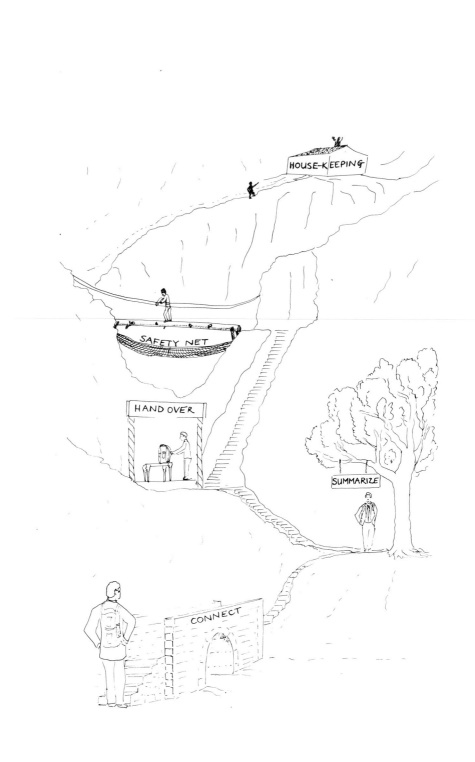

A6
Five 'en route' checkpoints

Is your journey really necessary?

Worl War II railway poster

This chapter describes the five checkpoints in more detail – what they are, why they are important, why you might like to use them as a route for the consultation. It begins with a 'question and answer' tutorial session.

Chris:　Why call them 'checkpoints'?

Me:　Because the word 'checkpoint' implies a temporary pause; somewhere to make for; a recognizable gathering place where you register that one stage of your journey is over and reorientate yourself to strike off in a fresh direction.

Chris:　Why are there *five* checkpoints?

Me:　When the Austrian Emperor Joseph II first heard Mozart's opera 'The Abduction from the Seraglio', he is reputed to have remarked, "Too beautiful for our ears, and too many notes, my dear Mozart." And, the story goes, the composer replied, "Just as many notes, your Majesty, neither more nor less, as are required."

The 'checkpoint' model represents the ingredients of a successful consultation in a form that's at the same time concise, comprehensive and practical. It just so happens that to include everything that's important needs more than four components, but not as many as six. A five-part model does have the advantage of being relatively easy to remember, particularly if you use the 'finger-labelling' gimmick as a mnemonic. Ultimately, of course, the test of any model is whether or not it proves helpful.

Chris: Why these particular checkpoints?

Me: Almost any encounter between two human beings, whatever the setting, goes through four stages. First there's a 'meeting' stage, then a period when the two parties work out what each wants, then there's a period of interaction while the necessary business is transacted, and finally there is a parting, with or without an arrangement to meet again. You can see this sequence happening when you go into a shop to buy something, or when boy meets girl, or when you play badminton with a friend. The first four checkpoints – **connecting, summarizing, handing over** and **safety netting** – describe these stages in the context of a medical consultation.

The names give a clue to your objectives at each stage. If you think of your first intention as being to 'connect' with the patient, you are reminded of the need, before anything worthwhile can happen, to greet, meet and join with the patient – not just at the superficial level of social politeness, but at a deeper level where you can communicate closely enough for real empathy to develop. 'Connecting' means being able to see the world as if through the patients' eyes; knowing how they are feeling as if inside their skin; telling how they think from the words that they use. When you communicate as closely as that with a patient, the rapport that develops has a richness which fertilizes the remainder of the consultation.

All doctors pay at least lip-service to the importance of understanding patients' reasons for coming to see them. How else, after all, can they offer what is needed? But how can you tell when that understanding has been achieved? 'Summarizing' – telling the patient the impression you've so far formed of his or her needs – is a good practical test of whether you've understood or not. If you direct your history-taking towards a point where you could confidently sum up the patient's worries and wishes, and say them out loud, you will find that you become more far-ranging and accurate in the assessments you make. If you get it wrong, the patient has the chance to correct or amplify your summary. If the understanding you display is good enough, the patient will feel ready to move ahead with you, in your direction and at your pace.

If summarizing is the test of whether you've understood the patient's needs or not, being able to 'hand over' is the test of whether or not you have adequately dealt with them. The patient comes into your consulting room a free but in some way troubled person. He hopes to leave it rather less troubled but equally free. In order to avail himself of your professional skill, the patient allows you for a time to direct his attention, guide his decisions, and invite yourself into his private world of thoughts and feelings. Without thus temporarily renouncing some degree of independence, the patient cannot benefit from his encounter with you. But before he leaves, you must make sure that you have fully handed back to him his sense of self-reliance and responsibility. Otherwise he has exchanged discomfort for inadequacy and dependency, which is a poor bargain. The 'hand over' checkpoint is the point at which the patient feels well enough equipped to depart – adequately informed and sufficiently confident of progress. As the doctor, you need to be able to navigate and steer to the 'hand over' checkpoint, and to recognize it when you arrive.

The key phrases in what I've just said are 'adequately', 'well enough', 'sufficiently'. In medicine, problems don't stand still long enough to be completely solved. We can never completely understand or satisfy or predict another person. We have to settle for what is 'good enough to go on with'. This leaves the possibility of mis-understanding or dissatisfaction or the un-predictable, all of which may have to be catered for. It is important for the peace of mind of both patient and doctor to anticipate what you expect to happen to the patient, and also what conceivably might happen, and to have some contingency plans formulated. The 'safety-netting' checkpoint reminds you to consider, before the patient leaves, a few "What if?" questions. "What shall we do if" the patient's symptoms persist or worsen? "What if" treatment doesn't work? "What if" the tests or X-rays show this or that? If you can think of questions like these as the consultation draws to a close, it's a safe bet that the patient is probably wondering much the same. If you can indicate that you too are thinking ahead and antici-pating various possibilities, the patient will feel reassured and appreciative, and is more likely to accept your sug-gestions and comply with any management plan you have agreed.

Moving in order through these four checkpoints will take your consultation from start to finish in a natural and comprehensive way. You will embed your clinical decision-making in a flexible context that honours the patient's human hopes and fears. But you the doctor are human too.

You also have hopes and concerns and feelings. Whatever they may have taught you at medical school, you cannot fail to feel some personal involvement in your patients' destinies, or to have some personal reaction to the demands general practice makes on you. You would be a lesser doctor and person if you did. Your most powerful diagnostic and therapeutic tool is you yourself – your intellect, your memory, your perceptiveness and your intuition; your two heads, the Organizer and the Responder. On this precision instrument, rust and dust tend to accumulate in the form of fatigue, boredom, stress, frustration, loss of concentration, the preoccupations of your private life, and a range of emotions from elation and joy to sadness, anger and guilt. So the final checkpoint, 'house-keeping', reminds you to attach no less importance to looking after your own physiological and mental health than you do to patients'. You need to attend to your own 'house-keeping' at regular periods: during the consultation, between patients, before and after surgeries, after particularly stressful incidents, and at intervals during the course of your career. This is not indulgence – it is part of professional competence. You need to be able to recognize the need for house-keeping, and to know some ways of doing it.

Chris: What about clinical medicine? In your descriptions of the checkpoints, why don't clinical investigation and management feature?

Me: You've had at least five or six years of full-time training in the clinical method, and you are practising it all the time. You couldn't forget it if you tried. But as a general practitioner you will know that the exercise of clinical skill isn't an end in itself. It goes on all the time throughout the consultation. Sometimes as soon as the patient walks in you recognize anaemia, or myxoedema, or depression. And on other occasions it isn't until the patient is just about to leave that you remember that the sore throat you've been treating could be glandular fever, or toxoplasmosis, or cyto-megalovirus, or AIDS. So drawing on your clinical knowledge is not something you only do after connecting and summarizing, but before handing over and safety-netting. If you ask, "Where does clinical problem-solving come in the model?", I would counter with, "Where doesn't it?" You don't need to dwell on it, that's all. Trust what you've learned already.

Chris: Quite a lot of this sounds familiar. Aren't many of these ideas similar to the other models we looked at in chapter A3?

Me: Yes. Figure A6.1 shows how I have included various elements from some of the other consultation models within the 'five checkpoints' model. My purpose in offering this new model is to help make the transition from models which are mainly

CONNECTING	Byrne and Long – Phase I Pendleton Task vii – establishing and maintaining a relationship HBM – personality, interest in health matters, educational level, perceived vulnerability Helman – "why me?", "why now?"
SUMMARIZING	Physical, psychological and social diagnoses Byrne and Long – Phases II and III Pendleton Task i – nature, history and effects of problem HBM – action-prompting factors; ideas, concerns and expectations Helman – "what has happened?", "why has it happened?"
HANDING OVER	S and D – management of presenting problems, – modifying help-seeking behaviour Byrne and Long – Phases III, IV and V Pendleton Task i – aetiology of problem Task iii – choosing appropriate action Task iv – achieving shared understanding HBM – perceived benefit/risk ratio
SAFETY-NETTING	S and D – management of continuing problems opportunistic health promotion Byrne and Long – Phases IV and V Pendleton Task ii – continuing problems, risk factors Task iv – use of time and resources Helman – "what might happen?", "what shall I do?"
HOUSE-KEEPING	Balint – use of doctor–patient relationship in diagnosis and treatment, – doctor as 'drug'

Abbreviations (full references given in Chapter A3)
Balint – *The Doctor, His Patient and the Illness* (1957)
Byrne and Long – *Doctors Talking to Patients* (1976)
HBM – Health Belief Model
Helman – Folk Model of Illness (1981)
Pendleton – Pendleton, Schofield, Tate and Havelock. *The Consultation: An Approach to Learning and Teaching* (1984)
S and D – Stott and Davis. *The exceptional potential in each primary care consultation* (1979)

Figure A6.1 The antecedents of the 'five checkpoint' model

descriptive to a model which is essentially practical. The 'checkpoint' model helps you 'think on your feet' while a consultation is proceeding, and, as you develop some familiarity with it, will guide you as you ask yourself "Where shall I go next?", "How shall I get there?", and "How shall I know when I've arrived?".

There are no new truths, but only truths that have not been recognized by those who perceived them without knowing.

Mary McCarthy

Sometimes it is a good idea to rearrange an old set of ideas into fresh combinations, so that new patterns and connections appear. Remember the story of how the organic chemist Friedrich Kekule, puzzling over the arrangement of the six carbon atoms in the benzene molecule, found his thoughts drifting into a reverie. He imagined a chain of carbon atoms turning into a snake, which then seized its own tail in its mouth and became a ring – the benzene ring.

Significance is in the eye (or more likely the right hemisphere) of the beholder. The same situation or set of circumstances can take on new meaning and new usefulness according to the context within which it is perceived.

An old Chinese story tells of a farmer in a poor district who owned a horse. One day the horse ran away. All the farmer's neighbours came to show sympathy for his misfortune, but the farmer simply said, "Maybe".

The next day the horse returned, bringing with it two wild horses. The neighbours rejoiced at this stroke of luck, but the farmer just said, "Maybe".

When the farmer's son tried to ride one of the wild horses, the horse threw him and broke his leg. Again the neighbours offered sympathy, and again the farmer said, "Maybe".

Soon soldiers raided the village to conscript young men for the army. But they did not take the farmer's son, because his leg was broken. When the neighbours told him how fortunate he was, the farmer simply said, "Maybe" ...

Look at picture A in Figure A6.2. What is it? Is it an old woman looking towards your left shoulder (B)? Or a young woman turning away from you (C)? It is both, or neither. If you want a picture of an old woman, or of a young woman, the picture will do for either.

One more Chinese story: a man who kept monkeys told them, "You get three acorns in the morning and four in the evening". This made

What is this a picture of?

A

B   **C**

An old lady   OR   A young girl
looking towards you?   looking away from you?

Figure A6.2

the monkeys very angry. So he said, "How about four in the morning and three in the evening?". With this the monkeys were happy.

So don't say "the five checkpoints are nothing new", and dismiss them. And don't, just because they *are* new, embrace them to the exclusion of everything else either. See what they have to offer you. If you like them and find them helpful, that's fine. And if you don't find them helpful, you can always forget them and find another way that suits better.

PITSTOP

Can you recall the names of the checkpoints 'imprinted' on the fingers and thumb of your left hand by the exercise in Chapter A5?

(If you didn't do the exercise then, please do it now.)

Please now turn back to Chapter A1, and read through the sequence of five case illustrations. I'm going to take those examples of consulting skills in action, and correlate them with the five checkpoints. The cases were:

young Jeremy Wriggler, with tonsillitis;
Mrs Timid, with the lump in her throat;
the new diabetic, Mrs Hogg;
Gary and Barry, two young men with probable glandular fever;
and that time-consuming marital couple, Mr and Mrs Battle.

Two different approaches to each of these clinical situations were given, and I hope you'll agree that in each case the second approach was more skilled than the first. In terms of the 'checkpoint model', the second approach successfully reaches one of the checkpoints, while the first fails to do so. We'll consider each case briefly, and ask ourselves two questions of each of the better consultations:

1. How do you get to the checkpoint?
and 2. How can you tell when you've reached the checkpoint?

JEREMY WRIGGLER – 'CONNECTING' CHECKPOINT – (LEFT INDEX FINGER)

Jeremy was three, if you remember, and his mother thought he might have tonsillitis. Doctor A succeeded only in antagonizing and probably frightening him. He used words like 'hurt', 'abdomen', and 'examine', which don't sound nice to three-year-old ears. He talked over the child's head, figuratively and literally, standing above him and being quick to resort to a forceful examination.

Dr B on the other hand spoke directly to Jeremy, calling him by name and using 'safe' language, like 'nice teeth' and 'tummy' in a way that implied approval. He literally got down to the child's level, and made sure that his first physical contact was non-threatening by playing with the child's fingers. His examination was disguised as a game.

How do you get to the 'connecting' checkpoint?

The doctor at the outset matched his own behaviour to the child's level. His language matched the child's; by kneeling down, he matched the child's physical position; and by playing, he matched the child's stage of development.

He led Jeremy into a series of positive responses. By playing with his fingers, he non-verbally drew a 'yes' from the child to the idea that the two of them might play. He used the 'game' of making a big mouth to get Jeremy to respond 'yes' to having his throat examined. In a jargon phrase, the doctor produced a 'yes-set' in his patient. He secured the child's acceptance of some initial moves that weren't directly relevant clinically, and thereby created a likelihood that his subsequent, more intrusive, requests would be accepted also. At this stage, the doctor and the patient have **connected**.

How can you tell when you've reached the 'connecting' checkpoint?

Dr B was looking throughout for signs that Jeremy accepted what he was doing. A 'yes-set' has definite physical signs, such as comfortable eye contact, a relaxed and open facial expression, willingness to communicate, willingness to approach and be approached. When he thought he detected some of these physical signs in Jeremy, Dr B tested his observation by asking the child to do something a little more threatening than previously, in this case asking him to come and sit on the doctor's knee while his stomach was felt.

So you can recognize the 'connecting' checkpoint by detecting the physical signs of rapport, and putting that rapport to a gentle challenge. In Chapter B2 we shall go into more detail about how to develop rapport, and how to recognize it when you've got it.

EXERCISE

As you read the sections on each checkpoint, I should like you to reinforce the association between the checkpoint names and the digits of your left hand. Visualize the words on each finger and thumb in turn as you come to the relevant case example, and give each 'labelled' finger an alerting tap with your right index finger. In this way you are programming your left hand to be a practical and ever-present 'aide memoire' for you to use when you yourself are consulting.

Please do this now for the 'Connect' checkpoint, linked to your left index finger.

MRS TIMID – 'SUMMARIZING' CHECKPOINT – (LEFT MIDDLE FINGER)

Mrs Timid presented with symptoms of intermittent dysphagia that might have had an important organic cause, but in view of the history were probably 'functional' or stress-related. Dr A was clinically perfectly sound, but he made several assumptions. He assumed that all Mrs Timid wanted from him was general reassurance and advice, and that what he had done was all that she had expected. But he didn't check to see whether he was right in these assumptions. By her request for an X-ray just as Doctor A thought the consultation had finished, Mrs Timid showed that he had given the impression of not having understood the full extent of her problem.

Dr B did not make the same assumptions. After taking a history, he summarized Mrs Timid's symptoms in a few words, and showed he suspected that something (as yet unspecified) about them was worrying her. Mrs Timid's nod confirmed that yes, the doctor had correctly understood her symptoms, and yes, she was worried. Since up to that point both doctor and patient had been vague about the exact nature of the worry, Dr B invited Mrs Timid to be more precise. She then disclosed a fear of cancer she had been too afraid or embarrassed to reveal previously. If Dr B were then to add to his first summary a rider such as, "– and you'd like me to make sure you don't have cancer?", Mrs Timid would have gratefully agreed, and the consultation would have moved swiftly ahead.

Dr A, being no fool, would also have considered the possibility of malignant disease, and excluded it because of the intermittent nature of the symptoms and the normal examination. But he gave no indication of his thought process. And because Mrs Timid, not being a mind-reader, did not know that he had indeed considered the very possibility that was worrying her, the doctor found himself under pressure to arrange an X-ray he thought was unnecessary.

How do you get to the 'summarizing' checkpoint?

In reaching the 'summarizing' checkpoint, the doctor has taken enough of a history to form a provisional assessment of the patient's presenting complaint. Diagnoses are made in physical, psychological and social terms, and patients have their own ideas, concerns, expectations and feelings about their problems. So the doctor's first evaluation should have regard to all these factors. But even the most comprehensive history is wasted unless the patient realizes what the doctor is thinking. There is no better way to indicate this than for the doctor to make a summary statement when he thinks he probably has enough to go on.

Summarizing is an aid to the efficient use of time. Since the possible range of a patient's ideas, concerns, expectations and feelings are legion, it saves time if the doctor offers a provisional summary and checks to see whether it is near enough to the mark to satisfy the patient. If it is, the consultation can proceed without more ado. If it is not, the patient's reaction to the summary will direct the doctor's attention to any relevant unexplored area.

How can you tell when you've reached the 'summarizing' checkpoint?

There are two ways. Both begin with directing your history-taking towards the point that you could, if you chose, make an explicit 'out loud' summary of why you think the patient has consulted you. The first way is then to go ahead and make your tentative summary, and observe the patient's reaction. (You may like to give a prompt, such as, "Have I got that right?") If the patient says "yes", you have reached the checkpoint. If the patient alters or qualifies your summary, you amplify the reply until you feel in a position to make another up-dated version.

If you don't feel inclined to make an explicit summary statement, you can test whether or not you are at the checkpoint in another way which is more subtle but can be less accurate. You move the consultation ahead as if your private unvoiced hypotheses were correct – by for example beginning a line of questioning to confirm or refute your provisional diagnosis. And you watch closely, looking for non-verbal signs of whether the patient is happy or uncomfortable with what you are saying. If you have understood the patient sufficiently, even though you don't show it in so many words, the patient will continue to react with non-verbal indications of rapport and acceptance, similar to the physical signs of the 'yes-set' that characterized the 'connecting' checkpoint. If you are working on incorrect assumptions and an inadequate summary, the patient will sense this, and display physical signs of losing 'connectedness' with you, such as fidgeting, hesitancy of speech, and reduction in eye contact.

Chapter B3 will give you more practical tips for reaching and recognizing the 'Summarize' checkpoint.

EXERCISE

When you feel happy that you understand the 'Summarize' checkpoint, reinforce its imprint on your left middle finger as before.

MRS HOGG – 'HANDING OVER' CHECKPOINT – (LEFT RING FINGER)

Mrs Hogg presents an example of a familiar general practice problem. We met her after a history had been taken and the organic diagnosis of non-insulin dependent diabetes mellitus made. The transition from this diagnosis to a fully-formed management plan involving medication, diet control, follow-up visits and routine surveillance is a familiar clinical reflex that takes a doctor only a few seconds of thought. Doctor A lost no time in trying to convey every implication of his assessment to Mrs Hogg. He spared her no scrap of information, overlooked no administrative arrangement – and failed to help her. Mrs Hogg was too shell-shocked to take any of it in.

Doctor B had different priorities. While his own medical agenda was no less comprehensive than Doctor A's, he had a keener awareness of Mrs Hogg as a person. He knew that she would be feeling afraid, swamped, unsure what to do, her mind reeling with disconnected ideas and emotions. By telling her that he was going to get her feeling better and would want to see her again soon, Doctor B gave Mrs Hogg an immediate sense of security. He told her what was from his point of view the single most important part of treatment, that he was going to prescribe medication. He then asked her to take a few moments of time to arrange her doubts and fears into questions which he could answer. He decided that considerations such as diet, health education, and the mechanics of follow-up could quite safely be left either until later in the consultation, or till another time. It is likely that Mrs Hogg will feel better cared for by Doctor B, and will understand and manage her diabetes better in the long run.

How do you get to the 'hand over' checkpoint?

To get to the 'hand over' checkpoint, the doctor brings the consultation to the stage where the patient's and the doctor's agendas have both been agreed and dealt with, so that the business of that particular consultation is concluded. Doctor and patient can now prepare to end their meeting. Three processes are involved in reaching this checkpoint – negotiating, influencing, and 'gift-wrapping'.

Negotiating – Both doctor and patient will have some priority objectives for the consultation, some things they will feel unhappy about if they fail to achieve. They will each also have some lower order objectives that can afford to be postponed, ignored or compromised. 'Negotiating' means reaching agreement on which objectives are to be met on this occasion and by what means. For the doctor, this may involve explaining possible diagnoses and management options. It may also mean that the doctor has to pay renewed attention at this point to the patient's needs and priorities.

Influencing – Usually the doctor has a more detailed and precise idea of his own objectives and priorities than the patient does. The patient may simply 'want to feel better', or 'need a certificate', or 'wonder what the tests showed'. The doctor may sometimes have to persuade, direct or manipulate the patient, perfectly benevolently, to settle for an alternative course of action, such as not being immediately cured, or seeing a problem as emotionally rather than physically caused, or making changes in a cherished life-style. To be able to exert influence responsibly and effectively is one of the hallmarks of skilled consulting.

'Gift-wrapping' – There are kind ways and unkind ways of saying things, helpful or unhelpful forms of words. Remember how in the advert it takes a 'best friend' to let someone know they need a deodorant toilet soap? The exact words a doctor uses when giving advice or explaining a diagnosis or making a criticism have an extremely important influence on whether his comments are accepted, understood and acted upon, or rejected. A skilled practitioner needs to be able to 'wrap up' what he has to say into a package that is sufficiently intelligible and acceptable to the patient that it actually produces the result the doctor intends. Experts in psycholinguistics have a maxim – 'the meaning of a communication is the effect it produces.' It is no use telling a patient, "There's nothing the matter with you", if the only result is that he or she goes off and sees another doctor about, say, psychosomatic symptoms. In this case, what you succeeded in 'meaning' was only, "Go away." Better to spend a little time 'gift-wrapping' your explanation, and saying something like, "Although your symptoms are real, we both have to face the fact that they're not caused by anything going wrong physically. I expect that puzzles you ..."

How can you tell when you've reached the 'hand over' checkpoint?

You can tell whether you have finished negotiating simply by asking. You might ask the patient, "Are you happy about that?", or "Is that clear?", or "Have we left anything out?", or "Is there anything else you'd like to ask me?"

It is a little harder to monitor the effects of your influencing and gift-wrapping. As a rule, say nothing to a patient that you wouldn't say to your maker, your mother, your spouse or your child. And watch the effects of what you say on the patient. There are physical signs of rapport. You have to notice changes in facial expression, body movements like nodding or restlessness, and you have to listen attentively to what and how the patient replies.

You will also be able to recognize the physical signs that indicate when it is time to end the consultation. Some of these are your own internal thoughts and sensations. And some of them are revealed in the patient's behaviour. Get into the habit now of noticing how people behave at mealtimes when they have had enough, neither too much nor too little. You will find that patients display similar indications during the consultation!

Chapter B4 goes into more practical detail about negotiating, influencing and gift-wrapping, and about recognizing the 'hand over' checkpoint.

EXERCISE

When you feel happy that you understand what I've said about the 'hand over' checkpoint, reinforce its imprint on your left ring finger.

GARY AND BARRY – 'SAFETY-NETTING' CHECKPOINT – (LEFT LITTLE FINGER)

Two young men went to see their doctors with what initially looked like bacterial tonsillitis, for which penicillin was prescribed. Since their symptoms worsened despite the antibiotic, each returned, and with hindsight it seemed likely that in fact they were suffering from infectious mononucleosis.

Gary, who consulted Doctor A, was not told what response he could expect to the penicillin if the diagnosis of bacterial tonsillitis was correct. When after a fair trial period Gary failed to improve, Doctor A sent a throat swab, presumably because he thought the causative organism might be penicillin-resistant. He may at this stage have considered mononucleosis, but decided not to test for it in view of the relatively short history. Because Doctor A had kept any doubts and uncertainties to himself, however, Gary interpreted the sequence of events as indicating incompetence on the doctor's part. He understandably felt indignant. Accompanied by his father, he consulted another doctor, who, by making what by then was an easy diagnosis, appeared to confirm Gary's poor opinion of Doctor A.

When Barry consulted Doctor B with identical symptoms, the doctor made the same provisional diagnosis as Doctor A, and gave the same prescription for penicillin. However Doctor B explicitly told Barry what results he might expect from taking the antibiotic, and mentioned the alternative diagnoses of viral illness or glandular fever. As a result, far from appearing to be caught unawares when symptoms of the true diagnosis appeared, Doctor B was credited with considerable foresight, and his relationship with Barry was enhanced.

How do you get to the 'safety-netting' checkpoint?

In order to reach the 'safety-netting' checkpoint, the doctor assumes that his assessment and management of the patient's problem have been correct and makes some predictions. He uses his knowledge of clinical medicine, pathology and epidemiology and anticipates the natural history of whatever disease is present. He draws on his knowledge of human nature in general and the individual patient in particular to predict how he expects the patient to respond. He thinks to himself, "If I am right, I imagine such and such will happen to this patient."

Because he knows that general practice is the art of managing uncertainty, a good doctor will also accept that things may not turn out as expected. His clinical knowledge will alert him to some of the more likely possibilities. He may also find that certain aspects of the present case remind him of occasions he can learn from in his past experience. He will make skilled use of that invaluable clinical instrument, the retrospectoscope. The doctor who is used to noticing his own thought processes will also be able to spot features in the presentation or in the patient's reactions that leave him feeling puzzled or slightly anxious. As a result, the doctor can think ahead to what he will do if the unexpected actually occurs. One essential difference between hospital medicine and general practice is that in hospital the aim is to prevent the unexpected from happening, whereas in general practice we learn to settle for knowing what to do next if it does! The central role of safety-netting in general practice is underlined by the caricature of the GP who only knows three diagnoses:

TALOIA-fever (There's A Lot of It About),

HIBAGIA-disease (you've Had It Before And you've Got It Again),

and "Come and see me next week if you're no better".

How can you tell when you've reached the 'safety-netting' checkpoint?

Your unconscious mind always takes good care of you. At this stage in the consultation, your own confidence and peace of mind are at stake as well as those of the patient. You find that quite automatically "What shall I do if ...?" questions begin to form themselves in your mind. You don't have to force them. The 'safety-netting' checkpoint is now at hand. When you notice these unbidden promptings of your unconscious mind, it is a good idea systematically to consider as many possible outcomes as you can imagine, and quickly think what you might do in each case.

You may find yourself wondering how much of your inner debate to tell the patient about. It is a matter of judgement how much you should share of a lengthy differential diagnosis, or the possible side-effects of treatment, or the fact that you haven't a clue what is going on and will have to ask someone else's opinion. The key sign of the 'safety-netting' checkpoint is when you ask yourself, "How much of my uncertainty shall I disclose to the patient?" It matters less what you decide to pass on than that you consciously consider it.

Chapter B5 will explain more about safety-netting.

EXERCISE

When you feel you have got the hang of the safety-netting checkpoint, strengthen the associative link to your left little finger as before.

THE BATTLES - 'HOUSEKEEPING' CHECKPOINT - (LEFT THUMB)

Last thing Friday evening is not a good time to see your doctor. Doctors, like many other people, hope to celebrate POETS day (Push Off Early, Tomorrow's Saturday). So Mr and Mrs Battle started their marital counselling session at something of a disadvantage. The quality of the attention their doctor was able to pay them was further jeopardized by the apparently destructive attitude of Mrs Battle, which Doctor A found hard to challenge effectively.

Doctor A seemed to feel himself bound by an unwritten rule which forbade him to express any of the personal frustration and resentment he felt towards this couple entrenched in their own war-game. He felt obliged, on the face of it at least, to deny his own strong feelings because they did not coincide with the virtuous and caring image he thought he should present at all times. His attention drifted away from the Battles and towards his own personal life, presumably to the detriment of any therapy. His thoughts ranged over the various culprits responsible for his discomfiture – his receptionist, the traffic, the unexpected extra patient, his partners who had managed to get away on time. In a version of the party game 'musical parcel', a large chunk of resentment was passed down a line from the Battles to the doctor, to the receptionist, and finally to the unsuspecting scapegoat, the extra patient who through no fault of his own received short shrift.

Doctor B, becoming equally aware of negative feelings that would, if they grew, quickly become destructive to the consultation, took a risk. Call it intuition or call it folly, he allowed himself to express his frustration in an authentic and spontaneous V-sign gesture. Mrs Battle was so startled at this response so apparently out of keeping with the context that she stopped short. She was strikingly confronted with the effect she was producing on a doctor whom she respected, and was able to make the imaginative leap that gave her an insight into her husband's feelings. The doctor's action cut across her well-established attitudes and provided a novel opportunity for her to appreciate her husband's solace. She was also able for once to show her own vulnerability with tears instead of her usual criticism. Doctor B experienced a powerful relief of his own tension, and as a result felt rather more warmly towards the couple. He didn't snap at his receptionist, and went home in a positive frame of mind.

(This example, like others in this book, is based on a real clinical case. The actual patient for whom 'Mrs Battle' is a pseudonym frequently refers to this incident, now several years in the past, as one of the most helpful things that any doctor ever did for her.)

How do you get to the 'housekeeping' checkpoint?

Like a car, a doctor needs regular attention to maintain peak performance. At periodic 'servicing intervals' he focuses attention on his own internal physiological and psychological states, noticing any pressing needs and deciding what to do about them. During a consultation he will from time to time ask himself, "What emotions, if any, are arising in me? Where have they come from? What, if anything, do I need to do about it?" Sometimes the doctor's feelings are unconnected with the consultation in progress, and have to be contained for the time being. At other times, however, the doctor may experience emotions which he has absorbed from the patient, such as anxiety, depression or anger. In this case, he may be able to make therapeutic use of the insight they provide.

It is a good idea between patients to check out, "In what state has the last patient left me, and in what state will the next patient find me?" It is quite possible for left-over feelings from a previous consultation to contaminate the doctor's handling of subsequent ones. Each doctor devises his own personal ways of dissipating job stress as it arises, such as having a cup of coffee, going for a short walk, or talking things over with colleagues. But often it is enough merely to notice how you are feeling; what is conscious can be dealt with, while what is unconscious may intrude.

How can you tell when you've reached the 'housekeeping' checkpoint?

All of us are aware of what for us are our normal 'good enough' moods, attitudes, and powers of concentration. As you become more effective as a doctor, you find yourself becoming more sensitive to those occasions when your internal state falls short of what patients deserve. You can calibrate your performance against your own optimum. You will recognize when 'unfinished business' gets in the way of paying full attention to the patient you are talking with. You have reached the 'housekeeping' checkpoint when you can answer "Yes" to the question "Am I in good enough shape for the next patient?"

Chapter B6 will say more about ways to look after your own housekeeping.

EXERCISE

Take a few moments to think about some of the sources of your own stress at work and some of your own feelings which can intrude into your consultations. Think how you recognize them, what effects they can have on your performance, and some of the ways you deal with them.

Then reinforce the connection between the 'housekeeping' checkpoint and your left thumb.

PITSTOP

A TUTORIAL CONCLUDED

Me: We've now reached the end of the first part of this book. Are there any questions you'ld like me to see if I can answer?

Chris: Yes. What's all this business with labelling my left hand with the names of the checkpoints?

Me: It's a technique which will make it easier and less intrusive for you to use the checkpoint model while you're actually consulting. It's a bit like having a reminder list, only this way it is literally 'always to hand'. While you are getting used to the checkpoint model, the finger labels will give you a prompt if you need one. Your intellectual left hemisphere – the 'Organizer' – will have learned the checkpoints as abstract concepts. Your more intuitive right hemisphere – the 'Responder' – learns things in a more concrete way; it will remember the visualized words on the fingers, the sounds of the checkpoint names as you say them aloud, and will be stimulated by the physical sensation of touch on the fingers.

Chris: Quite often as you were describing the checkpoints, particularly how to recognize arriving at them, you talked about the patient showing 'physical signs of mental states', like rapport, connectedness, agreement, dissatisfaction, and so on. That's a new idea to me.

Me: It may be new to learn that these physical signs are important in the consultation, but in fact you've been using them all your life. Whenever we're communicating with anyone, right from infancy, we respond to non-verbal signals such as facial expression and body language. They provide moment-by-moment feed-back about what the other person is thinking. You can tell, can't you, when someone is encouraging you to go on talking, or when they want you to stop so that they can have a turn, or when they find you interesting, or boring? All we'll be doing as you learn the Inner Consultation is discovering how to use these minimal cues to assist our progress from checkpoint to checkpoint.

You'll find also that developing an eye for these minimal physical signs helps overcome the paradox of having two heads. Section C will tell you more about that.

Chris: What next?

Me: Section A was called 'Goal-Setting'. I've shown you some reasons for using the checkpoint model as a route to skilful consulting, and given you a picture of what the checkpoints are like, so that you have an idea of what we're aiming at. In Section B, which is called 'Skill-Building', I shall try to make sure you are fully equipped with the navigational skills to move confidently from each checkpoint to the next. Both hemispheres of your brain need to be involved in this learning process; it forms the subject of the next chapter.

Section B
Skill-building

B1
How people learn

Men must be taught as if you taught them not,
And things unknown proposed as things forgot.

Pope

Dal dire al fare c'è di mezzo il mare.
(Between saying and doing there lies the ocean)

Italian proverb

Everything changes – a truth so simple that whole religions have been built upon it. Throughout the universe, matter is in a state of never-ending flux, from the dancing blur of sub-atomic particles to the evolution of galaxies so imperceptibly slow as to tease us with the illusion of permanence. In the living world too individuals and species are born, flourish and in their turn evaporate. Because we are sentient beings, we notice when it is us that change happens to. Because we are talking and thinking beings, we give different names to the process of change, according to how it affects us. When we like the way we're changing, we call it 'growing', or 'developing'. When we would rather not have changed, and we glimpse the beckoning finger of our own impermanence, we call it 'degenerating'. When we're not sure, we suspend judgement and use a neutral word like 'altering'. But when change takes place in the realm of what we can think or do, and especially if some person intends that it should occur, we call it 'learning'.

A phenomenal ability to learn is inherent in the human nervous system. Learning goes on all the time, whether we like it, notice it, strive for it, or whether we don't. A person can't not learn. Yet when you consider the vast financial, organizational and intellectual resources devoted to institutionalized education, you might wonder how anyone ever learned anything before there were teacher training colleges.

People learn in many ways. Learning some things – French irregular verbs, for example – feels like a struggle; other things, like walking and talking and finding your way around your neighbourhood, come effortlessly. Sometimes people don't know what they've learned until after they've learned it. (I know a young mother who had her first baby in an out of the way place. During her second pregnancy she went along to antenatal classes, and found she had been doing 'mothercraft' for years!) And sometimes you can be so preoccupied with trying to learn that you don't realize when you've finally succeeded. I'll bet you can't remember a specific day when you finally decided you knew how to do a routine physical examination. Learning often starts with trying, but doesn't end there. As a plant continues to grow long after you apply the fertilizer, change continues after the trying stops. The easiest sort of learning is the "Good Lord, how did I do that?" sort.

Some wag once observed that there are two kinds of people: those who divide people into two kinds, and those who don't. It seems also that there are two kinds of learning. Some skills are painstakingly learned in the full spotlight of conscious intention, while others seem to slip on board out of the shadows like stowaways while our conscious awareness has its back turned.

I'll call the first ('spotlight') sort of skills learning **conscious learning**. Conscious learning is predominantly the business of the dominant, speech-orientated cerebral hemisphere, the left in most people. Conscious learning usually proceeds by the 'Analysis, Practice, Feedback' cycle we discussed in Chapter A2. For it to succceed, the pupil has to try. The teacher supplies some instruction, theory, concept, analysis or model against which the pupil critically assesses his performance. He then tells himself what he thinks he should do to improve, and consciously tries to do it. Then someone tells him whether he has succeeded or not. Material which is intended to be learned consciously is presented in rational unambiguous language, precisely, explicitly, and in a sequence that makes logical sense. Conscious learning results in 'knowing' facts, or 'knowing about' a subject. In my 'two heads' analogy, conscious learning produces a clever Organizer.

Surreptitious skills learning of the second 'stowaway' kind I'll call **unconscious learning**. Unconscious learning invokes the special characteristics of the non-dominant hemisphere, usually the right, which thinks in a different language less exclusively reliant on words. The right hemisphere prefers handling patterns of sensory information to abstract concepts. It is more of an analogue computer, whereas the left hemisphere is digital. The right hemisphere 'sees' a joke; the left needs it explained. The intuitive right would be an artist, the analytic left a scientist. During unconscious learning, the right hemisphere makes symbolic and metaphorical 'as if' associations with the learner's past experiences. The results of unconscious learning are 'knowing in one's bones', flashes of insight, finding oneself spontaneously able to do something or unexpectedly reacting in new ways. It produces a skilful Responder.

Let me summarize this admittedly oversimplified distinction in two ways, themselves examples of the differences between hemispheric functions, so that the medium forms the message. The first (left hemisphere style) is a table of comparisons (Figure B1.1). The second way of illustrating the same point for the right hemisphere is in a story.

'CONSCIOUS' LEARNING	'UNCONSCIOUS' LEARNING
'Organizer' head	'Responder' head
mainly dominant (left) hemisphere	mainly non-dominant (right) hemisphere
thinks in words and concepts	thinks in images, sensations and associations
makes analyses	sees connections
thinks linearly and convergently	thinks laterally and divergently
teases ideas apart	puts ideas together
understands literal meanings	understands metaphorical and symbolic meanings
rational	intuitive
learns from instruction	learns from experiencing
learns by 'trying'	learns by 'allowing'
recalls by effort of will	recalls spontaneously
results in 'knowing' and 'knowing about'	results in 'reacting' and 'knowing how to'
comes up with explanations	comes up with insights
brainy	perceptive

Figure B 1.1 Comparison between conscious and unconscious learning

How a lion learned to be nice

One day Androcles was out walking with a friend of his, a professor of education, when they came face to face with a ferocious man-eating lion. "Leave this to me," cried the professor, and he strode forward and addressed the beast.

"Now see here," he told it, "you are not to eat us. Eating people is wrong, morally and nutritionally. For a start, human flesh is far too rich in saturated fatty acids. Let me give you the address of a very good vegetarian restaurant. It's high time you learned some self-control."

The lion looked unconvinced, and licked its slavering lips. Its tail lashed and its stomach rumbled.

"Shut up, by Jupiter," said Androcles. "Stop lecturing, and just look. Can't you see it's hurt its paw?"

And turning to the lion, he murmured soothingly, "Who's a poorly pussy then?", and gently pulled forth the famous thorn. A look of relief came over the lion's face. It gave Androcles a grateful lick, and purred itself to sleep.

As the two men chatted afterwards, the professor said to Androcles, "I see now what you were doing. You identified its needs and mobilized the available resources, using yourself as a role-model for non-aggresive interaction."

Androcles yawned. "Be that as it may," he said, "but lions don't always eat people. There's a nice side to their nature, if only you let them show it."

And we know, though Androcles didn't at the time, that the lion never forgot.

Let's make this talk of conscious and unconscious learning a little more concrete by seeing how it applies to consulting. Think of your own consultations. At the moment your personal method of consulting has certain hallmarks that are yours and yours alone; certain ways of talking, particular set routines of asking questions and carrying out examinations, your own particular mannerisms and rituals, your clinical and personal strong points and blind spots. All these things add up to what we might call your consulting 'style'. How did that style come to be formed? How did 'your way' become that particular way?

Many of the components of your present professional style were acquired as the result of planned tuition and conscious learning. The routines of taking a history, making a diagnosis, using a stethoscope and all the other clinical trappings were systematically taught you at medical school by teachers using mainly the 'Analysis, Practice, Feedback' cycle. After you graduated, you have been to courses, clinical meetings and case discussions where, on being told of some new knowledge or skill, you have thought to yourself, "I must remember that." And then you have come back to your own work and tried consciously to change your previous behaviour.

But many other facets of your style have been imperceptibly absorbed and pieced into the mosaic without you knowing exactly where they came from. To show you what I mean, let's look closely at the very first few moments of a consultation, when the door opens and a patient comes into your consulting room.

What are you wearing? Your choice of clothes for work might reflect your social status, the self-image you want to project, your income, the types of clothes your parents made you wear as a child, the types of clothes you opted for to show your parents you were grown-up now, your position on the 'conventional–dissident' political spectrum, your mood that day – and so on. Do you stand as the patient enters? Shake hands? Do you sit behind your desk, or beside it, or have no desk at all? What sort of chair do you have, and does the patient have? Does the room look like an operating theatre or more like your own living room? It is possible that you have consciously decided all these things after attending a course on non-verbal communication, but it's more likely that, without realizing it, you are following the example of particular doctors whom you respected, or reacting against the example of others you cared less for, or even basing your behaviour on your own non-medical likes and dislikes, such as what makes you feel comfortable when as a client you consult your own bank manager! Who speaks first, you or the patient? Do you say, "What can I do for you?", or "What seems to be the problem?", or "What are you complaining of?", or do you just wait in expectant silence? The attitudes that underly your preference for one or other opening gambit go way back and rest ultimately on the psychological motives and undercurrents that led you to become a doctor in the first place.

All these points of personal style, which significantly affect the quality of rapport you establish at the outset of the consultation, have been learned, but not in a class-room or lecture theatre. As an 18th century philosopher, Vauvenargues, observed, "The things we know best are the things we haven't been taught." The depressing or challenging fact is that these apparent stylistic minutiae have at least as much effect on whether patients *feel* you're helping them as does your clinical decision-making. Patients take the medical skills of their doctors largely for granted. Unfortunately, although traditional methods of medical education are good at teaching young doctors their purely clinical skills, the acquisition of any effective consulting style has tended, 'faute de mieux', to be arbitrary and fortuitous. It is only recently that the mechanisms of unconscious learning have begun to be better understood and can, therefore, form the basis of a systematic programme of tuition.

So far in this chapter I have used the phrases 'conscious' and 'unconscious' learning as if they were two distinct and perhaps mutually exclusive processes. This is not the case. Learning is one function of a brain that operates all of a piece; it is only because we are intellectual busy-bodies that we are tempted to impose the language of 'either–or' distinctions upon what is really an integrated process. So what is this unitary process of which 'conscious' and 'unconscious' learning are apparently opposite poles? Just as I have encouraged you to think of the consultation as a dynamic sequence of stages rather than something static and dissectable, so human learning goes through a series of stages, each of which we may be aware or unaware of.

Masters of Eastern philosophy – who understand better than most the indivisibility and interconnectedness of the world, and also the human compulsion to intellectualize and classify our experience of it – speak of three stages through which a trainee in Zen progresses towards enlightenment.

The first is **hearing with the ear**, (or, as we might prefer to say in the print-orientated West, 'reading with the eye'.)

This is followed by **pondering in the heart**. (In the East, as until recently in the West, 'heart' denotes the seat of insight and emotion. Nowadays we would render this as 'turning over in the mind', or, more prosaically, 'developing a gut feeling'.)

Finally there is **practising with the body**, without which the preceding stages are so many 'flowers in the empty sky'.

The early Christian mystics seem to have held similar notions of the three stages whereby God works upon the human spirit. God, they wrote, "primo singula creat, secundo rapit, tertio perfecit" – first He creates things to be seen in their uniqueness, then He claims them as His own, and thirdly He brings them to perfection.

The learning sequence to which these mystics figuratively allude runs as follows. The aspiring practitioner who wishes to transform his way of being in the world is first instructed about the possibility of such transformation through the spoken or written word. His curiosity is aroused, and he begins with an intellectual study of an established corpus of knowledge. If he is serious about his task, he allows this tentative theoretical understanding to interact with his existing knowledge, memories and attitudes. In so doing, a fresh repertoire of potential experience is created in his imagination – as it were, available but as yet unexpressed. Finally, the value and validity of his new state of mind are tested and refined in the uncompromising reality of everyday life.

It is important for there to be time and opportunity for the second stage of internal processing, grafting and refashioning to take place. Without it, the veneer of change is superficial and temporary.

Similarly, if the learning process stops short of physical expression, where is the point of it? A doctor whose stated credo for instance includes 'respect for the patient as an equal', but who fails to transfer that intention from head to heart and on into actions is like a certain Czarist Russian princess. A musical illiterate, she was persuaded by her friends one winter's night to go to a performance of 'Eugene Onegin' at the St Petersburg opera. Despite the cold, she ordered her coachman to remain seated on the box of her carriage while she was in the theatre. Inside, she was moved to compassionate tears by the tale of conflict between love and duty. Outside a blizzard raged. When the princess at last emerged, her heart thrilling to the new world of music and drama, she found her coachman frozen to death.

PITSTOP

THE THREE STAGES OF LEARNING

I want to develop more rigorously the idea that learning, particularly the learning of complex behavioural skills like consulting, takes place in three stages; and moreover, each stage requires different optimum educational conditions if the learner is to reach his or her full potential.

Please look at Figure B1.2 for a few minutes, to familiarize yourself with its layout. It summarizes the learning process in a combination of words and images.

The three stages are:

    (1)   the stage of **instruction,**
    (2)   the stage of **imagination,**
and   (3)   the stage of **expression.**

A proportion of any educational information presented passes through a kind of 'selection gate' as it enters the learner's central nervous system. In so doing it sinks beneath the 'threshold of awareness', with the effect that the learner remains largely unaware of how the information is being processed. The combination of new information with the learner's pre-existing knowledge and experience takes place in what the drawing depicts as a factory 'assembly shop'. Indications that a recombination process is going on emerge like smoke signals from the factory chimney and float into awareness in the form of thoughts, plans and internal dialogue. The products of the assembly line (freshly-acquired learning) are fed back into the store of

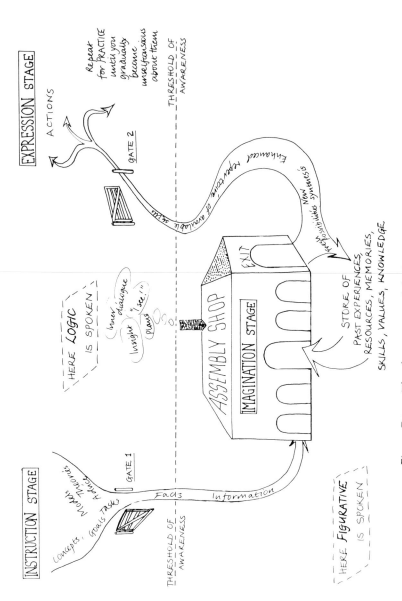

Figure B1.2 The three stages of the learning process

available resources. They also re-emerge through a second gate above the threshold of awareness in the form of an enhanced repertoire of actions in which the new learning displays itself. With practice, the new skills become gradually more automatic and 'second nature'.

The 'instruction' stage

This stage needs little saying about it, as it is the stage you are already most familiar with. Chapters A2 and A3 of this book have gone into it in some detail. Information which the pupil is intended to learn, and which it is hoped will ultimately produce a change in behaviour, is presented in the form of facts, concepts, models, theories, tasks, goals or advice. The language in which instructions are couched is usually 'logic'; instructions usually originate in the left hemisphere of the teacher, and are expressed in a linear sequence of words which makes most sense to the left hemisphere of the learner. The Zen monk mentioned earlier would in his own context call this the stage of "hearing with the ear", or "reading with the eye".

Gate 1

Sadly or mercifully, not all the information which arrives at our sense organs is admitted beyond the peripheral nervous system and brain stem. You'll recall from physiology the concept of 'efferent control' of sense organs, whereby the sensitivities of the eye, the ear and the assorted receptors in the skin are controlled via efferent fibres by higher cerebral centres, in order to protect the brain from stimulus overload. In the heat of battle, for instance, pain messages are filtered out; in a discotheque the ear is rendered relatively insensitive to quiet sounds, though you can still pick out your name softly spoken.

A similar 'filtering' principle operates also at a higher level of neural organization. In the educational setting, a person learns most effectively things which he knows he is ready to learn, material which interests and motivates him, which he already has some inkling of, and about which he feels curious to learn more. Depending on these various internal variables, one person presented with a set of new ideas might say, "This is irrelevant; I can't and I don't need to and I don't want to understand it," while a second, similarly instructed, might respond, "How fascinating – this is exactly what I need to know about." A process akin to this is seen operating in animals who have 'sensitive periods' when particular behaviours are preferentially learned, or in the ordered progression of a human baby from one developmental milestone to the next. It is as if our learning faculty knows in advance what fresh knowledge would make a timely and welcome addition to our existing store, and can close the gate on any material which doesn't seem likely to suit our purpose. My Zen monk would be familiar with a saying,

"When the Pupil is ready, the Master appears."

The 'imagination' stage

I use this label to describe those parts of the learning process that take place in the thoughts and imagination of the learner. Neurologically, the right hemisphere makes its major contribution at this stage. The role of the imagination has tended to be overlooked and undervalued by traditional educational methods, an imbalance I am trying to redress in this book. "Out of sight" does not mean "out of mind" or "out of reach".

Threshold of awareness

Of the information that gets through the first selection gate, not all reaches full conscious awareness. Some 'pre-conscious' thoughts and sensations are hovering just out of reach, in the wings whence they can easily be coaxed into attention if necessary. Until you read this sentence you were probably not aware of the sensations in your neck and shoulders, but now that I mention it, you are. Other 'subconscious' and 'unconscious' events take place in the shallows and the deeps of mental life, and can be detected or inferred only by the patient trawling of psychoanalysts. I use the term 'threshold of awareness' to indicate, as a frontier does, that there are two functionally distinct neuropsychological territories, with different languages and working methods.

'Figurative' language

Whereas 'logic' is the language of our consciousness, in the unconscious we speak 'figurative' language. Unconscious processes make their own kind of sense, which is different from the rational sense we aim for in everyday conscious activity. 'Unconscious sense' is the sense of the painter and the poet; of the mystic and the lover; of hypnotists and comedians; of advertisements and dreams. 'Figurative' is the brain's language for handling memory, fantasy, intuition, art and humour.

Although by definition we cannot as educators have direct access to the unconscious, we can nevertheless influence it indirectly. It is possible to structure the form and format of information presented to consciousness in such a way that, once past the selection gate, it is processed unconsciously in ways likely to produce the response we seek. The right hemisphere can, as it were, be seduced into co-operation, but not forced.

For example, if I wanted to teach you how important it is for parents to demonstrate a consistent moral stance, or what is meant by sublimation of the sexual impulse, there are several textbooks of child psychiatry to which I could refer you, and which you might or might not read. Alternatively, to make the same points I could take you to a performance of Peter Shaffer's play 'Equus', about how it comes about that a young man puts out the eyes of six horses. You would find that more memorable.

Here are some examples of figurative language forms with which we can communicate with the unconscious. You will recognize some of them already from this book.

- The association of ideas, e.g. linking the five checkpoints to the fingers and thumb of your left hand;
- Images, e.g. the two heads, Organizer and Responder, taking it in turns to sit on your shoulders;
- Metaphors and analogies, e.g. the consultation being like a journey;
- Puns and wordplays, e.g. the R. D. Laing 'Knots';
- Proverbs and aphorisms;
- Jokes and cartoons;
- Poetry;
- Fantasies, visualizations and daydreams, e.g. the 'picture yourself consulting skilfully' exercise in chapter A1;
- Neologisms, e.g. 'checkpoints';
- Myths and folk tales, e.g. the stories of the Trojan horse, or Androcles and the lion;
- Models (in the sense of illustrative role-models), e.g. Doctors A and B in chapter A1;
- Verbal ambiguities that make you wonder exactly what's meant, e.g. does 'nothing acts faster than Anadin' mean that Anadin acts faster or slower than nothing?

Resource store

> There is a concealed strength in men's memories which they take no notice of.
>
> Thomas Fuller, 1642

We don't understand how memory works. Some experimental evidence suggests that specific memories are located in specific points of synaptic patterns in the brain. Other evidence inclines to the view that memory works as if the brain were a giant hologram, with each part possessing to some extent all the qualities of the whole. How neuroanatomy and neurochemistry interact remains unknown. What we can say with certainty, however, is that the mind of each of us contains an immense storehouse of resources – past experiences which we draw upon in order to understand and adapt to our ever-changing circumstances. Whenever a learning task confronts us, our minds automatically turn to whatever previous learning resources will assist us.

By 'learning resources' I mean the stored traces of past occasions when we have learned and displayed to some degree qualities which will be useful in the present. A large proportion (some would say the whole) of everything we ever learn remains available to recall. Learning acquired in one context can, given the right reminders, be nudged into accessibility and made use of in a different context. This 'transfer of learning' operates as a labour-saving device for the memory. Learning resources include previously acquired knowledge, behavioural sub-routines, skills, attitudes, perception sets, memories and feelings. They make a contribution, imaginary at first but later practical, to the way we handle new information. An example might make this clear.

Suppose I want to teach you how to inject the shoulder joint with hydrocortisone, a skill which at the moment you don't possess. I can tell you the indications, point out the anatomical landmarks, describe the injection technique, and refer you to a textbook of physical medicine. This would constitute the 'instruction' stage. But in learning this new skill you wouldn't be starting from scratch. You would probably already possess some of the necessary component knowledge, skills and attitudes which, if you could link them in, would make the task easier. Useful resources in this case might include:

– your recall of that excellent lecture–demonstration you attended recently by a consultant rheumatologist, (previous knowledge, role-models);

– having previously learned to aspirate the knee joint, (existing skills);

– already knowing how to draw up and prepare a syringe for intravenous injection, and use sterile procedures, (behavioural sub-routines);

– your willingness to try out new procedures, as you've been doing throughout your medical career to date, (attitude of being open to new learning);

– the gratitude of Mr and Mrs Biffen, with whom last week you first tried your hand at marital counselling, (attitude of anticipating a successful outcome);

– your experience, learned the hard way, that it's normal and necessary to feel nervous before attempting something new, but in hindsight, it usually proves to have been worth it, (being able to overcome anxiety);

– your personal career goal of developing your professional skills as far as possible, (motivating effect of self-image).

Some of these resources – the knowledge and technical skills – you would employ consciously. On the other hand, you might not realise the resources you already possessed in the areas of attitude, feelings and motivation. The desirable resources listed above might well be mixed up with others less helpful, such as the fear of failure, or doubting whether injecting shoulders should be part of a general practitioner's repertoire. Any skill I had as a teacher would lie both in the clarity of my instructions and also in my ability to evoke learning resources appropriate to the task in hand.

'Assembly shop'

During the learning process, two sources of information combine their contributions: new material coming from the outside world, and your own personal store of resources. New learning is never taken on board as completely and uncritically as the instructor hopes. There is always an interaction with what the learner already knows, remembers, thinks and feels. The evocation of the learner's internal resources happens automatically, and is usually below the threshold of awareness. But by the skilful use of figurative language the teacher can evoke particular resources more likely to help learning than hinder it.

For instance, if I now quote an aphorism of G.K. Chesterton,

"You can only find truth with logic if you have already found truth without it",

your right hemisphere will quickly spot that it makes some kind of sense, figuratively if not logically. I hope it will evoke in you a degree of willingness not to be too critical too soon of what I am currently writing about, and make it slightly more likely that you will recognize that what I'm saying is something you knew all along.

The products of the assembly shop are "possibilities". When you combine fresh instructions with existing resources, what you produce are blueprints for new experience. To the unconscious mind, the equation

$$PAST + PRESENT = FUTURE$$

is a simple truth. You create some new ideas that might or might not prove fruitful; or an attitude shift that may or may not last; or a picture of a situation that hasn't yet happened; or the prospect of a new piece of behaviour you haven't yet tried. Because at first new learning exists only in the imagination, in a latent or potential state, I call this the 'Imagination' stage of learning. It corresponds to the 'pondering in the heart' stage of the Zen monk's apprenticeship.

Although the association process in the assembly shop is an unconscious one, we do receive conscious indications that something is happening. These come in the form of the thoughts that arise while we are coming to terms with the new information. We find ourselves thinking "Oh I see what that means," or "I don't accept that." We might get a sudden sense of things falling into place. Something might unexpectedly strike us as odd or funny. We might inwardly begin an imaginary conversation. Or we might find ourselves 'miles away', thinking about something apparently quite unrelated. In Figure B1.2, I've shown these indicators as smoke-signals floating up into awareness from the assembly shop chimney.

The 'expression' stage

> At the day of judgement we shall not be asked what we have read but what we have done.
>
> Thomas à Kempis, c. 1420

Instruction and imagination combine to bring about a state of readiness – 'learning on the verge of action'. The process is completed by being expressed in practice, a final stage that both reinforces the learning and ratifies its value. This is the 'practising with the body' demanded of the young Zen monk.

Gate 2

The association process in the 'assembly shop' produces a range of possible new responses in the learner. These possibilities may remain unexpressed; in this case they are nevertheless not forgotten, but are stored as future resources. However, newly-learned skills can be imagined as gathering at Gate 2, awaiting an opportunity to be used in the real world.

Sometimes it is circumstances that open the gate: a child runs out in front of the learner driver, who without a second thought does an emergency stop for the first time. Not until afterwards does the driver realise the connection between a reaction that seemed automatic and the instructor's tuition that had preceded it. At other times, the decision to expose the fragile wings of the newly-emergent butterfly to the wind and sun is consciously taken. After reading this book, you might consider trying out the 'connecting' skills I'll be describing in the next chapter. Before your first attempt you will probably rehearse in your mind's eye and ear how it might turn out, and you will know when it is that you consciously decide to 'connect' with the next patient.

In practice, Gate 2 is never completely closed. There is always a certain amount of 'leakage'; once learning has refashioned the network of your unconscious associations, you can no longer revert exactly to the pre-learning state. When someone has taught you how not to lose at noughts-and-crosses, you can never again naïvely play the game.

Practice

All new behaviour, whether consciously or unconsciously learned, intentionally or accidentally performed, feels unfamiliar and therefore a little frightening at first. Like a small child who has just learned how to tie a shoelace, we are 'all thumbs'. At this stage, we are very aware of our two heads; the Responder feels clumsy, and the Organizer nags incessantly. You will know from many examples in your own experience, however, that without having to force the process, we gradually become less and less self-conscious about it, until awkwardness slips away. The inner dialogue quietens. If asked how we managed to learn, we reply, "I'ld have to think about that; and in any case, it's nothing special."

HOW THIS BOOK IS HELPING YOU LEARN

We have seen how human learning involves the intellect, the imagination and the body – in that sequence, but with all three faculties making equally necessary contributions to the overall process. The role of the intellect is to select what the imagination will learn. The role of the imagination is to rehearse what the body will express. And, to complete the three-part symmetry, the role of the body is to keep the intellect rooted in reality – its feet on the ground and its head out of the clouds. The three major sections of this book exactly parallel the three stages of learning as I have described them. Section A (GOAL-SETTING) is the equivalent of the Instruction stage. The remaining chapters of Section B (SKILL-BUILDING) are the Imagination stage. Section C (GETTING IT TOGETHER) helps you (as far as any printed material can!) with the Expression stage.

Section A (Goal-setting)

The foregoing chapters have set out what it is I am endeavouring to teach you: that there are such things as consulting skills; that you can recognize them when you see them; that analysis, modelling, and traditional educational methods are helpful but insufficient means of instilling consulting skills; because consciously trying to improve can result in distracting inner dialogue; that skilled consulting can be simplified into a progression along a route with five checkpoints.

Section B (Skill-building)

In the remaining chapters of this section, my aim is to equip you with the skills necessary to move from one checkpoint to the next – in other words, to make sure that your learning resource store contains the necessary components. Sometimes it will seem as if new skills are being installed, and at others merely old ones evoked.

Section C (Getting it together)

At the end of Section B you should find yourself 'on the verge of action'. The only barrier will be how to overcome the intrusive 'inner consultation' and give full attention to what you're saying and doing to the patient. Luckily, there are some simple techniques for achieving this, and Section C will tell you about them.

B2
Checkpoint 1 (Connecting) – rapport-building skills

Only connect!

E.M. Forster (Epigraph from *Howards End*)

Very early in my general practice career I was lucky enough to learn something very important. I belonged to a case discussion group of doctors, relative strangers to each other, led by a distinguished GP for whom we felt an admiration we would die rather than admit to. One member in turn would present a patient, and then the rest of us, affecting the insight of Freud, Pasteur and Madam Arcati all rolled into one, would vouchsafe our elaborate and penetrating inter-pretations. We would then sit back and preen, waiting for the presenting doctor to gasp with belated admiration at how clever we were. If you were the doctor in the hot seat, it seemed the only way you could avoid humiliation was to spin out your presentation so interminably that there was a chance the others would lose the thread. People would sometimes go cyanosed with the effort of trying never to pause for breath.

Then the leader changed the rules. Instead of allowing a long case presentation to grow ever more convoluted, he would interrupt the presenting doctor after literally a sentence or two with a cry of "Stop right there! Now then, the rest of you, what's this patient's real problem?" We would of course protest that we hadn't yet heard enough to go on, but the leader insisted. The presenter might begin, "I saw a lady last week, Babs, known her for fifteen years, and she wanted to know whether I thought hormone replacement therapy might help her..." The leader would interject, "Right, what's the prob-lem here?", and one by one we would jump to our premature conclu-soions – frigidity, intermenstrual bleeding, doctor-worship, or whatever titillation we thought might be good for an hour's discussion.

At first we thought this was just a game that the group leader would quickly tire of, but he said no, he was there to help us help our patients, not to inflate our egos, and he wanted us to concentrate our attention where it would do most good. The first few moments of the consultation, he explained, the opening exchange of remarks, contain far more information than ever we realize. In ten or twenty seconds the patient's problem is displayed for us in microcosm, if only we can focus our eyes and attune our ears to be sufficiently perceptive. And time and time again he would ask, "What did the patient actually say? What were the actual words, the actual tone of voice?"

"Well," the luckless presenter, whose name was Keith, began. "She told me she'd seen an article in a magazine..."

"What were her actual words?"

"Er – something like – 'I've been reading this piece in the waiting room while I was waiting that says you can get something nowadays for hot flushes and that.'"

"And her voice was quiet, like yours was just then? Fine. Was that the first thing she said? No greeting?"

"Dammit, I don't know if I can remember that", says Keith, mentally peering at what by now is a very faded memory. "She might have said, 'Hallo, doctor, I hope I'm not wasting your time.'"

"Good", says the leader. "And your first words were...?"

"Evening, Babs."

"Do you call all your patients by their first names?"

"No, just people I feel I know well, and children of course."

"And she called you 'doctor', didn't use your name?"

"Yes. No. I think so."

"So she came in, and you said, 'Evening, Babs', and she said, 'Hallo, doctor, I hope I'm not wasting your time, I've been reading this piece in the waiting room while I was waiting that says you can get something nowadays for hot flushes and that.'"

And turning to the rest of us, the leader asked again, "What do you think is this lady's problem?" For some reason, we weren't as eager as before to chip in with our twopennyworth. "I'll tell you what I think", he continued, acquiring in a single bound a prodigious reputation as a psychic. "I think this lady's husband is having an affair – am I right?"

"Perfectly", gasped the awe-struck Keith, whose surname would have been Watson if the leader's had been Holmes. "It took me upwards of twenty minutes to get that out of her."

"All the clues were there in the first two sentences", said the leader. "Let me explain."

"We know that this lady was uncertain how to tell Keith about her problem, because she only finally decided how to begin while she was sitting reading in the waiting room. When patients say 'I hope I'm not wasting your time', it often means they're not sure whether you can help, or that coming to see you might be a waste of their own time. She implies there is a problem with her sexuality, because she asks about something not just for her hot flushes, but for her 'flushes *and that'*. And she hasn't fully declared her hand, because so far it's the magazine article she's asking about, not herself.

"Keith found himself addressing her in the same way he talks to children. Babs kept him at arms length by using his professional title 'doctor', not the greater intimacy of his real name. We know this was an appointment in the evening, usually a time for being with the family, so it's likely that she may have to – or want to – explain to her husband where she's been, and why.

"So here is a lady who, getting on towards bed-time, comes to a fatherly figure, reluctantly hinting in quiet downcast tones at an inadequacy in her sex life; and moreover she's not quite sure whether she ought to be telling a man about this at all. I think she's just found out her husband is having an affair."

A TUTORIAL

Chris, when I told this story, said it was the sort of smart-alec stuff that gets some doctors a bad name.

Chris: Don't you think you risk making some awful gaffes if you read too much into every little nuance? That patient could perfectly well have wanted nothing more than a diuretic.

Me: You're absolutely right. But let's not confuse two situations. It's one thing to jump to conclusions in a discussion group, where the worst that can happen is that some of your peers have a laugh at your expense. It would have been another matter altogether if Keith had actually said to his patient, "You don't need to tell me any more – I presume your husband's having an affair." That would have been dangerous, rude, insensitive, and quite possibly wrong.

Nevertheless, the patient does communicate an enormous amount of information at the very start of the consultation, and a doctor who lets it go by unnoticed misses a great opportunity. The point is, the doctor needs to do lots of *noticing*, but as little as possible *evaluating* or *judging*. In the 'two heads' analogy, at the beginning of the consultation we want to keep the Responder in charge and at maximum sensitivity, and to keep the Organizer on a tight rein. Its time comes later, once all the necessary information has been collected.

So if Keith had been able to detect rather more of the

information that was embedded and concealed in Babs' words, and been content just to notice what was there with an open mind, without immediately trying to make it *mean* something – how do you think the consultation might have gone on?

Chris: I can imagine he might have got to the root of her underlying problems rather more quickly. He would probably have come over to the patient as easy to talk to, intuitive, sympathetic.

Me: In a word, they would have established a good *rapport*. What do you understand by that word, 'rapport'?

Chris: It's a feeling that builds up between two people as they begin to trust each other's company, like being on the same wavelength.

Me: So rapport is a part of the process of communication – probably the most fundamental part. When two people communicate, they alternately transmit and receive information, like two radio-telephones. Developing rapport is like making sure both sets are tuned to the same frequency. If the sets aren't in tune with each other, messages either don't get through, or are distorted by interference. In the consultation, it ought to be the patient who 'selects the frequency', so the doctor has to be able quickly to 'tune himself' to catch the patient's signals.

Chris: That reminds me of an aunt of mine who went on a trip to Japan. Everyone else was buying the cheap electronic goods, radios and such, but she wouldn't. She said she didn't want to listen to Japanese radio programmes when she got home to Basingstoke. She didn't believe you could tune a Japanese radio to British frequencies.

Me: I'll bet you've met doctors who were like foreign radio sets without a tuning facility. Let's think a bit more about what rapport is...

Rapport is –

- the 'sine qua non' of effective communication;
- two people being mutually responsive to each other's signals;
- showing that you understand what the other person is communicating;
- not the same as liking someone;
- part of what a doctor owes a patient;
- a process, not a state: something you actively *do*, like tuning a

116

frequency dial, not something you passively hope might happen;
- the route to the **connecting** checkpoint;
- reading the physical signs of someone's mental state;
- often established at an unconscious level;
- something you can nevertheless consciously practise, by developing greater sensory awareness of the minimal cues by which people signal their thoughts and feelings.

Chris: I think you'll need to tell me a bit more about what you mean by 'sensory awareness of minimal cues', and 'reading the physical signs of someone's mental state', and how I can practise them.

Me: The obvious way we communicate our thoughts and feelings is by speech. But as you know, a proportion – probably the greater, and certainly the more honest part – of our communication is non-verbal. Non-verbal communication includes speech-related 'paraverbal' things like tone of voice, rate, pitch and volume, and other 'body language', which includes such things as posture, gesture, facial expression and eye movements. Because some 'cues to meaning' are often not referred to consciously, but instead are perceived and reacted to subliminally, we call them 'minimal cues'. You can quickly train yourself to develop a greater awareness of them. First, we'll look at what minimal cues are there to be noticed, and then, as your powers of observation improve, I'll tell you how to use them in the consultation to establish rapport.
         Let me tell you about gambits and curtain-raisers ...

Gambits and curtain-raisers

In chess, some of the opening moves are called 'gambits'. One player makes a move calculated to draw a particular response from the opponent, which the gambit-maker hopes can be turned to his own advantage. Patients make opening gambits too. The first thing a patient says is the only part of the consultation he or she has much control over. In all the later stages the patient is very much reacting to you, the doctor. While patients are awaiting their turn to see you, they are usually silently rehearsing exactly what it is they are planning to say, how they are going to begin, how they are going to explain their symptoms or their requests. You'll know yourself how you do this on your way to an interview with, say, your bank manager to ask for a loan. But once the patient finally enters your room, the intended opening gambit sometimes gets modified by a spontaneous response to the way you look, or the things you say. So you often find patients coming out with an unrehearsed and unscripted remark which betrays a lot about their state of mind or the way they perceive you. I call these unguarded remarks 'curtain-raisers'.

For example, let's imagine Mr Gall, a businessman aged forty, who over several weeks has developed post-prandial epigastric pain. He decides to consult you, and plans to begin by saying, "I've been getting these stomach pains; I expect it's just indigestion." By calling it 'indigestion' he probably hopes that you'll think he's a stoical sort of chap, and that if that's all it turns out to be, he can claim it was someone else who made him come. But when he enters your room, his planned opening gambit is prefaced by a curtain-raiser:

"You're a difficult man to get to see – anyway, I've been getting these stomach pains. . ."

The curtain-raiser "You're a difficult man to get to see" immediately adds several possible layers of meaning. Is Mr Gall criticizing your surgery arrangements? Has he had a disagreement with a receptionist? Is he flattering you by implying you're worth waiting for? Does he want to show you that his time is no less important than yours? Is he an aggressive, adrenalin-addicted and ulcer-prone individual? Would he like to be treated privately? You don't yet know, and it would be foolhardy to respond prematurely. But it would be equally clumsy if you failed to register that the curtain-raiser contains some message about his attitude or expectations. All you can do – all you need to do – at the outset is to notice, and suspend judgement.

Here are some other curtain-raisers which might have preceded the same "indigestion" gambit. Give each a moment's thought, and notice what possible underlying issues they might reflect.

"I can't remember when you last saw me up here. . ."
"I don't think we've met – I usually see the other doctor. . ."
"Hullo, Doc, how's the new car going? Had your holidays yet?. . ."
"I can't afford any time off, but. . ."
"Don't go giving me any pills or anything, but. . ."
"I don't know where to start. . ."
"Erm . . ." (long silence)
"I'm sorry to be a nuisance. . ."
"I don't like coming here. . ."
"Is it all right if we both come in?. . ."

Sometimes the curtain-raiser may be absent, or redundant in terms of information, a little piece of purely social ritual that softens the

"Is it all right if we both come in?"

impact of the opening gambit. During the course of a single surgery session you will find examples of non-existent, redundant and highly significant curtain-raisers. I've just looked through a video tape of a morning surgery, and noted the following selection of curtain-raisers and gambits.

"I only just woke up." (curtain-raiser) "I just want some more pills." (gambit)

"You're very kind. Thanks ever so much." (curtain-raiser, on being invited to sit down) "Andrew's had these warty things on his hand." (gambit)

"You're busy this morning." (curtain-raiser) "I don't seem to have the energy I used to." (gambit)

"Peter, I told you not to bring that in with you! Aren't they the limit?" (curtain-raiser) "It's his ears again." (gambit)

"You'll be getting fed up with me." (curtain-raiser) "I don't know what we're going to do about my knee." (gambit)

"Aren't they the limit?"

I also noticed, looking at the video, how easily the doctor can inadvertently suppress a curtain-raiser by imposing his own opening ritual on the consultation. If you begin "Hallo, Mrs X, come in," and then pause expectantly, you leave the space for a curtain-raiser unoccupied, and the patient will usually supply one. In contrast, a doctor who begins "Hallo, Mrs X, come in, what can I do for you?" moves the patient immediately on to their opening gambit, crowds out a curtain-raiser, and in so doing may miss the opportunity to pick up valuable indications of the patient's state of mind at that moment.

Me: There used to be a choral programme on the radio called "Let The People Sing". That would be a good motto for the start of the consultation. If I could risk some definite advice, it would be:

Leave room for the patient's curtain-raiser. Don't swamp or rush the patient with your own opening ritual. Pay close attention to the exact content and manner of the patient's first remarks. Trust the Responder in yourself to alert you to anything of particular significance. Try to let nothing escape your awareness.

120

EXERCISE

In your next surgery session, as each patient leaves the room, write down, verbatim, that patient's opening gambit, and curtain-raiser if there was one.

Do nothing more than that. Don't try to make any clever inferences or sweeping generalizations. That would be your Organizer muscling in on the Responder's act. It is enough for you just to notice. By setting yourself the task of having to remember the curtain-raiser and gambit until the end of the consultation, in order to write them down, you will be training yourself in the uncritical awareness which is all that's needed at this stage.

Please DO this exercise. Don't just mean to, or think you could if you wanted to. You need actual experience of the focused concentration it will produce.

PITSTOP

MINIMAL CUES – THE PHYSICAL SIGNS OF MENTAL STATES

Anyone can swallow with his ears; if you're smart, you listen with your eyes.

It's surprising how much you can tell, not from *what* people say, but from how they look and sound while they're saying it. Maybe you've had the experience of viewing television in a country where you weren't fluent in the language, or watched a video of a medical consultation with the sound turned down. Anyone deaf or blind will tell you that, to compensate for the particular sense that is lost, the acuity of those remaining becomes enhanced.

On the evolutionary scale, receptivity to non-verbal messages long antedates the development of formal language. Our present human consciousness so centres around the spoken and written word that we often underestimate the importance of non-verbal language. Yet our capacity to detect and respond to non-verbal signals is anything but vestigial. Everyday social life is full of examples: gaining the attention of a shop assistant, making our way unjostled down the street, or cottoning on to the fact that a close friend is worried about something.

Join in this 'thought experiment' with me.

Some people accept every invitation to a party in the hope of meeting someone they'll really get on with. Other people never go to parties, in case they meet someone they don't really get on with. Most

121

people find, when they've been to a few parties, that they know how to tell who's 'simpatico' and who isn't.

Imagine you're going to a party where you won't know anyone at all. The only thing is, as the result of participating recently in a pharmaceutical trial, you're completely invisible. Invisible, that is, until you crack open and swallow the ampoule of antidote hanging invisibly round your neck. You slip into the room where the party is in full swing, and look about you, wondering where and when to materialize. How will you decide? You start to notice the tell-tale signs of the other guests' backgrounds, moods and personalities.

Some of these are obvious. Age and sex are discernible at a glance. From people's styles of dress and material accoutrements you quickly draw inferences about their income, their social background, their attitudes and values (although you might well be wrong about these). The exercise becomes rather more interesting if you try to assess how people are feeling and behaving in relation to the others around them. In that small group over there, who's the dominant centre of attention? – the person animatedly gesticulating, leaning slightly back on confidently-planted heels, with a louder voice and more widely modulated vocal range, holding eye contact longer than others in the group. You can spot the subservient ones from their frequently down-cast eyes, and by the way their personal space is often encroached upon by the others. Their contributions to conversation are sparse, hesitant and sporadic, and their voices soft and lacking much tonal variation.

Who's bored – the person making frequent half-suppressed restless little gestures with hands and feet, looking in every direction but at their present companion, saying "Mm, mm" a bit too often and in the wrong places in the other's flow of speech. And who is the bore whose unconscious mind either hasn't seen these signals or has been overruled by an insensitive conscious ego?

How can you tell that the couple over there are comfortable in each other's company? Their personal spaces are beginning to merge. Their body postures and gestures complement each other, and the choreography of their eye contact is synchronized. Little that's happening nearby distracts them.

Can you tell who is enjoying the music. Who has taken trouble over the way he or she looks? Who is feeling relaxed, and who is ill-at-ease? Who is hoping for greater intimacy, and who is looking for an excuse to leave? It's time for you to swallow the contents of the ampoule and make your appearance in the company of the person in the room with whom you feel the closest rapport.

Figure B2.1 gives a more systematic display of the verbal and non-verbal indicators of people's thoughts and feelings. Awareness of them is essential for building rapport. Taken together, these 'minimal cues' constitute the patient's 'language of self-expression'. To build effective rapport and achieve the **connecting** checkpoint, the doctor has at the start of the consultation to obtain a working knowledge of the patient's language of self-expression, and, initially at least, talk to the patient in his or her own language.

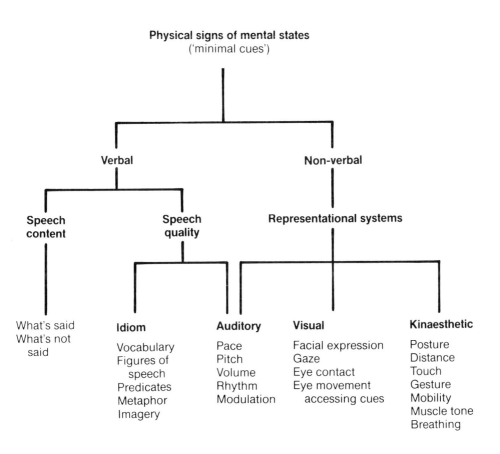

Figure B2.1 The physical signs of mental states

Many of the items in this diagram you will be perfectly familiar with. I should like, however, to explain its general concept, and some of the items which may not at first seem relevant. Many of the ideas it incorporates have been extensively developed in a therapeutic approach called 'Neuro-Linguistic Programming (NLP)[1].

What's said and what's not said

The most obvious way to discover what people are thinking and feeling is to ask them to tell you. Unfortunately, this is also the least reliable way. How many times have you heard a variation on the following snatch of dialogue played out, at home, on television, and not least in the surgery?

"How are you?"
"Fine."
"Sure?"
"I said so, didn't I?"
"Anything wrong?"
"No!"
"Oh for God's sake!" (slam)

I don't wish to suggest that patients try wilfully to mislead their doctors. Almost invariably the patient is genuinely concerned to waste no-one's time and to provide whatever information the doctor needs. But you take a risk when you tell another person about yourself. Patients come to doctors because they feel vulnerable. Disclosing that vulnerability, although essential to its resolution, initially adds to the sense of risk-taking. By being frank, you might talk your way into some unpleasant treatment, or find yourself getting upset, or having to worry about a possibly serious diagnosis, or revealing something you feel ashamed of.

As we speak, it is as if there was a pre-conscious 'censoring mechanism' monitoring what we say just before we say it, and making sure that we won't talk ourselves into trouble – rather like a Government press spokesman issuing a prepared statement and declining to comment on matters his boss doesn't yet want to be publicly known. So whenever we are on the verge of saying something that might present us in a bad light, or that breaks some taboo, or carries the risk of rebuff, our 'censor' steps in with the intention of protecting us. Instead of coming out with whatever was on the tip of our tongue, we might hesitate in mid-sentence and then go off at a tangent, or change the subject, or wrap up our meaning in vague and ambiguous language and hope the listener is good at mind-reading.

Hesitations, omissions, vaguenesses and non sequiturs are the clinical signs that speech is being censored, and that the speaker is saying less than he or she might. When as a doctor you hear a patient hesitate, or come out with a non sequitur, or try to avoid being specific, or leave out something that seems obviously relevant, then is the time to turn up the sensitivity of your ears, and listen to what is *not* being said. It is highly likely that, because your own conversational danger zones are different from the patient's, you will be able to detect what is not being said, and, if necessary, help the patient find a safe way to express it. For example:

Patient: I've been getting some bleeding from my rectum; I thought it might be piles, or constipation, er, or something I was eating, or …

Doctor: Maybe you were also worried it might be something serious, cancer even.

Patient: Everything's fine; kids are settled at school, we've no money worries, I've got a good steady job, nice car, the house is paid for …

Doctor: You didn't mention your wife. How do you and she get on?

Patient: Well, you know how it is, when you've been married a long time, I mean men and women are different, aren't they, and, er, of course, we're very happy in all sorts of other ways, so I mustn't complain …

Doctor: Sometimes when people talk like that, it's because they're having some difficulty in a sexual relationship.

It is important to be able to spot when something is being left unsaid, for two reasons. The first is that the information being suppressed may well be clinically the most important of all. Secondly, if you can help a patient put into words something he or she was finding hard to tell you, the patient will feel a great sense of relief that contributes significantly to the rapport developing between you.

The spoken part of a communication is a compromise between truth and safety, between the need to reveal and the instinct to defend the self-image. There is however always a 'leakage' of non-verbal cues which either support or give the lie to what is being said. Non-verbal cues, because we are less consciously aware of them, are less strictly censored and therefore more reliably reflect our true thoughts and feelings.

The distinction between verbal and non-verbal cues, though obvious, is not wholly correct. In verbal communication, the speaker's meaning is conveyed by the choice and sequence of words, so that a listener could understand it with the eyes shut. The non-verbal components are expressed through the musculo-skeletal system, and are detectable by someone with eyes open but ears stopped. But there is an overlap. Certain qualities of the voice – listed in the 'Auditory' column in figure B2.1 – carry useful information independent of the words being spoken, and are thus more akin to non-verbal messages.

Representational systems

The significance we ascribe to every object and experience we encounter – from an egg to a symphony – is based solely and ultimately on the physical sensations the object or experience originally produced in our various sense organs. An egg has no 'meaning', no quality of 'eggness', beyond its oval shape, its pale brown colour, the cool satiny texture we feel as we weigh it in our hand, the cracking sound its shell makes before we taste it, the feel of soft-boiled yolk on the tongue, and the way our mouth waters as we smell the accompanying scent of breakfast coffee. Mahler, composing his complex and sublime Ninth Symphony, did nothing more nor less than discover those particular sequences of notes, rhythms and harmonies which reproduced for him the self-same tears, the actual aching sensations of numbness and weariness he had previously endured when his eldest daughter died. The listener, aware of a moistening of the eye or a tightening in the throat, is feeling the memory of his or her own pain, not Mahler's. An innocent who had never wept for loss of a personal treasure would hear the symphony unmoved.

The brain encodes all experience in terms of visual, auditory, kinaesthetic and, to a lesser degree, olfactory information. 'Kinaesthetic' experience includes feelings arising from the skin, proprioceptive information derived from muscles, and the subtle combinations of sensation that signal to us our emotional state. Each of us has a preference for one or other of the three main sense modalities, sight, sound or feeling. Some of us think mainly in pictures, others think in sounds and imaginary conversations, while others work things out by reliving the memories of bodily and emotional feelings. Experts in neuro-linguistics[1] speak of three corresponding Representational Systems:

Visual (V),
Auditory (A)
and Kinaesthetic (K).

We tend to couch our perceptions, memories and descriptions in terms of one preferred Representational System rather than another. For example, ask three people what they liked best about a coach trip to the seaside. The 'Visual' person will tell you about the scenery on the way, the light shimmering on the sea and the sand, and the colours of the boats in the harbour. The Visual's memories will consist mainly of images and pictures. The 'Auditory' person will remember more of the conversations, the fairground music and the sound of the waves on the beach. The 'Kinaesthetic' may find it harder to put his or her recollections into words, but will easily recapture in imagination the warmth of the sun, the feel of sand underfoot, and the relaxation of sunbathing on a comfortable air-bed.

Knowing about Representational Systems is of more than academic interest if you want to connect with a patient and achieve empathy. Identifying the patient's preferred system, and consciously matching your own choice of words to that system, is a short-cut to rapport. The patient, without quite knowing why, will feel intuitively understood. The pair of you will, quite literally, be speaking the same language. So you need to be able to recognize Representational Systems quickly and easily.

Predicates

Many of the verbs, adverbs and adjectives used in the course of everyday speech have Visual, Auditory or Kinaesthetic associations, and indicate the Representational System the speaker is predominantly thinking in at that moment. Words that act as marker flags (V), or warning bells (A) or pointers (K) in this way are called 'predicates'. Here are some clinical examples:

"You may need an operation. How do you *view that prospect?*" (V)
"How does that *sound* to you?" (A)
"How do you *feel* about that?" (K)

"I'ld like you to *look at* this rash." (V)
"I'ld like you to *listen* to my chest." (A)
"I'ld like you to *feel* my pulse." (K)

"I'm *off colour.*" (V)
"I'm *off key.*" (A)
"I'm *off balance.*" (K)

"I *see* what you mean." (V)
"I *hear* what you're *saying.*" (A)
"I *grasp* what it is you're *going through.*" (K)

127

"Let's *look into* this." (V)
"Let's *talk* this over." (A)
"Let's *get to grips* with this problem." (K)

"Let me make this *clear*." (V)
"Let me *spell* it out." (A)
"Let me *lay this on the line*." (K)

"The future *looks* bleak. My life's a *mess*." (V)
"We're not *in tune* with each other any more. We just *row* and *clash*." (A)
"I don't know where to *turn*. I feel *stuck in a rut*." (K)

"The *outlook's brighter* now." (V)
"Life's *quieter* now. Things are more *harmonious*." (A)
"Things are beginning to *fall* into *place*." (K)

EXERCISE

Once you've got the hang of this, it can be quite entertaining to spot (tell, latch onto) the predicates in people's everyday speech. In order to train your powers of observation you can do either or both of two things.

Mentally translate what you've heard into its equivalent in another Representational System, e.g. "I haven't *seen* you for ages", could become "I haven't *heard* from you", or "We've rather lost *touch*."

Reply using the same Representational System as the speaker, e.g. "Things are *getting on top* of me." (K) "So you feel under *pressure*?", or, "I had a *call* from Bill." (A) "Bill? Name *rings a bell*."

In establishing rapport, the doctor is trying to understand how the world appears to the patient. What other ways are there to get inside someone else's eyes, ears and skin, and get a sense of how the world appears to another person? One way is by listening attentively to the imagery, figures of speech and metaphors patients use to tell you about themselves. Another way – which surprised me the first time I heard about it, but it works – is from the directions in which people's eyes are constantly moving as you talk to them.

Imagery, figures of speech and metaphors

Luckily, people don't converse all the time in the logical, no-nonsense language of scientific papers. The reason such formal language can become boring after a while is that it has been intentionally pruned of all traces of the speaker's individual personality. However much we might wish, while trying to establish the exact history of an abdominal pain, that a patient would 'stick to the point', everyday speech is enriched and enlivened by a generous sprinkling of idiosyncracies. Spoken language is full of ambiguities, favourite vocabulary and images, metaphors and analogies which tell the alert listener a great deal about the speaker's thought processes. Again you will find if you keep your ears open that the three categories of Visual, Auditory and Kinaesthetic are useful.

Here are three patients beginning to tell you what's worrying them. First, the Visual, full of 'seeing' words and colourful imagery:

"I thought I'd look in and see you, doctor. I saw my sister last week, I hadn't seen her for ages, and we had tea at that new place just opposite the church, where they have all those cakes in the window. Anyway, I put on a blue dress I'd had since last summer, and my sister took one glance at me and said I looked like something out of Belsen, I'd got that thin . . ."

Next, the Auditory, full of 'saying' words and accounts of previous conversations:

"Doctor, I just want you to tell me I needn't worry. I read this article that said if you thought you were losing weight and couldn't explain it, you should go and ask your doctor. When I told my husband about it, he said, 'Okay, love,' he said, 'if you think it sounds like it might apply to you, go and ask,' he said . . ."

Finally the Kinaesthetic, using 'feeling' words, both sensory and emotional, to describe her situation. She might well begin with a handshake or a touch on the doctor's arm:

"I'm hoping you'll be able to take a weight off my mind. Actually I've been worried sick – when I stood on the scales it was as if someone had knocked the stuffing out of me. I've gone down over a stone, and I've got a good appetite. So I turned round and told my husband . . ."

Eye movement accessing cues

You're bound to have noticed how people's eyes flick about in various directions while they're speaking and thinking. But did you know that these involuntary eye movements form patterns that tell you whether a person is at that exact moment thinking in pictures, or words, or feelings? I don't know why – I don't think anyone does – but you can check this out for yourself, and you will find that it's by and large true.

People glance *upwards* when they are remembering or imagining a
visual image.

They glance *to the side* when remembering or imagining *sounds or
words.*

They glance *downwards* when experiencing or remembering a *feeling.*

The direction of the eye movement, left or right, is also significant.
A more complete description of the eye movement patterns, (called
'Accessing Cues' because they are cues to which of the three
Representational Systems the person is accessing at that moment), is
as follows:

Eyes **up** and **to the left** – **remembering** a **visual** memory
Eyes **up** and **to the right** – (VR)
constructing an imaginary
visual image (VC)

Eyes **horizontal** and **to the left** – **remembering** an **auditory**
memory, recalling a previous
dialogue (AR)

Eyes **horizontal** and **to the right** –**constructing** an imaginary
auditory event, thinking what
to say (AC)

Eyes **down** and **to the left** – carrying on an **internal
auditory** dialogue, imagining
a conversation (AI)

Eyes **down** and **to the right** – having or remembering a
kinaesthetic experience, a
bodily or emotional feeling
(K)

These directions are the ones usually found in right-handed people,
and in left-handed people with the left hemisphere as the dominant
speech hemisphere. In a minority of left-handed people the directions
left and right are reversed, but not the ups and downs. Figure B2.2 is
an 'aide-memoire' for spotting these accessing cues.

It is easy to 'calibrate' a speaker's eye movement accessing cues by
asking a short series of questions that require particular thought
processes to answer. For instance:

"What colour are the sheets on your bed?", or "What did you have
for breakfast this morning?" will activate a visual memory (VR) and
the eyes will usually flick up and to the left just before the reply
comes.

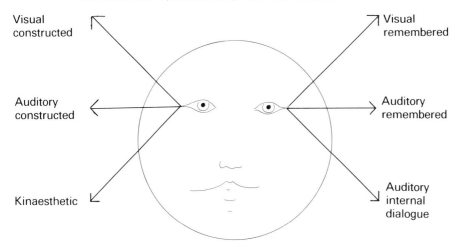

Figure B2.2 Eye movement accessing cues

"Can you imagine how traffic lights would look if the colours were upside down?", or "How would you look from my point of view?" requires the construction of an imaginary picture (VC), and the glance is usually up and to the right.

"What's your favourite type of music?" – Auditory Remembered (AR), eye movement horizontal and to the left.

"How would my voice sound if I pinched my nose?" – Auditory Constructed (AC), eye movement horizontal and to the right.

"What question would you most like to ask the Prime Minister?" – Auditory Internal dialogue, (AI), eye movement down and to the left.

"How are you feeling at the moment?", or "What's it like to have cramp in your leg?" – Kinaesthetic (K), eyes down and to the right.

Figure B2.3, illustrates this.

EXERCISE

You now know three ways of recognizing when someone is thinking Visually, Auditorily or Kinaesthetically:

    (1) by the verbal predicates he or she uses;
    (2) by the imagery, metaphors and figures of speech;
and (3) by the eye movement accessing cues.

Make yourself a copy of Figure B2.2, preferably by hand so that making the copy helps you to remember it. Put it on your desk in a position where you will notice it periodically during a consultation.

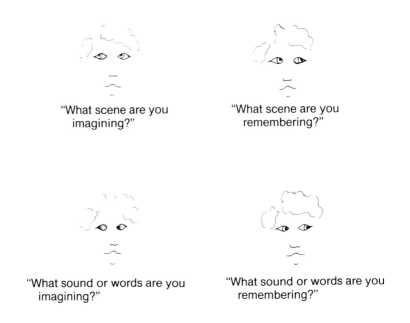

"What scene are you
imagining?"

"What scene are you
remembering?"

"What sound or words are you
imagining?"

"What sound or words are you
remembering?"

"What are you feeling?"

"What are you imagining
yourself saying?"

Figure B2.3 Calibrating accessing cues

Two or three times during each consultation, remind yourself to 'listen between the lines' of the patient's speech, and, using any or all of these cues, decide which Representational System the patient is at that moment using.

(There will be times when this is obvious, and other times when you can't decide, either because there seem to be no cues, or because cues from all three systems are all mixed up. This does not matter – it just goes to show how complex human beings are. As with the 'gambits and curtain-raiser' exercise, the object is primarily to improve your noticing ability.)

So far we have thought about what patients say, what they don't say, and the linguistic and eye movement cues to their preferred sensory modalities. The remaining minimal cues I want to discuss – the indicators of mental states – are the purely non-verbal ones, listed in the 'Auditory', 'Visual' and 'Kinaesthetic' columns of Figure B2.1. These require little explanation from me, as you have been perceiving and responding to them all your life. Let me repeat that all you have to do at this stage is to discriminate them: to know that they are there and notice them. You don't have to try to interpret them, or read a complicated message into every little twitch the patient makes.

Auditory cues

Pace: Does the patient speak fast or slowly? How fast or slow? If you understand musical terms, is the tempo marking adagio, andante, moderato, allegretto, allegro, or presto?

Pitch: Is the voice predominantly high-pitched or low-pitched? Treble, soprano, mezzo-soprano, contralto, alto, tenor, baritone or bass?

Volume: Is the voice quiet, so soft that you have to lean forward and strain to hear it? Or is it loud, making you want to back away? Or is it quite comfortable?

Rhythm: Is the flow of speech regular and rhythmic? Or broken up, irregular and sporadic? Are some parts of the sentences given emphasis?

Modulation: How much do the other speech qualities – pace, pitch, volume and rhythm – vary? Does the speaker's delivery stay much the same all the time? Or are there times where the voice quality changes abruptly? Are there some topics that are discussed in one tone of voice, and others where another voice is used?

Visual cues

Facial expression: The power of the human face to convey nuances of emotion is legendary, and would not be so unless we were all innately able to recognize the various patterns. What mood or emotion does the patient's face convey? Does it vary? Is the facial expression appropriate to the subject being discussed?

Gaze: Where is the patient's gaze mainly directed? At you, or down at the floor, or over your shoulder, or at objects in the room? Does it seem a warm, comfortable gaze? Or are there qualities of distress, or coldness, or flirtatiousness?

Eye contact: Does the patient maintain a comfortable degree of eye contact with you? Or is eye contact held only briefly? Who usually breaks eye contact first? Do you find yourself wanting more or less eye contact with this patient?

Eye movements: Are the patient's eye movements on a large or small scale? How easy is it for you to recognize the eye movement accessing cues? Does there seem to be a lot of internal imagery before the patient speaks, or a little?

Kinaesthetic cues

Posture: Does the patient sit erect or slumped? Lean forwards or backwards in the chair? Is the posture open, with hands relaxed, arms unfolded and legs uncrossed? Or is it closed and inhibited, with hands clenched, and arms and legs crossed?

Distance: What seems to be the 'right' distance between you and the patient? Does the patient seem to want to sit closer to you or further away? Does either of you move the chair to alter the separation between you?

Touch: How comfortable does the patient seem with physical contact? Was there a handshake or mutual touch as the patient entered the room? Does the patient flinch and tense at your touch? Or is it accepted and welcomed? Does the patient sometimes initiate physical contact between you?

Gesture: Does the patient use a lot of gesturing, or seem relatively restrained? Magnus Pyke or Queen Victoria? What part of the patient's body is the most expressive?

Mobility: Are the patient's posture and gestures constantly changing, or relatively static? Are the changes natural or contrived? Do they seem to result from high energy levels, discomfort, or restlessness?

Muscle tone: Is the patient relaxed or tense? If tense, which muscle groups contain most tension? Is it the hands, or the abdomen, or the neck and shoulders? Are there any topics which when discussed affect the patient's tension level?

Breathing: How fast is the patient breathing? Deeply or shallowly? At a steady rate, or with variation? Is the breathing mainly abdominal or thoracic?

PITSTOP

A note of re-assurance: this is a long chapter, the longest in the book. And it's only about the very beginning of the consultation! Do not despair. Although the chapter so far has reviewed and presented a great deal of information, making use of it to connect with the patient is quite easy. Furthermore, a grasp of the ingredients of rapport makes all subsequent stages of the consultation much easier.

LEARNING AND SPEAKING THE PATIENT'S LANGUAGE OF SELF-EXPRESSION – MAKING USE OF MINIMAL CUES

All the verbal and non-verbal cues that we have so far considered can be regarded as physical signs reflecting the inner world of the patient's thoughts and feelings. They constitute the patient's 'language of self-expression'. We have seen (heard, gathered!) that there are three 'sub-languages' or 'dialects' of this largely unspoken language. The question now arises of how to use this understanding to further our aim of establishing rapport with the patient on the way to the CONNECTING checkpoint.

Just as in the clinical realm, symptoms and signs cluster together into syndromes, so there are particular clusters or combinations of minimal cues which have particular meanings. There are three such clusters of minimal cues indicating three mental processes which it is important to be able to recognize in the consultation. You need to know how each patient looks when he or she is engaging in each of these three thought processes. Once you know them, you will find it quite simple to establish and maintain rapport. They will also provide invaluable feedback for you later in the consultation. You could think of them as three stock phrases in the language of self-expression. I think that, having been alerted already to the spectrum of minimal cues, you will quickly recognize these three states as I describe them. The three cardinal mental processes, each with characteristic physical signs, are:

- speech censoring;
- internal search;

and – acceptance set.

The first you know about already.

Speech censoring

In the section on 'What's said and what's not said', I described the pre-conscious censor whose motto is 'think before you speak', and who, to coin a phrase, closes our mouth before we put our foot in it. Look back now and re-read that section if you need to. The linguistic signs that some act of internal censorship is going on include:

- *hesitating* in mid-sentence or mid-paragraph;
- *omitting* some piece of information that common sense suggests should be included;
- being persistently *vague* in descriptions, and withholding specific details of sensitive issues;
- raising sensitive issues obliquely, by *hinting* and *implication*;
- skipping in a *non sequitur* way from one idea to another not obviously linked to it, so that the listener has to guess at the connection.

Pause now for a moment to see whether you have a mental picture of the way someone looks and sounds while the censoring process is at work. Maybe you can think of a specific example, or perhaps you have already noticed this process accurately enough to be able to generalize. You might, for instance, hear a slight change in the tone of voice, or a nervous clearing of the throat. You might notice a temporary loss of eye contact, and a restless shift of position or slight 'backing away' movement.

Internal search

Try this thought experiment. You and I are sitting talking. A video camera is recording us. I ask if I might put a question to you. You tell me I may. I ask you, "What was the most embarrassing thing that ever happened to you?"

You think for a while, your mind racing. Why's he asking that? Why should I tell him? What will he want to know next? What *was* the most embarrassing thing, anyway? Ah yes, I remember. Goodness, that was embarrassing. It makes me squirm even now, just to think about it. No, I couldn't tell him that. Maybe I could pick some other occasion instead. How about ...? Yes, that'll do, I'll say that one.

And you open your mouth to speak. Before you can say a word I cut you off, and instead we rewind the video tape and watch on the monitor your behaviour from the moment I asked the question until the moment you were on the point of replying. What shall we see on the screen?

What the video camera would have picked up are the physical signs

"What was the most embarrassing thing that ever happened to you?"

of 'internal search'. The lengthy pause while you thought, which looked like silence from the outside, was in fact a time of intense mental activity. You were thinking, pondering, and puzzling things out. Various old memories – scenes, people, conversations – were being dredged up, and, to some extent old emotions were being restimulated. You were searching inwardly through all the information you needed to decide how to answer my question, weighing up the pros and cons of several possible replies.

On the video, we would probably see you become comparatively immobile, your position frozen and any gesturing halted. There might be some increase in muscle tone around the hands, forehead and neck, There might be a transient change in your respiration rate, were we able to observe it, your pulse rate too.

Your eyes would be particularly revealing, especially the pattern of eye movements. Two things may happen: there may be a period of very rapid eye movements, upwards and to the left and right, indicating that you were remembering and imagining a series of visual memories and fantasies, alternating with movements down and to the right, as you recalled various emotional feelings. We would also notice that for a while your eyes become very still and defocused, as your attention was directed inwardly rather than towards your surroundings. Although you might still be looking towards me, your gaze would seem to be directed through me or beyond me, and not at me. Depending on the emotional associations of your memories, there might be a misting or a moistening of the eyes as well. Then, just as you were about to speak, your eye movements would probably change to horizontal, or down and to the left, as you planned exactly what to say. Your eyes would abruptly refocus, there might be a slight smile on your lips, and you might shift your previously still position.

These minimal cues, particularly the lack of movement and the defocusing of the eyes, are indications that a person is doing some serious thinking. When you see these signs of internal search, do not interrupt. You may destroy a line of thought that is particularly productive. Signs of internal search are the equivalent of a 'Do Not Disturb' notice. Only when you see the refocusing and the resumption of mobility that mark the end of the internal search should you say anything at all. Respecting the privacy of times of internal search is a powerful aid to rapport.

Acceptance set

It is very helpful to know when the patient is agreeing or disagreeing with you, accepting or rejecting what you say. It's not too cynical to observe that patients sometimes tell you, "Yes doctor, I will doctor, that's right doctor, I understand doctor," when in fact, as their future actions will confirm, the opposite is true. The non-verbal signals of agreement or disagreement are more reliable than the verbal. So at all stages of the consultation you need to be able to detect non-verbally whether or not the patient is genuinely happy with whatever is going on. The frame of mind of being willing to accept and welcome another person's ideas and information, feeling honestly inclined to say "Yes", is called the 'acceptance set'. The face and body language reveal when someone is in an acceptance set.

Unlike the previous two cardinal processes, speech censoring and internal search, whose physical signs are much the same in all people, the physical signs of an acceptance set vary between individuals, and at different times in the same individual. Most of us nod our heads slightly, and make the little "Mmm, mmm," noises that mean "Okay so far, go on." Most people maintain a steady eye contact and an attentive posture. But beyond that there is great individual variation in the minimal cues signifying acceptance.

Some people keep their faces blank; others wear a slight frown, or purse their lips, or open their eyes wide, or close them a little. Some people join in what the speaker is saying, echoing particular words or finishing his sentences for him; others stay resolutely silent.

Luckily, there is an easy way to 'calibrate' each patient's acceptance set at the start of the consultation. Once you have seen it, you will recognize it whenever it reappears later on. All you have to do is to ask a few questions to which the answer is bound to be "yes", and make a few comments the patient is sure to agree with, watching while the answer comes. What you see then is that patient's acceptance set on that particular occasion.

Here is a short piece of fictitious dialogue to illustrate this simple process.

Doctor: Hallo Mrs Nod. Come in.
Mrs Nod: Morning, doctor. Gosh it's cold today. (curtain-raiser, with no particular hidden meaning).
Doctor: You're right. You have to wrap up warm. (*)
Mrs Nod: Mmm. (†)
Doctor: I haven't seen you for a long time. (*)
Mrs Nod: No, over a year, probably. (†)
Doctor: Anyway, ...
Mrs Nod: What I came about was this elbow. (gambit)
Doctor: The right one? (*)
Mrs Nod: Yes. (†) It's mainly when I lift.
Doctor: Or carry something? (*)
Mrs Nod: That's when I feel it most. (†)

Notice how at the places marked (*) the doctor asks a question or makes a comment to which Mrs Nod is likely to respond in the affirmative. At the places marked (†), the alert doctor will see Mrs Nod demonstrate the minimal cues – the facial expression, the body language – which, for her on that day with that doctor during that consultation, will denote an acceptance set. (Notice also that even when Mrs Nod, in her third speech, says "No," she is nevertheless agreeing with the doctor's previous comment, and her body language will still say "Yes"). Later in that consultation, when the doctor wants to propose some medication, or to inject her tennis elbow with a steroid, he will know he has Mrs Nod's true and valid agreement when he sees her again exhibiting these minimal cues of acceptance. Without them, he may well embark on a line of management which his patient will not feel satisfied with. The acceptance set is the patient's signal to the doctor that it is safe to move on.

EXERCISE

If you have an old video recording of some consultations, your own or anybody else's, watch some of it with the aim of spotting the three cardinal cue clusters. Make three columns on a sheet of paper, and head them 'censoring', 'internal search' and 'acceptance set'. Make a tick in the appropriate column whenever you think you recognize examples of these three processes.

How to establish rapport

You now have everything it takes to achieve a rapport with your patients, even the ones you don't initially warm to.

You know how important the opening moments of the consultation are, and how much information is there for the taking;

you know about curtain-raisers and opening gambits, and how important it is not to interrupt or distort them;

you know how to listen between the lines of what the patient says, and catch the things that aren't said;

you know about the three Representational Systems, Visual, Auditory and Kinaesthetic, and people's preferences for one or other of them;

you know how to notice speech predicates, the use of imagery and metaphor, and the eye movement cues that tell you which Representational System the patient is using;

you can recognize a good range of visual, auditory and kinaesthetic minimal cues;

and you know how to recognize speech censoring, internal search, and an acceptance set.

You also know that rapport is something you *do*, something you work at, not something you just live in hope of. Here's how to 'do rapport'.

AT THE START OF THE CONSULTATION, LEARN, THEN SPEAK, THE PATIENT'S DIALECT OF SELF-EXPRESSION

Learn, then speak, the patient's dialect of self-expression. How, exactly?

You and the patient start with your own different and personal ways of thinking and feeling. These differences in your knowledge, thought processes, attitudes and beliefs are revealed verbally and non-verbally in all the minimal cues we have studied, which together amount to a language of self-expression. We have learned how people have their own personal dialect of self-expression, their own personal non-verbal vocabulary and grammar. Because you are the doctor, the knowledgeable professional, and the patient is the customer, the person with a claim on your skill, it is your job to communicate in the patient's own language and not expect the patient to be fluent in yours. You have to match your verbal and non-verbal language to the patient's.

Here's how to learn the patient's dialect of self-expression. Although when written down this may look complicated, it all happens in a few moments, and once you've done it consciously a time or two, you will find you are doing it quite automatically. Believe me, you can trust your powers of unconscious learning!

Initially just be quiet, listen and watch, with as much attention as you can muster.

Notice, but don't try to interpret, the patient's curtain-raiser and opening gambit.

When you get the chance, say one or two things that the patient will agree with. Watch as closely as you can how the patient's acceptance set looks, as if you were a camera taking a photograph of that moment.

Listen for any speech predicates, imagery and metaphors in the patient's speech. Just allow them to register; don't at this stage rush to draw any conclusions.

Likewise, try and notice some of the patient's eye movement accessing cues.

Allow yourself to notice the patient's non-verbal minimal cues, non-judgementally, as if you were a camera or a tape recorder. This is best done systematically, looking at the eyes and facial expression, then at the rest of the body for the kinaesthetic cues, then listening to anything that strikes you about the patient's tone of voice.

You really can do all this while still attending to the clinical content of what the patient is saying. Part C of this book will further reassure you on this score. What happens in real life if you try to let all this information register is that before long some of the patient's minimal cues begin to stand out more noticeably than others, and your attention is drawn towards the more obvious ones. You find yourself thinking, "This patient is speaking particularly loud and fast," or, "what a lot of visual allusions there are in this person's speech, and aren't there a lot of upward-going eye movements?" or, "this patient keeps crossing and uncrossing her legs." In other words, from all the information that was there to be noticed, your Responder has quickly and effortlessly picked out a few salient cues and directed your awareness towards them. This process happens quite automatically. Subjectively, it seems to you as if all that has happened is that you tried to take in a lot of details about the person before you, and soon found that a few prominent features stood out. It's as simple as that.

When you are struck by such a thought, you are ready to complete the rapport-building process by speaking the patient's dialect. How is that done? Even more simply.

You intentionally adjust your own behaviour so that it more nearly resembles those aspects of the patient's which you have particularly noticed. You might match your imagery and speech predicates to the patient's, and/or your voice delivery, and/or your posture and gestures, so that a third party observing the pair of you would be struck by the similarities between your own minimal cues and the patient's.

The key concept here is 'matching' – some writers use the terms 'mirroring' or 'parroting' to describe the same thing – and it needs a little explanation.

Matching

Some doctors, when it is suggested that they try and speak or sound or look like the patient does, protest that it's just mimicry, and if they are rumbled the patient will feel insulted. But there is a difference which anyone can see between matching a patient's minimal cues and taking the mickey. One is done subliminally, beneath the threshold of conscious awareness, motivated by a genuine concern to put the other person at ease. The other is exaggerated, a caricature, done in order to be noticed, and intended to unsettle.

Go back in your imagination to the party you attended as an invisible guest, and picture in your mind's eye a couple whom you can tell are getting on well together. (Chatting, just chatting!) How do you know they are in rapport? They are talking about the same topic in similar terms, understanding each other's nuances and idiosyncracies, using awareness of each other's eye contact and speech inflexion to synchronize their conversation. Their voices will be similarly paced and pitched, matched for volume, rhythm and modulation. In their facial expressions, their hand movements, the alignment of their torsos and the disposition of their limbs they closely resemble each other. Yet neither of them would have consciously noticed the matching, nor be offended if it was pointed out.

"Aha," says the sceptic, "are they in rapport because their behaviour is matched, or is their behaviour matched because they already have rapport?" Rapport may result in matching, but does matching induce rapport? It seems that it does. I think it works in two ways. Firstly, just as when you try to speak French to a Frenchman he feels more inclined to be friendly, so by expressing yourself in the patient's verbal and non-verbal dialect you make yourself more comprehensible to the patient, and communicate your good intentions in an immediately perceptible way. Secondly, the mere act of trying to achieve a match, the mere fact that you are willing to shift towards the patient's way of thinking has an effect on your own attitude that makes empathy and understanding emerge more easily. Wanting to connect and trying to connect achieves the connection.

How do you know when you have rapport?

How do you know when you have reached the CONNECTING checkpoint? How can you tell when the noticing and matching process has achieved a good enough rapport for the consultation to progress? The question is more theoretical than practical. It's your Organizer asking; your Responder knows perfectly well. The same subliminal awareness that identified the patient's matchable cues will automatically let you know when connection between you and the patient is strong enough to take the strain of developing the consultation.

What happens is that at the start of the consultation your Responder noticed the patient's acceptance set (or if there wasn't one, imagined one of its own), and fixed that pattern like a Polaroid photograph. As the consultation goes through its early stages and as you make some 'matching' moves, the Responder continues to observe the patient, and checks whether the acceptance set persists or not. If your Responder senses that you've lost the patient's acceptance, and rapport is precarious, it signals to you in the form of a sense of slight unease. When the patient's acceptance set is firmly established, the Responder sends you a feeling of being ready to move on.

You begin to develop the consultation along whatever lines seem clinically relevant, selecting some aspects of the history and discarding others, and asking for details the patient had perhaps not expected.

143

This is rather more challenging to the patient. If he or she does not feel ready to move ahead with you, you will lose the signs of the acceptance set and instead notice minimal cues of discomfort and reluctance. If you have established a firm enough rapport, the patient will trust the direction you are taking, and continue to manifest the signs of acceptance. All this boils down to a single pragmatic and reassuring statement – when you're doing it, you just know!

A TUTORIAL CONCLUDED

Me: Chris, I'm sorry this has been a long session. What are your thoughts at the moment?

Chris: I'm feeling a bit swamped, particularly by the material about Representational Systems and eye movement cues. I'm not sure whether they really matter.

Me: Keep an open mind about them for the moment. Now that you've been made aware of them you'll gradually form your own opinion of their relevance. What else?

Chris: I have two main worries. The first is, while I can understand in principle about observing and matching the patient's minimal cues, I'm not sure whether I could intentionally do it in practice. There's so much else to think of at the start of the consultation, clinical things mainly. Secondly, the idea of changing my way of talking or imitating the patient's non-verbal signals, even if it's done very subtly, sounds artificial and calculating, like play-acting. I think building a good working relationship with a patient should be a spontaneous thing.

Me: To take your last point first, it's indeed very pleasant if rapport comes spontaneously. But it doesn't always happen, and in those cases you have to know what to do about it. In fact you don't have to do the full 'observing/matching/check-ing for acceptance' process every single time. With some patients you hit the right wavelength automatically (though even then I think it's because your dialect and the patient's happen to coincide). Also, with patients that you see fairly frequently, you can quickly resume the degree of rapport you established the previous time you saw them. There is a difference between knowing how to do something but choosing not to, and not knowing how in the first place.

As to whether you can find the mental space to do the CONNECTING process as well as pay attention to the clinical problem, try it and see. You'll find that you can. Your clinical skills have been so rigorously instilled into you during your medical training that you couldn't overlook them if you tried! And in fact you are already doing several mental tasks at once while consulting. Your Organizer, like a frisky puppy that wants to pull you in different directions at once, is constantly at work trying to structure your thoughts, like it or not. We've discussed the distracting 'inner dialogue' in an earlier chapter. By consciously setting yourself the clear task of observing, matching and checking for acceptance, you are in effect providing a rein on your wayward Organizer and giving it a single relevant goal to aim for. You'll find that this is an aid to concentration, not a distraction. We'll be thinking more about this in Part C.

The question of whether intentionally matching the patient's cues is too artificial is one of attitude. It's to do with how comfortable you can feel suspending temporarily your own ideas of how you want the consultation to proceed, and allowing the patient to make the running at first. The notion of methodically working at rapport is an alien one only if you're the kind of doctor who likes or needs to preserve a dominating role. You have to feel comfortable with a neutral, non-judgemental accepting frame of mind at first: later on in the consultation you can lead the patient through your own agenda, but not to start with. I think it helps if you can understand that, however bizarre or quirky or puzzling or inappropriate the patient's form of expression appears to you, it is for the patient the best available way he or she has been able to come up with of communicating with you.

Chris: If I want to put this into practice, what's the best way to start?

Me: You already have started.

Chris: How?

Me: Merely having read and discussed the ideas in this chapter will have changed the way you think about meeting a patient. Unless you have total amnesia, you are bound to enter each consultation now with a different awareness of what there is to be noticed. And that shift in awareness means that you will see new things and hear new things, and will therefore begin to respond in new ways. Do you remember how we imprinted the names of the five checkpoints onto your left hand? Look at your left index finger now. Can you still visualize the word on it?

Chris: CONNECTING.

Me: The index finger is a physical mnemonic, reminding you to

Chris: You described a great many minimal cues. How do you decide which ones to match?

Me: The immediate answer is, "Match the cues you notice." That advice is less glib than it seems. I'm suggesting that you consciously try to notice as many cues as you can. In fact only some cues register at all strongly. The selection of those particularly noticeable cues is made at an unconscious level, and the innate wisdom of your unconscious mind will choose the cues that the patient will most readily respond to. Remember to make the matching subtle and covert, though, below the patient's conscious awareness.

In practice it turns out that the most effective cues to match are:

- body and limb postures;
- speed, volume and modulation of speech;
and - predicates and imagery: use the patient's own favourite metaphors and descriptions.

Chris: You've laid great emphasis on noticing minimal cues. Is that warranted?

Me: I think so: especially the three cue clusters of speech censoring, internal search and the acceptance set. These three are going to recur constantly as you improve your consulting technique – they provide the main source of non-verbal feedback from the patient that helps you monitor how the consultation is progressing.

The other reason for emphasizing awareness of minimal cues is that it nudges you away from the idea of striving to keep control of the consultation, and towards the frame of mind where it's enough to settle for accurate observation of what's going on. It's non-judgemental awareness that gets you onto the patient's wavelength, not effort; then the rest of the consultation proceeds much more smoothly.

EXERCISES

There are two exercises I'm going to propose you do, in order to guarantee your effectiveness as a builder of rapport. The first is a consciousness-raising exercise, and the second a way of practising matching.

I-Spy

For this exercise, you need to be able to observe some consultations without participating in them. One way is to use video-tapes; another is to sit in as an observer with another doctor.

Copy out the following list on the left-hand side of a sheet of paper:

Curtain raiser
Opening gambit
Acceptance set
Speech censoring
Internal search
Predicates:
  – Visual
  – Auditory
  – Kinaesthetic
Eye movement accessing cues:
  – Visual (upwards)
  – Auditory (horizontal, down left)
  – Kinaesthetic (down right)

As you observe each consultation, the aim is to spot at least one example of every item on the list. Check them off as you notice them until the list is complete.

Playing cards

Prepare 7 small cards; box-index cards are ideal. Write one of the following on each card:

Posture
Gestures
Change of body position
Rate of speech
Speech volume
Speech modulation
Representational system

Before you start a surgery session, shuffle the pack of cards and place them face down on your desk. Just before each patient comes in, turn over the top card. You are to match at least two examples of the cue described on the card before the end of the consultation.

I have already quoted Heinz von Foerster's aphorism:
If you desire to see, learn how to act.

I should like to add a rider:
If you desire to act, learn what there is to see.

"I've always been a lovely little mover, but I'm hopeless on my stomach."

B3
Checkpoint 2 (Summarizing) – listening and eliciting skills

I'll tell you why I've come, Doctor. I've always been a lovely little mover, but I'm hopeless on my stomach.

           – my favourite opening gambit from a patient.

This is also a true story. I had spent the day examining at the Royal College of General Practitioners in London. Walking towards the Underground station, I succumbed to the temptation to take a passing taxi to Euston. The driver wasn't the strong silent type. Opening the sliding glass panel intended to prevent our germs and philosophies from intermingling, he inhaled mightily on a roll-up and let fly. Apparently the heat (or was it the cold?) was playing havoc with his sinuses. The resulting congestion had the finest medical brains in the country baffled. Harley Street, it seemed, was gibbering in bewilderment. I tried to imagine how anyone except a doctor would look, and to look like that.

"What did your own quack say it was?", I asked as nonchalantly as I could manage.

"Oh, some rubbish about tubes," he said. "Anyway," he went on, earning himself a tip for services to me he never knew he'd rendered, "you don't go to the doctor's to find out what's the matter – you go to tell him what *you* think's the matter."

"Really?", I yelled. (I thought if I spoke louder he wouldn't have to keep turning round so often to make sure I'd heard him above the whizzing traffic.) "So what did you tell him?"

"Not a lot," said my informant. I didn't believe that for a start, but he continued. "When you go to the doctor's, you don't want to tell 'em everything at once. If you give 'em too much to go on they only jump to conclusions and give you a lot of fancy advice about smoking and that. No, you want to let it out a bit at a time – that way you keep one jump ahead of them."

I must have looked too interested. "What line are you in then, squire?" came the fateful enquiry.

"Oh, er – I'm in, er, in education, actually."

"Great," he said, "I've got this daughter, twelve she is, hates school..."

After CONNECTING, the next checkpoint to make for in our journey through the consultation is SUMMARIZING.

To stress the importance of finding out exactly why the patient has come to see you needs no justification. A logical prerequisite of giving satisfaction is to know what would satisfy. The patient usually needs little in the way of encouragement, once the social preliminaries are over and while you are still observing and matching minimal cues to heighten the rapport between you, to embark on a description of the problem in his or her own words.

As we have noted, the patient's choice of language and its non-verbal accompaniments are the culmination of that individual's upbringing, education and personal history to date, all his or her thoughts, attitudes and feelings, remote and recent: that person's whole world in a fragment of speech. Communication – two people sharing their experience – can only proceed if there is sufficient overlap between their respective world views, and if the language they have in common means the same thing to each. The last chapter described how the process of learning the patient's language of self-expression begins in general terms with non-judgemental awareness of verbal and non-verbal cues, so that a general feeling of understanding emerges which we call 'rapport'. That same process now continues in much more specific terms as the patient's particular areas of concern become clearer.

The official language of the consultation – the framework within which cause and effect are understood and decisions are made – is 'medical'. Unfortunately, whereas doctors speak it fluently, patients' command of medical language is often at the novice or phrase-book level. Patients speak mainly in 'vernacular' language. But luckily, doctors are bilingual: they can speak both 'medical' and 'vernacular'.

The early part of the consultation is taken up with gathering information in 'vernacular', and in translating it accurately into 'medical' so that the doctor can bring his professional skills to bear. Traditionally, this is called 'taking a history of the presenting complaint'. (How many patients, on being asked in 'medical', "What are you complaining of?" have mistranslated the question back into 'vernacular' as, "What have you got to grumble about – you should count your blessings."?) A better word for discovering the 'what?' and 'why?' of the patient's concern is 'eliciting', from a Latin root meaning 'drawing forth'.

The process of eliciting the full extent of the patient's worries and translating them into 'medical' is usually led by the doctor, and only the doctor knows when the process has gone far enough for a provisional assessment to be made. However, unless the patient also knows when that 'point of sufficient understanding' has been reached, two possible dangers arise. First, the patient will not know when to stop, and may continue to supply redundant information to an increasingly impatient doctor. Secondly, the patient will not know whether the translation from 'vernacular' into 'medical' has been accurate, and may therefore find it hard to accept and trust the doctor's responses. So it is not enough for the doctor to understand everything the patient means; that understanding must also be explicitly demonstrated so that the patient can check it.

When the leaders of the USA and the Soviet Union meet, they have a professional translator. In fact, so important is it to avoid misunderstanding and to foster trust that they have two translators, each checking the accuracy of the other's version. In the consulting room, doctor and patient have only themselves to give and receive feedback. At this early stage in the consultation the main direction of information flow is from patient to doctor, and the translation is from 'vernacular' into 'medical'. (Later on, at the HANDING OVER checkpoint, the directions will be reversed.) The best way for the doctor to allow his translation to be checked is to SUMMARIZE – periodically to offer the patient a paraphrase or précis of his current understanding. A summary provides the patient with a clear signal as to whether the doctor needs any more clarifying information, and also gives the opportunity to correct any misinterpretations.

The key question for the doctor to keep in mind while taking a history is, "Could I show this patient that I have sufficiently understood why he or she has come to see me?" When you can answer 'yes' to this question, you are at the SUMMARIZING checkpoint.

The route to the SUMMARIZING checkpoint is illustrated in Figure B3.1.

The part of Figure B3.1 below the dotted line represents what goes on in the doctor's mind as he inwardly translates the patient's story into 'medical' language and evaluates it, comparing what he has gathered so far against what he needs to know in order to make a provisional assessment or management plan. If the doctor doesn't have enough information to go on, he returns to the patient for more. If on the other hand the doctor reckons he has enough information to make his next decision, and feels ready to move on, he makes a

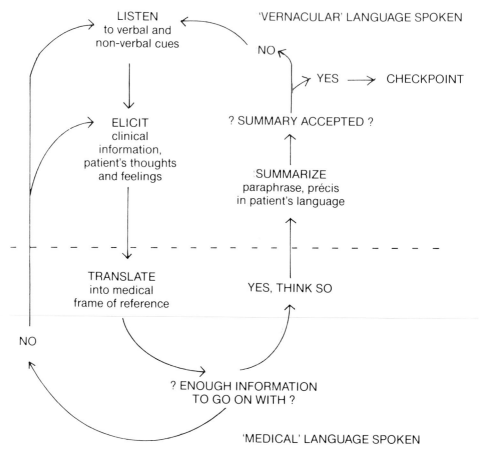

Figure B3.1 The route to the SUMMARIZING checkpoint

summary statement and sees whether or not the patient accepts it. If so, the consultation can advance; if not, again the doctor goes back to listening and eliciting until he feels ready to try another, updated, summary.

Having been practising medicine for some time, you are thoroughly familiar with the translating and evaluating phases of the clinical process. They are not the subjects of this book. What I should like to offer at this stage is some help with what and how to elicit, and some advice on the phrasing and timing of effective summaries.

WHO NEEDS SUGGESTIONS?

There is no shortage of advice in the literature about what information a general practitioner ought to elicit from his patients, nor of suggestions about how to do it. We considered some authors' ideas in Chapter A 3, 'Models of the Consultation'. The consensus seems to be that the doctor should broaden his enquiries beyond the purely clinical to encompass the Psychological, Social and Family factors in the patient's predicament as well as the Physical. Another convenient framework, if a framework you need, is:

Ideas – what ideas does the patient have about the reasons for his health problem?
Concerns – what aspect(s) of the problem is the patient chiefly concerned about?
Expectations – how does the patient expect the problem to be tackled?
Feelings – what emotional reaction does the patient have to the situation?
Effects – what consequences of the problem can the patient foresee?

As to the tactics of eliciting, Byrne and Long (op. cit.) offer many suggestions, which were summarized in Figure A3.4. Their categories of the techniques they observed doctors using include: 'encouraging', 'clarifying', 'reflecting', 'exploring', 'challenging'; and a range of questions variously described as 'direct', 'correlational', 'open-ended', 'concealed', 'closed', and 'self-answering'.

And yet I have a sense of unease. If the basic principle – "find out what your patient has really come for" – is so obvious, the aide-memoires so familar, and the theoretical approaches so exhaustively documented, why do we all so frequently fail to uncover the factors in the patient's situation that would have made sense of otherwise inexplicable presentations? If we don't always do a good job of eliciting, it certainly isn't because no-one has told us to. Do we really need to be taught how to ask someone a question?

The trouble with exhortation as a means of changing behaviour is that it doesn't work. The more someone nags us to do something, the more reasons we can think of for not doing it. We discover that we feel more ambivalent towards the task than we realized; a significant part of us is against the whole idea. Logically, we ought to elicit our patients' views about their problems as assiduously as a medical student preparing to present a case on the Professor's ward-round. But we don't. Why not?

Some of the reasons are practical: perhaps the models and frameworks are too imprecise, too lacking in detail to lead any further than good intentions. Or perhaps we feel that time is too short in most consultations to go into the more far-flung ramifications of patients' concerns, so that we are content to explore only a fraction of the potential information. Besides, a good many of the problems we deal with are sufficiently mundane to be adequately dealt with in a limited context. Do we really need to worry over the existential implications of every ingrowing toenail? Surely face value is sometimes enough?

But I think that constraints of attitude lie nearer to the real reasons for any reluctance. The suggestion is that the consultation should start with a determined effort by the doctor to enter briefly but completely into the patient's world; to imagine her pain, to sense the extent of her distress, to understand just what it is that frightens, bewilders and saddens her – in a word, empathy. Put that way, though, empathy doesn't sound like a lot of fun. It sounds draining, uncomfortable, and, we imagine, a threat to our own peace of mind. We flatter ourselves instead with the comforting conceit that we already 'do enough empathizing', neither too much nor too little, by common sense and native intuition. So why bother to make an issue of eliciting? And since there is no point in checking on what we know to be the case, why waste time reiterating summaries of what the patient has already told us? The silent smile on our faces as we listen to each tale of woe is reassuring, not complacent. And while we're about it, the earth looks flat.

This subversive line of self-questioning carries us a step nearer to the ultimate professional heresy. If the charge of sometimes insufficiently identifying with our patients is levelled, we risk having to make the most shaming confession a doctor can contemplate: nostra culpa, nostra maxima culpa – we don't actually *like* all our patients. And while we're about it, did you know Queen Anne was dead?

WHY ELICIT?

The same mismatch between patients' 'lay' understanding and our own 'professional' one, which can cause such confusion, is often also highly amusing. I heard a sociologist once give a lecture to an audience of doctors (no, that's not the joke). He had studied the health beliefs of a class of six-year-olds to investigate the origins of adult misconceptions about common medical topics. One such was the notion of 'germs'.

Six-year-olds know about germs. Germs are what some people have, and give you, and you get ill. The trouble was, that group of children, avid television watchers, had formed their concepts of what a germ looked like from a TV commercial for a toilet cleaner that was certain death to all germs. As a result, the children also 'knew' that germs were about an inch across, bright blue, and went 'pop' in the lavatory pan when you sprinkled stuff on them. No wonder, then, that they looked askance at their mothers when told to wash their hands before meals 'to get the germs off'. No use telling them not to play with Johnny while he'd got chicken pox – you could *see* he didn't have germs on him. And they fell about with laughter at the idea of cold germs coming out of people's noses into the air you breathed.

Remember this story next time a patient tells you they've got rheumatism, or a chill, or you put something down to a virus, or your lengthy explanation of psychosomatic illness gets taken to mean you think the patient's just imagining things.

It's the more incongruous mismatches that stick in the memory. Another of my personal favourites was a lady patient whose opening remark, the gambit she had presumably been honing to perfection while she waited, was, "Doctor, I think I've got a hormone imbalance, and they've all gone over to the left."

I think you know what the point of eliciting is – not least, it's to explain odd remarks like that and translate them into cries for help. What I hope you are now more interested in is how to do a good job of eliciting. The hallmark of good eliciting is the ability to base an accurate summary on it. Be reassured that 'good' eliciting doesn't have to mean exhaustive. It means appropriate, well-directed, sensitive and efficient. Common sense and native intuition will of course carry us a long way. But I happen to believe that educated common sense is better, and that native intuition can get rusty if it's not practised. In the next sections we'll consider how to keep your eliciting on track.

PITSTOP

It will help if at this point you would take a little time to retrieve from your memory your own anecdotes about the bizarre, puzzling and amusing things patients say, to cap mine. I expect you can also remember the apprehensions and misapprehensions that lay behind them. And I'll warrant that, once you had unravelled the surface incongruities and discovered the vulnerability within, you felt much more sympathetic to the patient.

Here are two excerpts from a ten-minute drama I've already referred to. The cast consists of Mrs Wystful, aged 46, a teacher of English to overseas students; and me.

Act I, scene 1. A consulting room.
Enter Mrs Wystful, carrying a book.

Mrs Wystful: I brought 'Pride and Prejudice' along with me, in case I had a long – in case you were snowed under.

Me: At least it wasn't 'War and Peace'.

Mrs Wystful: Doctor, I think I've got a hormone imbalance, and they've all gone over to the left ...

Act I, scene 2. The same, four minutes later.

Me: So, just to recap, you've been getting pains in the left side of your stomach for several months which are worse around period time; and for about the same time your left ankle's been swelling; and you wondered whether this might be the start of the menopause, particularly since you don't feel as – shall we say? – feminine as usual.

Mrs Wystful: Yes. I expect you'll need to examine me now, won't you?

The only rule about how to elicit is that there are no rules. Whatever works, does. In Zen, if you ask a Master how to lead a perfect life, you are likely to be told, "First make yourself perfect, and then live naturally!" As long as you are clear what you are trying to achieve, and have your resource store well stocked up, you can rely on your unconscious mind to put the right words into your mouth when the need arises. I propose, therefore, rather than produce a table d'hôte menu of eliciting skills, to lay before you a buffet from which you can make a personal selection. There are four courses to this meal:

> What you might elicit;
> When you should elicit;
> How you could elicit;
> and When to stop eliciting.

I have a 'greed' problem. (Doesn't that sound nicer than "I'm greedy"?) Recently I went to a training workshop about 'Strategies of Brief Psychotherapy'. Lunch that day was a cold buffet. We participants formed a salivating queue. Long before I reached the serving counter a rather bored waitress caught my eye and called, "Do you want chicken?" I was still too far away to see what the chicken looked like, or what else was on offer that I might prefer, so I hesitated. I didn't want to miss out on some even more delicious alternative, but suppose chicken was all there was. Then I had a brainwave. "Would you like to fix me the meal you think I'ld most enjoy?", I suggested. It was magnificent. No chicken, but lobster, spiced beef, a nut and lentil salad, asparagus. Some of my fellows, their own plates crowded out with chicken and lettuce, eyed mine with envy. I felt pleasantly special, cherished. I also couldn't help noticing that the waitress no longer looked bored. She was smiling.

WHAT YOU MIGHT ELICIT

Two fields of enquiry exist, which may or may not overlap. One is the doctor's need for the clinical information required to make a diagnosis and management plan. The other is the need the patient feels to impart information which, if suppressed, will produce a sense of having been inadequately attended to. True to my theme, I am not going to presume to give you advice on the clinical process. Clinical assessment, though often difficult, is seldom a problem. You know how to go about it.

I am more concerned that you develop a feeling for the contexts in which people's health problems arise, and which they in turn affect. We are all impelled to try and attribute meaning and significance to the events that befall us, including ill-health. Whenever something unexpected happens, we are inclined to ask ourselves, "Where does this new experience fit into my personal scheme of things?" Without such a sense of meaning, a sense of understanding how the various parts of our lives interconnect, we feel unsettled and prone to anxiety. As a doctor trying to assess a patient's presenting complaint, it is helpful to keep asking yourself, "What does this problem mean to this person?" That curiosity, combined with the human and cultural heritage we all share, will increase the relevance and efficiency of your history-taking.

The same organic malfunction can take on entirely different meanings for different patients, who will each therefore have different hopes and expectations of the doctor they consult. Let's take a common example – a soft tissue strain in the lumbar region – and imagine its implications for five individuals.

For the wealthy retired stockbroker, obtaining relief of the pain is his main priority; apart from that, his life continues much as before.

For the fitness fanatic who trains three nights a week, it means a blow to his pride and self-image; he can handle the pain, but not the embarrassment.

For the busy mother of three young children, who has to 'keep going at all costs', it means she'll have to ask her mother to come and help out, and that will cause friction, and her husband will storm out to the pub, and then there'll be violence.

159

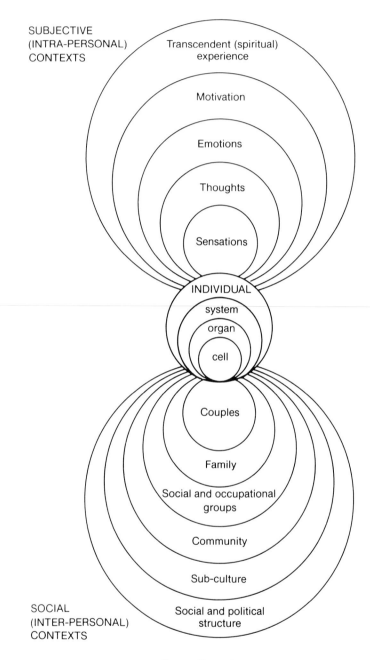

SUBJECTIVE
(INTRA-PERSONAL)
CONTEXTS

Transcendent (spiritual)
experience

Motivation

Emotions

Thoughts

Sensations

INDIVIDUAL

system

organ

cell

Couples

Family

Social and occupational
groups

Community

Sub-culture

Social and political
structure

SOCIAL
(INTER-PERSONAL)
CONTEXTS

Figure B3.2 Contexts

For the depressed clerical officer who keeps missing out on promotion, it's just another example of life kicking you when you're down; it's bound to drag on, and then it'll be hospitals, and operations, and probably paralysis.

For the teenager, doing boring work on a noisy and impersonal production line, it's a god-send; with a bit of luck it'll mean at least two weeks off work.

May I share with you three simple schemes that I have found helpful in alerting me to some of the possible meanings I could consider when eliciting? They deal with contexts, motivational needs, and understanding. In the individual case you might use one of them, or none of them or some parts of each.

Contexts

The universe, from quarks to quasars, is hierarchically organized into interlocking systems with different levels of complexity, like a nest of Chinese dolls within dolls. At each level in the hierarchy different properties are displayed and different phenomena emerge. Applied to human beings, this concept describes how atoms form molecules, which form cells, which form organs, which form functional systems, which make up the individual person. Each level in the organization depends on the integrity of the level beneath, and in turn contributes to the effective functioning of the level above.

As Figure B3.2 shows, the individual is the starting point for two such hierarchies. Expanding the contexts outwards into social realms, the individual is intimately involved in a number of two-person relationships, for which the family group is the natural setting. The individual also functions within larger groups for work and leisure, themselves part of wider communities, sub-cultures and political structures.

There is also a hierarchy of subjective experience within the individual's consciousness, ranging from raw sensations, progressively organized into thoughts, emotions and motivational drives, and culminating (as the next section describes) in transcendent spiritual or religious experiences in which the sense of individual identity is outgrown.

This model is a reminder of how the individual person is the point of expression of biological, sociological and psychological events. It illustrates graphically how disturbances at one level can have an impact at all the others. The traditional emphasis of clinical medicine has been at the level of biological events within the individual organism. Most GPs feel decreasingly competent the further removed from this level a problem takes them. Politics and religion are usually as taboo in the consulting room as they are at the dinner table. Yet our patients do have genuine concerns in these more remote contexts. Give yourself permission to think about them sometimes!

Self-actualization needs	self-transcendence self-actualization realization of potential self-expression
	self-esteem self-respect self-confidence
Esteem needs	esteem status approval recognition
'Belongingness' needs	love intimacy someone to confide in
	acceptance affection friendship company
Safety needs	boundaries predictability freedom from fear and anxiety protection stability security roots
Physiological needs	sex sleep optimum physiology food water air

Figure B3.3 Hierarchy of human needs, after Maslow[1]

Motivational needs

Figure B3.3 shows a way of thinking about human needs and motivation, adapted from the original model by Abraham Maslow, which I find enormously helpful [1]. Maslow, an American psychologist who was one of the inspirations for the humanistic psychology movement, based his work on a novel premise. Whereas most psychologists have turned to psychopathology and abnormal development in their search for insight, Maslow elected instead to study healthy individuals who seemed to represent the best and most fulfilled in human achievement.

He concluded that human beings have an intrinsic drive to grow and develop towards the fulfilment of their inherited capacities, provided certain environmental and psychological conditions are met. As personal growth occurs, the individual feels motivated to meet a succession of needs. These needs and their corresponding motivations form a hierarchy. If the needs at one level are adequately met, the person is 'released' to seek satisfaction at the next level up. On the other hand, if the necessary conditions to satisfy one level of need are not met, the individual's motivation tends to persist at that level, leaving the higher ones unfulfilled.

At the bottom of the hierarchy is the need for physiological stability. This includes the drives for oxygen, food, biochemical homeostasis, sleep and sexual release. These are the most powerful instincts, and, when felt, take precedence over any others. Someone who hasn't eaten for days, or whose bladder is bursting, is in no mood to discuss the weather. If these needs are sufficiently met, the next level of need we experience is for 'safety', both physical and psychological. This need is the next most pressing after the physiological; we seek shelter, security, freedom from the unknown and the unpredictable, to know where our roots and boundaries are. Third in precedence come what Maslow calls 'belongingness' needs – the urge we all feel for close human relationships in the form of friendship, love, intimacy and knowing someone cares.

If by and large our needs at these three levels are well enough satisfied, a need for the 'esteem' of a wider circle of people makes itself felt. We seek recognition, respect, status and approval beyond our immediate circle. Experiencing the love, respect and esteem of other people seems to allow us to feel worthy of that love and esteem; so we develop self-esteem, self-respect and self-confidence. Those lucky individuals whose psychological growth has been fostered to this degree finally become motivated to discover and express the full range of their own potential and talents, a process Maslow terms 'self-actualization'. This may take the form of artistic, creative and intellectual endeavour, or the search for self-transcendent experience of a religious or mystical kind.

As a description of the human condition, this model rings true to me. The upward progression is evident in the normal development through childhood and adolescence. Organizations, marriages and careers go through similar processes of unfolding, and can be stunted by equivalent deprivations in their own contexts. The model also has some practical application in the consulting room. I expect you can recall patients who have brought to you their needs at all levels: seeking relief from pain or discomfort (physiological need); seeking reassurance and explanation (safety need); wanting someone to talk to and confide in (belongingness need); seeking your sanction or permission for changing jobs or divorcing (esteem need); and for counselling at a time of life crisis or to rethink their values and life-styles (self-actualization need).

It can be helpful to ask yourself, "What level of need on the hierarchy is the patient using his or her problem in an attempt to fulfil?" If, for instance, you can recognize that a chronic varicose ulcer is serving to bring some conversation and human contact (belongingness) into an otherwise lonely life, you might decide not to refer for a surgical opinion, but instead ask your nurse to treat 'it' with regular dressings and Tender Loving Care. Or you might care to treat your esteem-deprived chronic requester of inappropriate house calls with the accolade of calling by special arrangement once a week for a cup of tea.

Understanding

Finally in this section on 'what you might elicit', I want again to commend to you Helman's 'Folk Model of Illness', referred to already in Chapter A3. It pulls together a number of theoretical strands, has the stamp of common sense about it, and is small enough to be written on a card and put on your desk as an aide-memoire to good eliciting!

Whatever the problem and whether or not they ask you in so many words, everybody who consults a doctor wants to find out:

What has happened?
Why has it happened?
Why has it happened to *me*?
Why has it happened *now*?
What would happen if nothing were done about it?
What should I do about it?

Knowing that later in the consultation the patient will appreciate answers to these questions, you can use your eliciting skills to gather the information you will need in order to reply.

WHEN YOU SHOULD ELICIT

How do you decide, in the first few minutes of the consultation, what information and which areas of concern you need to clarify and explore in order to offer your patient a balanced and empathic summary of the presenting problem? As the previous section has shown, the possible ramifications of almost every problem are practically boundless; yet some of them matter acutely to the individual patient, while others can safely remain unexplored. How can the doctor focus down selectively but appropriately, and time his eliciting questions to best effect? Let's see how far common sense will take us.

There will be some points that you, the doctor, decide you need to know more about. For instance, you might be looking for precise clinical details in order to make a diagnosis or management plan. When your need is for hard medical data, you won't need any prompting to elicit it, any more than a terrier needs persuading to chase a cat! Other occasions when you might take the initiative would be when you had formed a hunch – perhaps from something the patient had said, or perhaps as a result of thinking about contexts, or motivations, or the Helman questions – that a particular area was worth investigating. So you would simply go ahead and ask (or, as we have to say nowadays, 'test your hypothesis').

More nebulous but no less important are those occasions when the patient signals to you that they have something significant to impart, even if you had not realized it. When the patient signals overtly, it's easy. No doctor who is still reading this book will overrule a remark like, "Excuse me doctor, if I could interrupt, but can I also say . . .?" But, as you will recall from the previous chapter, communication also comes covertly in the form of minimal cues, verbal and non-verbal. Let's consider some of the more subtle ways you might tell that significant information was ripe for eliciting.

Incongruities

Any remark that leaves you amused or nonplussed – like the one which opened this chapter, or Mrs Wystful's hormone imbalance – probably does so because some of the mental steps that make it logical to the speaker have been left out of the transmission. So you have to try to fill in the gaps, which is hard, since your thought processes are different from the patient's. The strain of trying to impose sense on absurdity is either funny or irritating. So when you feel the start of a smile or a frown coming on, it's because your Responder has subliminally detected some 'missing links' which might be worth investigating. It transpired that the 'lovely little mover with the hopeless stomach' was worried by the discomfort in her abdomen when her regular dancing partner held her tightly. The diagnosis turned out to be diverticular disease.

I once had on my list a man who had devoted (and I mean devoted) twenty years of his life to baffling every conceivable specialist with his head pains, as a two-inch thickness of letters in his notes bore witness. One day, frustrated to the point of devilment, I announced that there was only one way to establish the cause of his symptoms. "What's that?", he asked. "An autopsy", I told him. "Anything, anything," he cried, "I'll even go private!"

Speech censoring

The last chapter alerted you to the hesitations, vaguenesses and non sequiturs which indicate that a speaker is holding back from saying something risky or important. When you notice these signs, you have the option of either making a mental note of what you guess the sensitive topic might be, or gently prompting the patient to reveal a little more.

Deletions, distortions and generalizations

These are three specific types of speech vagueness which indicate the conscious or unconscious suppression of relevant information. (The process of analysing someone's spoken language to infer and treat psychological problems has been extensively developed in a therapy method called Neuro-Linguistic Programming [2]. Despite its name, this system has some very helpful ideas to offer – including how to deal with deletions, distortions and generalizations.)

As I have previously said, the basic ingredients of everyone's understanding of the world are the raw sensations arising from our various sense organs. In order for us to function at all, our brains take short-cuts, and simplify this overwhelming complexity into patterns and concepts and rules and principles. We gradually build up our own personal expurgated version of how we perceive the people and events in our world, and react to them as if our simplified model was true. Unfortunately, we can sometimes over-simplify and mis-represent, and hence mis-understand. Sometimes the eye-shades we don to protect us from the glare turn into blinkers.

A man wanted to hang a picture, but had no hammer to drive in the nail. Then he remembered that his new neighbour had one, if the sounds of hammering that had been coming from the house next door were anything to go by. In fact, since whoever it was had moved in a

166

week ago, it seemed to have been nothing but bang, bang, bang, at all hours of the day and night. What sort of inconsiderate swine was it who didn't know people needed their sleep? And you'd have thought he'd have popped in before now to introduce himself. Stuck-up bastard. Probably rich enough to afford two hammers. Is that the sort of chap I want to be beholden to? He'd never let me forget it. He'll always be on the scrounge for something. Just my luck. The last lot were no better, but at least they'd tried to be friendly. This used to be a nice neighbourhood, but look at it now. He marched round to his neighbour's house and knocked on the door. When a smiling young woman opened it, he shouted at her, "And you can keep your bloody hammer!"

Deletions, distortions and generalizations in someone's speech are the signs that an over-simplification process might be going on, and that these are points where a misunderstanding could occur.

'*Deletion*' means that some details essential to a complete understanding have been left out. Here are some clinical examples of deletion:

"It's no better." (What's not? No better than when?)

"Something will have to be done." (What will have to be done? Who should do it?)

"We're worried about Jane." (Who's worried? How worried? Worried about Jane doing what?)

"I know my husband doesn't understand how I feel." (What feelings, exactly, doesn't he understand? How do you know he doesn't? What would he have to do to show that he did?)

'*Distortion*' means turning actual behaviour and events into abstract concepts, as if concepts had a material reality of their own. Distortion can be a means of staying uninvolved. Here are some examples:

"I need help." (What do you mean by 'help'? In practical terms, what would someone have to do in order for you to feel helped?)

"I lost my temper." (What's a 'temper'? Actually what happened was that you shouted and swore, and slammed the door.)

"I'm suffering from anxiety." (Does that mean, "When I go out or meet strangers, I feel my heart pound and my palms sweat and I want to hide."? Or does it mean that you borrowed one of a friend's tranquillizers, and felt a bit better?)

"I feel a failure." (What, precisely, have you failed to do? What feelings do you have when you remember those occasions?)

"I don't like his attitude." (You may not like his aftershave, but what's an 'attitude'? What exactly does he do or say that makes you feel upset?)

167

'*Generalization*' means arguing from the particular to the general in such a way as to rule out any possible exception to the rule you infer. Generalizations like 'all', 'never' and 'every' make it difficult to countenance change. For instance:

"I don't like hospitals." (Every single hospital? Under all possible circumstances? And you never will?)

"No-one understands me." (So am I wasting my time trying to?)

"I always get a cold throughout the winter." (Every winter? The same cold lasts from October 1st till March 31st?)

"Your receptionists are rude." (Which receptionist said what to you, when, and in what circumstances?)

When you notice deletions, distortions or generalizations, it can be a good idea to see if you can get the patient to tell you the exact feelings or the precise words or the specific behaviour being referred to. Feelings and behaviour are easier to imagine and understand than abstractions and attitudes. Castles in the air are built of concrete.

So far we have considered the language cues that tell you when you could do some eliciting. Non-verbal signals can also help. The most important of these is 'internal search', which you already know about from the previous chapter.

Internal search

Remember how people look when they are thinking about something important. The attention is directed inwards while thoughts and memories begin to associate in the imagination. The body becomes relatively still; the eyes become defocused, and sometimes move rapidly as they scan the images projected in the mind's eye. Almost invariably the end result of this internal search is something significant – a new insight, or a relevant memory, or a possible link between two previously unrelated ideas.

These signs indicate that the patient is either seriously considering what had just been said, or opening up a new line of thought. Either way, you ought to know. Wait until the internal search ends, and the patient 'comes back into the here-and-now'. Then find out. Sometimes you can guess from the preceding context. Or the patient might tell you. Alternatively, should you need to, you could make a prompting remark such as, "What were you just thinking about?"

Sometimes an apparently straightforward remark or question unexpectedly starts a lengthy internal search. You might innocently ask whether an abdominal pain feels better or worse after a meal, and find that the patient ponders far longer than you had anticipated before replying, "worse". Seeing the signs of internal search should make you lift your level of attention up out of 'idle' setting, and have you listening for the answer with all antennae at maximum sensitivity. It may simply be that the relationship to meals had never crossed the patient's mind till then. Or it might be because the patient is remembering how his father used to get pain after his meals, and didn't tell the doctor, and when they finally found his cancer it was too late, and maybe he's got the same, and now you're about to confirm his worst suspicions. Internal search is your opportunity to find gold nuggets near the surface; don't waste it.

EXERCISE

To practise spotting deletions, distortions and generalizations, watch a few video-recorded consultations, preferably not your own, so that you can concentrate more on the patient. Make three columns on a sheet of paper, and head them 'Deletions', 'Distortions' and 'Generalizations'. Listen carefully to everything the patient says. Don't try to analyse the problem in medical terms, or imagine how you yourself might have handled the consultation. Just keep a listening ear for imprecisions and evasions in the patient's account, and make a tick in the appropriate column. Do this for several consultations, so that you can recognize different patients' styles.

HOW TO ELICIT

Most doctors find their first experience of watching themselves consulting on video rather unnerving. "Whatever has become of the perceptive and friendly me," they complain, "who in 'real life' untiringly combines penetrating clinical acumen with abundant confidence-inspiring humanity? The camera and microphone, although the makers claim they do not lie, have somehow failed to pick up the soft glow of saintly light that normally illumines my face; the neatly-crafted dialogue that wings the consultation like an arrow towards its target has been edited out, and replaced with animal noises and gibberish." Then pride picks itself up, brushes the dust off, and starts to apply cold compresses to the bruising. "Of course, what I knew all the time was … a particularly difficult patient, that … and that consultation was only a small part of a much longer involvement … the camera angle couldn't quite see all the non-verbal

169

communication." And the best excuse of all: "knowing how much the patients would hate the video camera, I was too concerned for *their* embarrassment to be my normal self. That wasn't my *usual* style."

Yes it was. Byrne and Long, in *Doctors Talking to Patients*, seemed to establish that individual doctors do indeed have a particular consulting style, by which they meant that we each have our own favourite place in the 'doctor-centred/patient-centred' spectrum, and our own personal well-worn repertoire of verbal techniques for eliciting and explaining. Unfortunately they found little evidence of stylistic flexibility; apparently we aren't too good at varying our approach for the particular patient. Their observations seemed to confirm the proverb about old dogs and new tricks. Nevertheless, let's look on the bright side; since so many of our brain cells die every day, for us even to stay the same means that millions of new synapses must be capable of developing to compensate. So although you might consciously wonder whether you could ever in your maturity learn new ways of consulting, neurophysiology and the power of unconscious learning are more than equal to the task.

Just as there are no rules about *what* to elicit, only reminders, so there are no fixed schemes of *how* to elicit, only suggestions. Here are some ideas for you to pick and choose amongst, and some triggers for further thought. Some will not be news to you; others might. You don't want steak and chips every meal; why not be adventurous next surgery?

Speak the patient's language

By now you are familiar with the rapport-building effect of sharpening your listening ear for the patient's favourite words, images, metaphors, predicates and representational systems. Try to speak the same dialect of self-expression yourself. If a patient says a pain is 'like a knife going in' (Kinaesthetic), you might ask whether the knife feels sharp or blunt, hot or cold, a slow twist or a quick stab. If you suspect a peptic ulcer, and want to elicit any underlying stress factors, you might continue the same 'knife' analogy and enquire whether the patient has any 'wounded feelings', or is feeling 'cut up' about anything, or is the 'injured party' in any family disagreements. You might find the patient had more faith in a surgical operation rather than oral medication. It would be more reassuring for you to say, "I think we can get this sewn up quite easily", rather than, "I don't think this sounds too bad," (Auditory), or, "The outlook's good," (Visual).

The patient is always right (to start with!)

In the Oriental martial arts, I understand the knack is to maintain your own physical and mental equilibrium, and then, staying completely absorbed in the present moment, you divert the energy of your opponent's movement so that his momentum topples him off-balance. He makes the first move; you, by your superior skill, redirect his impetus to your own advantage. You appear to retreat before his advance, but in fact this is only an illusory set-back – who yields, wins. The French express the same tactical paradox in a saying, 'reculer pour mieux sauter' – 'draw back, the better to leap forwards'. In a strong wind, the unbending oak is uprooted, while the flexible reed springs back.

The consultation is not supposed to be a judo contest, with a winner and a loser; but if you fail to redirect the energy of a patient's presenting problem into directions that you can influence, you have done that patient no professional service. However much the patient blows a gale of what in your book is hot air and baloney, you will be better placed to translate it into your kind of medical sense if you initially accept it as meant – a genuine indication of the patient's experience. It is very easy to interrupt a stream of hyperbole and non sequiturs and say, in effect, "I don't want this, this is a red herring – tell me something different." The effect of too early a confrontation is likely to be that the patient, not knowing your preferences, will suppress the relevant along with the irrelevant. It is better to say "Yes" at first, to accept and agree with the patient's opening gambit, no matter how bizarre the description or how inappropriate the request. Your skill comes in being able to help the patient refine the description and redefine the request. 'Accept first, qualify second' makes a good working rule.

Here are three brief examples of productive and unproductive responses to gambits many doctors find provocative.

Patient:	My back's gone again. I know you can't do much, so I'll just have a certificate for a fortnight off work.
Doctor 1:	I'll be the judge of that!
Doctor 2:	Yes of course, if it takes that long. Let's just see if there isn't something more we could do

Patient:	I've had this cold nearly a week now. Something must be done!
Doctor 1:	You can't expect a cold to be gone as quickly as that.
Doctor 2:	They can seem to drag on, can't they? What have you tried?

171

Patient: Those iron tablets you gave me are making me tired.

Doctor 1:   It can't be those; it'll be your anaemia, which was the reason I prescribed them in the first place.

Doctor 2:   We certainly can't have that. Tell me a little more, so that I can see whether or not they need changing.

The patient goes first

When eliciting a patient's views about the causes and effects of her problem, it is a good idea to ask for her ideas first before you offer your own. Patients usually feel (or at least act) deferential to doctors' opinions, and are to varying degrees inhibited from putting up for consideration ideas they believe the doctor will dismiss. The flowering of the patient's imagination produces blooms which can easily be made to pale in comparison with the doctor's hothouse specimens. Admirers of Charles Schultz' 'Peanuts' characters may remember a strip which showed Linus, Sally and Charlie Brown lying on the ground, looking up at the sky and seeing pictures in the cloud formations. Linus says he can see a map of the British Honduras, a profile of Thomas Eakins the famous painter and sculptor, and an impression of the stoning of Saint Stephen. Sally asks, "What do you see, Charlie Brown?" Charlie Brown replies, "Well I was going to say I saw a ducky and a horsie, but I changed my mind!"

You can offset this reticence (which could result in a serious loss of information) by inviting the patient to tell you what he makes of the problem before you give your own assessment. There are some additional tactical reasons for letting the patient go first. If you know what ideas, concerns and expectations the patient has considered, you can:

(1) concentrate your own remarks on topics you know to be relevant to the patient;

(2) match your own explanations and advice to his theories of how his body works or his problem has arisen;

and (3) reassure on particular points that were worrying the patient, while not introducing doubts in areas that were not.

Beware of overdoing the "No, no, after you" approach, however. Too bald a "What do *you* think it is?" may elicit only the well-deserved riposte, "You tell me, you're the doctor." Soften the invitation with a hint of, "I'll show you mine if you show me yours." You might, for instance, say, "I've had several thoughts about what might be going on here, and I dare say you did too – what were your own ideas?"

Explain why you're asking

It is human nature (and one theme of this book!) to try to make sense of what people say to us. Just as we doctors try to understand the wider implications of what patients tell us, so also do patients try to fathom out why we are asking them for particular information. You are more likely to get the information you want quickly and honestly if you explain why you need it, rather then leave the patient guessing. Otherwise, the patient will fantasize about the 'real' reason behind your enquiry, and possibly answer a quite different question from the one you actually asked. For example:

Doctor: (wondering whether this 'tonsillitis' could be glandular fever) Have you noticed any lumps apart from the ones in your neck, or lost any weight lately?
Patient: (who has some inguinal lymphadenopathy, but who recently read a newspaper article about AIDS) No, certainly not.
Doctor: Do you mind if I just do a blood test, nevertheless?
Patient: I'm not homosexual, you know.

Better would have been:

Doctor: I was wondering whether this might be glandular fever after all. Have you noticed any lumps, or lost any weight lately?
Patient: I haven't lost any weight, but I feel a bit tender just here.
Doctor: That might fit in with glandular fever. I'ld like to do a blood test to check for that.
Patient: Fine.

Don't interrupt internal search

I've alerted you already to the physical signs of serious thought – reduced body mobility and defocusing of the eyes, with or without rapid eye-movements. When you see these signs, even if you are in mid-sentence or mid-paragraph, shut up. Wait until you see the refocusing and renewal of eye contact that indicate the end of the internal search. Then, and only then, invite the patient to tell you what had been going through his mind.

Statements make good questions

Some questions, known as 'closed' questions, are intended to elicit specific factual information. Question – "Did your knee hurt at all before you played football last Saturday?" Answer – "No, it was fine till then." Question – "What have you taken for the pain?" Answer – "Paracetamol." Such questions pre-suppose a limited range of possible answers; the only issue is which is the correct one, like a multiple choice examination question.

Other questions, called 'open-ended', acknowledge that the range of possible answers is greater than the questioner might suppose. They are intended to open up previously unconsidered areas for discussion. Question – "What is the pain like?" Answer – "It throbbed all the time at first, but now it feels it might give way when I walk." Question – "What have you tried doing about it so far?" Answer – "I rested it for a day, and put a bandage on, and took some paracetamol, and told the coach to leave me out of next week's game." Open-ended questions are like those questions in exams that begin, "Write short notes on ..."

But the best questions of all can be statements. If you've ever had to give evidence in court, you'll know that by carefully phrasing his questions a barrister can elicit answers which, though not untrue, are so incomplete and wrongly emphasized as to be seriously misleading. Barrister – "Were you driving in a reckless fashion, with flagrant disregard for the safety of other road users, or not?" Witness – "It wasn't like that. I was starting one of my migraines." Judge – "Just answer the question."

By asking questions, you inadvertently close off certain responses by presupposing the overall form of the answer. You risk suppressing the elaborations and qualifications which might have conveyed a more complete account. A better, though covert, way of asking questions can be to make a statement, and invite the patient's comments on it. Suppose you have diagnosed an uncomplicated upper respiratory tract infection, and are wondering whether or not the patient expects an antibiotic. You could ask a closed question, – "Do you want me to prescribe an antibiotic?" – or an open-ended question, – "Is there any treatment from me that you think might help?" Alternatively, you could make a comment-inviting statement, such as, "It's sometimes difficult to know whether or not to prescribe antibiotics for colds," and sit back and observe the response. One patient might say, "If that's all it is, I don't want to take any drugs for it." Another might say "With me, colds usually go onto my chest and I have to come back and get penicillin." A third might say, verbally or non-verbally, "Oh really, doctor?" This is your cue to elaborate on the various pros and cons of antibiotics, and do a little 'patient education'.

This way of asking questions is like the exam question that begins, "Antibiotics are over-prescribed in general practice. Discuss."

Two particular forms of 'question in a statement' are worth

mentioning in their own right. If you practise these surreptitiously, you will quickly discover their power. One technique is 'conjecture', and the other is 'my friend John'.

Conjecture

'Conjecture' statements begin, "I was wondering whether ..." or, "It occurred to me that ..." or, "One possibility might be ..." or, "Sometimes I find ..." The rider, "What do you think about that?" can either be added or implied, so that the patient is invited to comment, or not, as he chooses. This way of making an enquiry implies that the topic is safe to consider, but at the same time is free of implied value-judgements which might inhibit an honest response. Your conjecture might be rejected, or taken up and developed by the patient if it is relevant; either way, you learn something.

'My friend John'

'My friend John' statements are so-called after a favourite technique of an American master-therapist, Milton Erickson. He would describe the patient's problem or his own thoughts, as if talking about someone else. Instead of asking, "Has unemployment made you impotent?", or even the gentler conjecture, "I was wondering whether losing your job might have had any effects on your sex life", Erickson might say, "My friend John went through a bad patch after *he* lost his job. He finally plucked up courage to tell his doctor he had become impotent. He had some therapy, and is fine now." The patient then is free either to admit his own similar predicament, or, if it doesn't apply, to say in what ways his own case is different. The 'distancing' effect of this technique places a safety barrier between the patient and a potentially threatening question. From this dissociated position he can safely assess the doctor's intentions and decide whether or not he wants to identify himself with 'John's' situation, without any loss of face in either case.

Examples of the 'my friend John' technique suitable for general practice include:

"Some people ... (wonder about side effects but don't like to ask.")

"I had a patient once who ... (was very worried she had multiple sclerosis.")

"I can imagine many people in your situation ... (would get quite depressed.")

"I've known cases where . . . (an osteopath has proved very helpful.")

"If you had a friend with a problem rather like your own . . . (what would you advise?")

"You wouldn't be the first person to have wondered . . . (whether his doctor was keeping anything back.")

Dealing with deletions, distortions and generalizations

In the section on 'When to elicit', we reviewed these three indications of suppressed information. Turn back now to the examples of each, and read them again. In brackets are some possible ways of retrieving the missing details. The principles will be obvious to you.

If you were able to do the exercise in spotting examples of these processes in video-recorded consultations, go through one consultation again, this time deciding what you could say to the patient in order to get clear exactly what sensory experience underlay the simplification.

The NLP practitioners have a fully-fledged model of how to do this comprehensively, and how to make therapeutic use of the information you glean. It is well worth studying if this interests you at all [3].

57 varieties of "Go on"

Whenever I watch myself consulting on film, I am amazed how often I say, "Uhuh, uhum, yup, right, no, yeah, mm," with endless variations. At the same time my head goes up and down like one of those nodding dogs you see on the rear luggage shelf of Ford Cortinas. Two observations console me. First, every other doctor I've observed does the same. Secondly, the patient doesn't seem put off by this – rather the reverse.

It seems that all but the most egocentric of us need constant encouragement from our listeners to go on talking. Much of the information we seek to elicit from patients is personal, painful and awkward to put into words. So part of a doctor's professional skill is the ability to say 'go on' when necessary without becoming repetitious. There is a range of ways of doing this, from the imperceptible to the irresistible.

The commonest 'go on' device of all is simply to pay full and genuine attention to the other person. By consciously fostering rapport, as described in the chapter on 'Connecting', you will have developed this ability to a high degree.

Next come all the non-verbal and semi-verbal signs of encouragement – the nods, the mm's. These have their verbal equivalents in quietly spoken remarks like, "Really? … go on … I know what you mean … what happened then?"

A little firmer encouragement can be given by direct instructions, such as, "Tell me more about that … Don't stop there … I'ld like you to enlarge on that, please."

These variants of 'go on' are part of everyone's everyday speech, and need no elaboration. Two specific techniques – 'echoing' and 'checking' – may seem a little more artificial, but are worth trying out.

Echoing

You'll remember the 'censor in our head' that stops us taking too many unwitting risks in what we disclose. An abrupt pause in the flow of speech indicates that the censor is at work. It is as if the stylus on a record-player had suddenly jumped out of the groove. An extremely powerful yet almost invisible way of nudging the stylus back into the track is to 'echo' back to the patient the last significant word, phrase or idea that was spoken immediately before the pause. This seems to catch the censor off guard, and to help the patient recover the confidence to continue. I am always surprised at how this technique – sometimes called 'mirroring', 'parrotting' or 'reflecting' – is almost never detected in use (though it is easy to spot and laugh at in training workshops!) Here is a brief example, which is far from exaggerated.

Patient:	I haven't seen you for ages. Anyway … (*pause*)
Doctor:	Anyway …
Patient:	Anyway, I've got this rash. (*pause*)
Doctor:	Rash?
Patient:	Well, it's more of a spot.
Doctor:	A spot, eh?
Patient:	On my leg. My husband said I ought to show you. (*pause*)
Doctor:	He thought you should come?
Patient:	In case it was anything serious. (*pause*)
Doctor:	How do you mean, serious?
Patient:	Well, you hear about moles, don't you?
Doctor:	What have you heard about moles?

And so on. Try it: it works.

Checking

'Checking' is an extremely good way both to draw further relevances from the patient and also to see if you are anywhere near the 'SUMMARIZING' checkpoint. Whereas 'echoing' is reiterating the patient's last idea, 'checking' is reiterating the patient's story so far in a short précis statement. This gives the patient the chance to correct any wrong impressions, and, if satisfied with your understanding, to continue if necessary. Checking is presenting a 'mini-summary'. If you are at the 'SUMMARIZING' checkpoint, the patient will accept your checking statement without amplification, and indicate that you can proceed. A little later in the example above we might hear:

Doctor:	So you've found this spot that your husband thought just might be a melanoma?
Patient:	Yes. Shall I show you?

'Hunting, shooting and fishing' questions

Asking questions is a vegetarian form of blood sport. The questioner is pursuing a quarry that might or might not be visible, might need several techniques to catch, and which might not even be there at all.

In hunting, you are looking for information which you believe exists, but is either lying hidden or running away from you. Your aim is to bring it into full view.

In shooting, you can see the target quite distinctly. Your skill consists of being able to hit it 'dead centre', bringing down the answer quickly and cleanly, rather than limping off wounded into the undergrowth.

In fishing, you are looking for what may not exist at all. You spend a long time with your hook dangling in the stream, patiently watching the float for signs of a nibble. Then you have to be able to coax the fish to the shallows and land it.

Thinking of your questioning techniques in this metaphorical way can help make eliciting a living and exciting activity. As an exercise, look back through the preceding sections and decide whether the various suggestions and examples are hunting, shooting or fishing questions.

PITSTOP

TUTORIAL

Chris: You've talked about the what?, when? and how? of eliciting, but they were only three of the four courses you promised for your buffet. Right now I'm quite interested in leaving room for the last one, which was 'when to stop'.

Me: I doubt you've often found that a problem in real life. What tends to happen is that we drift from history-taking on to examination and decision-making almost without noticing. Sometimes, though, we are jolted back again to elicit more information, as for example when we discover the physical signs don't tally with the history we had taken, or when the patient says, "And there's another thing, doctor." It's usually more obvious when we *haven't* done enough eliciting than when we *have*.

Chris: So how can I recognize the 'SUMMARIZING' checkpoint?

Me: Look at the middle finger of your left hand. Can you still visualize the word SUMMARIZE on it? Give that finger a tap with your right index finger to get the associations flowing.

Chris: Got it.

Me: Good. When you've arrived at the 'SUMMARIZING' checkpoint, two things coincide. One is that you as the doctor feel you've got enough information from the history to work on; and so you feel ready to proceed to examine the patient, or to formulate a management plan – whichever is clinically appropriate in the particular case. The other is that the patient believes you have understood enough of what was worrying her for her to feel ready for the consultation to proceed. You have to ask yourself two questions, and get a "Yes" answer to both. The first is, "Have I got as much clinical information as *I* think I need?" The second is, "Have I picked up enough of the information *the patient* wants me to have?"

Chris: How can you tell?

Me: As to when you've got enough clinical information to go on, only you can tell at the time. The way to tell when you've sufficiently grasped the patient's concerns is to make a summary of the problem, from the patient's point of view, and test the summary for accuracy and completeness.

Chris: How?

Me: You can test your summary either explicitly or implicitly. Explicitly first: in a sentence or two, you try to encapsulate the key features of the patient's problem, including any significant ramifications your eliciting has uncovered. You present it to the patient, saying something like, "As I understand it then, ...", "So, if I could just recap ...", or, "Let me see if I've got this straight ..." Then you make your summary. Then you ask, "Is that right? Have I left out anything important?" The patient will tell you, and will show the non-verbal signs of the 'acceptance set' which we discussed in the chapter before this.

Chris: Sounds easy enough.

Me: Tying your shoelaces once looked hard. The other way of testing your summary less directly is to notice how the patient responds if and when you attempt to move the consultation on to the next stage. If, without actually saying so, the patient shares your sense that you've grasped the problem, the patient will be as ready as you are to move on, and will show this in various ways. Sometimes the patient will say, "Do you want to examine me now?", or, "So what do you think then?", or, "So where do we go from here?" At other times, the patient's satisfaction will be signalled non-verbally. You'll again be hoping to detect the 'acceptance set'. You'll be able to tell if the patient is happy to co-operate with you, or still appears reluctant.

Chris: A bit earlier, when you were asking why doctors sometimes skimped on the eliciting process, you said it was more a question of attitude than lack of skill. You've told me a lot about the scope and methods of eliciting, and it seems to involve giving the patient's feelings greater priority than one's own, at least in the history-taking stage. But, as you rightly said, I don't always feel as much genuine curiosity and goodwill to every patient as I seem to need. Are there any ways of overcoming this?

Me: Yes. Sometimes the best way to change a negative attitude into a positive one is initially to make yourself behave – play-act, if you like – as if you already had the positive attitude. Just because you wouldn't choose a particular patient for your close friend doesn't prevent you from doing a competent professional job of venepuncture; nor need it hinder your eliciting. If, with some of the patients you find difficult to empathize with, you 'pretend' to show more interest than at first you feel, and deploy your eliciting skills willynilly, you will find that the insights generated by your technique will leave you feeling more genuine warmth towards them. Then a process of positive feedback takes over.

I remember one patient whose tone of voice and

mannerisms irritated me almost beyond endurance. I was so keen to conclude each consultation that I never went beyond the surface of her numerous complaints, which luckily for both of us were never very serious. Then, apparently out of the blue, she made a suicide attempt. One of my partners learned of this and asked if I knew she had had a still-birth ten years previously. I hadn't known. Although at first I didn't want to, I steeled myself to ask her about it. When it had happened, ten years earlier, she had been unmarried and far from home. She had no friends. She knew that her mannerisms, which she put down to shyness, put people off. She had coped with her baby's death by "pushing it out of her mind and putting a brave face on." Over the years, the mask had worn thin; she had overdosed on her dead son's birthday. Somewhere in the course of listening to this story, I found myself involuntarily warming to her. That warmth still endures. It was one of those cases when, if you change the behaviour, the attitude changes itself.

Rapport, as you know, comes down to non-judgementally observing the patient's minimal cues. You'll find, when you do this, that paying such close attention leaves less room for your own prejudices. The closer you notice the other person, the more clearly you see a real human being, not a Frankenstein's monster of your own creation.

Chris: Amen.

Me: Well, you asked. Here's another instant way of modifying any negative feelings that get in the way of relating to a patient. Search for any one single feature about the person that you *can* appreciate. It might be the deep blue of her eyes, or his choice of tie; her scent, his smile; the texture of a sweater, the sound of a regional accent – anything. Allow your attention to linger on this 'oasis of acceptability'. Think to yourself, "That's nice." Very quickly you'll notice some of your initial antipathy evaporating.

Chris: So, he said, tapping his left middle finger, if I could just summarize. To get to the 'SUMMARIZING' checkpoint, I have to translate the patient's presenting complaint from 'vernacular' into 'medical' until it makes sense to me; I want to go into the motivational needs and living contexts that might make the problem especially significant for that patient; and I know some of the indications and methods of eliciting. Then when I think I understand, I make a summary and see whether it's accepted. Is that right?

Me: Spot on. Shall we move on now?

181

EXERCISE

As in the exercise at the end of the previous chapter, get some blank box-index cards and make yourself another pack, this time of eight cards. Write on them, one trigger phrase per card:

The patient is right (to start with)
Explain why you're asking
Statements make good questions
Conjecture
My friend John
Deletions, distortions or generalizations
Echoing
Checking

Re-read the relevant section if you need to, so that you understand what eliciting technique each trigger refers to. Place the pack of cards face down on your desk, and turn one up before each patient enters your room. Whatever else you do, use that eliciting technique at least once during the consultation.

When you have been through the pack, shuffle the cards, and then turn them up two at a time, then three, so that you increase your ability to vary your techniques to order.

B4
Interlude – the clinical process in general practice

The Ballad of Doctor Busy

Good morning, Mrs Hill, do take a chair.
Now what's the trouble? Stomach hurting? Where?
    There's a soreness down below
    And it hurts you when you go –
No bleeding though, as far as you're aware?

I diagnose cystitis, Mrs Hill.
This prescription's for a most effective pill.
    Just swallow down a capsule
    Four times daily, and perhaps you'll
Feel more like it by the weekend – course you will.

What, back again already, Mrs Hill?
The underneaths are troubling you still?
    Could be thrush or gonorrhoea,
    (I'll just take a peep down here)
Though it probably is just a bladder chill.

The water test shows everything's alright.
Yes, *what* a puzzle. There we are then. Quite.
    That the lot then for today?
    Sorry, what's that "by the way"?
You're moody, tired, depressed, no appetite?

Hub's marital advances get declined?
I'm sure it's only something in the mind.
    He's been *how* long - er – without it?
    You must tell me all about it;
Not today though, as I've got a bit behind.

Hello again. A talk? Yes, fire away.
"Much better out than in," is what I say.
    I've the tolerance of Gandhi
    And a box of Kleenex handy
And some brandy if we need it (and we may)...

183

My stomach's rumbling; must be time for food.
So, just recapping, what can we conclude?
    The symptoms that you mention
    I would just put down to tension
And a rotten marriage. Sorry to be rude.

Maybe your sense of failure as a wife
Is bound up with your frightful family life;
    But at half past six I'ld rather
    Hear no more about your father
And your aunty and your cousin up in Fife.

You may be right: you may have lots to gain
From working through your existential pain,
    But the sad and sorry fact is
    That in busy general practice
We must concentrate on matters more mundane.

So just to tide things over, Mrs Hill,
Because we've each been somewhat through the mill,
    I think that I'll advise a
    Teeny weeny tranquillizer
Which'll help us *both* get by – pray God it will!

It's a chastening thought that, for every patient in the United Kingdom who presents a health problem to a general practitioner, about nine other people turn for advice on minor illness to retail pharmacists. In thousands of chemist's shops all over the country, endless variations on a familiar scenario are being enacted:

"Yes madam?"
"Got anything for a cough?"
"Moist or dry?"
"Dry."
"Try this."
"Ta."

Banal though it may seem, the process underlying this transaction is the same whether the customer is shopping for a cough mixture or a heart transplant. Notwithstanding all the analysis and navel-watching that doctors do (and to which this book is contributing), the consultation in the surgery is in principle no more sophisticated than the one across the pharmacy counter. It's just that pharmacists haven't yet got round to making such a fuss about it. The pharmacist finds out what his customer wants, satisfies himself that he knows what he's dealing with, thinks for a moment, then makes a selection from the preparations on his shelf and hands over the one he thinks will suit.

That's all the clinical process is – finding out what you're dealing with, thinking for a moment, choosing something off the shelf. To do that competently you trained at least five years.

So far in this book we have dealt with how to find out more thoroughly what it is you're dealing with. Subsequent chapters will consider how you hand over the treatment you recommend, and make sure that it suits the patient's needs. About clinical decision-making – the moment's thought and the choosing from the shelf – I want to say very little. You've been exhaustively trained in this already, and are not short of other opportunities to improve your diagnostic and therapeutic skills. I propose merely to remind you of the ways we in general practice go about our decision-making, so that you can see how the separate skills of consulting dovetail into the overall clinical process.

As the consultation progresses, the initiative gradually shifts from patient to doctor. In the early stages, as we have seen, the patient is the main source of information and director of events. Before long, however, the doctor takes more of the initiative; it becomes his turn to generate information and suggestions. This is, after all, why the patient came in the first place. From the patient's point of view, a consultation with a doctor is a straight swop. The patient expects to exchange a problem for a solution.

How does the doctor decide what advice to give; in the analogy, which of the many bottles on his shelf is he to recommend? It was drummed into you at medical school – diagnosis first, treatment second. The slogan 'diagnosis before treatment' is a dogma which may put a brake on the therapeutic zeal of an inexperienced or over-confident young doctor, but it is only a slogan. It doesn't work in real life. Real life's too short; you often have to make decisions about problems you don't fully understand. Many young general practitioners find it very hard to betray their cherished ideal of making a diagnosis in every case. Yet general practice is the art of managing uncertainty, and in an uncertain world sometimes you can make a diagnosis, and sometimes you can't.

If you can make a sound clinical diagnosis, in biochemical or pathological terms, so much the better. Imprecision in general practice is a fact of life, not a virtue. How are diagnoses arrived at?

At medical school you were taught the diagnostic process like a catechism – presenting complaint, history of presenting complaint, past medical history, an incredibly long list of enquiries about specific symptoms, system by system, family history, social history; then examination, complete and thorough, inspection, palpation, percussion, auscultation; then finally special tests, almost as many as you could think of, leaving one or two for your immediate superior to take the credit for suggesting. At the end of all that, a bell marked 'diagnosis' was supposed to ring. And of course, in the last resort, diagnoses can still be made in this way in general practice when we are genuinely puzzled.

Doing a complete history and examination is only one way of reaching a diagnosis, however, and in the real world it is the least frequently used. Many diagnoses are made by 'pattern recognition', on the 'once seen, never forgotten' principle. Examples of diagnosis at a glance include Down's syndrome, cleft palate, psoriasis and many other dermatological conditions, Parkinson's disease, opthalmic herpes zoster – the list is extensive.

Another short-cut approach to diagnosis is the clinical algorithm, where you gradually whittle down the number of possible diagnoses by asking a structured series of 'either–or' questions. For example, in an antenatal clinic, part of your assessment might go: Are the dates certain? If 'yes', does the fundal height correspond to the dates? If 'no', is the uterus larger or smaller than expected? If 'larger,' has multiple pregnancy been excluded? If 'no', can you feel more than two poles? If 'yes', refer for ultrasound scanning to confirm multiple pregnancy. This approach is eminently suited to diagnosis by computer, or the computer-like brains of ultraspecialists. It also affords a method of deriving management protocols for common problems which can then be delegated to ancillary staff in the surgery, or to lay personnel in the Third World.

But the bread-and-butter method of diagnosis throughout medicine is 'hypothesis testing'. As Noel Coward might have sung:

Registrars, consultants and GPs do it,
Even wet-behind-the-ears trainees do it;
Let's do it, let's . . .

. . . well, if not fall in love exactly, at least admit that most of the time we make our diagnoses by checking out our hunches. 'Hypothesis testing' is a fancy way of saying that we gather a certain amount of information, then make our best educated guess at the one, two or three most likely explanations. Then we look selectively for one or two cardinal signs or characteristic features which would confirm or refute our working hypothesis. In general practice, as someone once observed, the bird chirping on the telephone wire is more likely to be a sparrow than a canary. The child whose mother says he's had a cold and has been up all night crying that his ear hurts is most likely to have otitis media. A glance through the auriscope reveals a red drum – and from then on we will act as if the diagnosis of otitis media is established. Only if the drum is surprisingly normal will we fall back on the 'complete history and examination' routine.

The 60-year-old man who collapses with sudden chest pain is 'diagnosed' as having a myocardial infarct until proved otherwise. Only after emergency resuscitation if necessary, and if the ECG shows no ischaemia, will we begin seriously to entertain alternative diagnoses like pulmonary embolus or pathological fractured rib. Likewise the young woman whose period is overdue and who develops right iliac fossa pain and vaginal bleeding has an ectopic pregnancy until proved otherwise. If we delayed admitting her until we were absolutely certain of the diagnosis, there would be some avoidable tragedies.

There are two general points to make about this process of diagnosis by 'checking out a hunch'. The first is that it carries a greater risk that we might make a wrong diagnosis and jump to the wrong conclusion, so that we have to have some fail-safe strategies for detecting errors. Chapter B 6 will consider these.

Secondly, it behoves us to be as careful as possible in our choice of the discriminating signs we use to confirm or refute the hunch. Looking at the throat is not a good way of confirming glandular fever; a blood film and Monospot test are better ways. An excellent review of the hallmarks of a good discriminating test, and of many other features of the diagnostic process, is contained in a recent Canadian book, *Clinical Epidemiology*, by Sackett, Haynes and Tugwell [1].

I think the most important feature of the clinical decision-making process in general practice is to be found in its end result. In general practice we are frequently unable to make a diagnosis, at least in traditional terms. We nevertheless must, and always can, make a management plan.

The usual job definition acknowledges that a GP "accepts the responsibility for making an initial decision on every problem his patient may present to him..." [2]. If to some problems we can attach a formal diagnosis, that's a bonus: what we must always do for every problem, diagnosed or not, is **decide what to do about it**. Not knowing what something is doesn't stop us knowing how to act. What's a diagnosis, after all? – a concept, an inference, a convenient one-word pseudo-explanation for a composite set of sensory experiences. Have you ever seen a schizophrenia, or heard a migraine, or felt a bronchitis? You've seen people behaving in certain ways, and heard them telling you about certain feelings, but you've never met an explanation face to face. Yet there are doctors who, on seeing footprints in the snow, never seem to tire of chasing the Yeti.

A diagnosis is a model, like all the other models we have considered in this book. It's only worth having as long as it's useful. If something else is more useful in a given situation, use that. Labels like 'schizophrenia', 'migraine' and 'bronchitis' are useful solely if they help you decide what to do for the person you've tied the label on. GPs are sometimes teased for knowing only three diagnoses:

(1) There's a lot of it about;
(2) You've had it before and you've got it again;
and (3) If it's not better next week, come and see me again.

We should take pride in this taunt; it's really a compliment on the priority we give to making management plans.

Other examples of management plans might include:

- Deciding to do any tests necessary to establish a diagnosis;
- Trying some treatment and observing the response;
- Deciding to do nothing for the moment and see what happens;
- Asking someone else's opinion;
- Spending more time on another occasion going into further details;
- Dialling 999;
- Asking other family members to participate in the assessment;
- Redirecting the patient to some other avenue of help.

I find it helpful, in formulating management plans, to do it in two stages, on different time scales. The first is to consider, "what am I going to do right now, during this consultation?" This involves deciding immediate priorities, meeting your own and the patient's most pressing needs. The second thing to be clear about is, "what is the plan after the patient leaves the room?" This second phase involves thinking of follow-up arrangements, referral, routine surveillance, managing the course of the problem on a longer time-scale.

So, returning to the image of the pharmacist reaching for the appropriate bottle off his shelf, make sure that the label on the bottle you hand to the patient after your clinical deliberation reads 'MANAGEMENT PLAN'.

I used to have a senior partner who was much loved by his elderly patients. Soon after he retired, I went to see one of his 'regulars', a lady with what seemed to be nothing worse than indigestion. "Yes, my old doctor thought that's all it was," she agreed. I suggested I might prescribe some 'white indigestion mixture' for her. "Oh, I've got some already," she told me, showing me an unopened, dust-covered bottle occupying pride of place on her mantel-piece. "It doesn't look as if you've taken any of it," I said. A dreamy, far-away look crept over her face. She belched quietly. "Oh no, I couldn't, Doctor Macarth gave me that," she murmured. "It's been ever so good."

B5
Checkpoint 3 (Handover) – communication skills

> On several occasions I have been with my brother Herodicus or some other physician to see one of his patients, who would not allow the physician to give him medicine, or apply the knife or hot iron to him; and I have persuaded him to do for me what he would not do for the physician by the use of rhetoric.
>
> From *Gorgias*, by Plato (c. 428–c. 348 BC)

We are often told, in one of those irritating truisms that introduce television documentaries, that we live in an 'Age of Communication'. Perhaps it is for the lack of much true intimacy in the midst of life's jostling anonymity that we have lowered the art of conversation to an academic discipline, systematized and certificated it, and called it 'interpersonal communication skills'. In therapy sessions and management training courses, patients and salesmen who never dreamed they could be tongue-tied are taught how to give their speech an irresistible veneer. (In much the same way is Cling-film used to refresh a tired sandwich and so lure the passer-by with an implied promise, "You'll like me when you unwrap me.")

All this talk about talk – I think it's the sort of thing that gets language a bad name. Actually, I shouldn't say 'I think'; today's communicators say, 'I Feel', with a capital F. If you tell someone you think they're boring, that makes you a snob. But if you tell them you Feel they're boring, you become a therapist. We don't have 'wants' any more – that would be selfish; instead we have 'Needs'. Even the two-year-old daughter of some friends of mine was quick to get in on the act. She would insist, plaintively and publicly, that what she Needed – and whereof denial would therefore damage her irretrievably – was a biscuit. In the Society for Treading on the Tails of Sleeping Dogs (motto – 'candour at all costs') we don't even have to (sorry, we are free to choose not to) disagree with anyone any more. Instead we can say, "I'ld like to share with you that right now I feel a negative response to how you're expressing where you're at." Isn't that disarming?

To be serious though, this is all rather fun. More than fun – it's a way of acknowledging the latent power of even the most apparently simple turn of phrase. This whole book, its content and its methods, is about the ability of words to convey a meaning over and above, within and beneath, their literal sense.

Surrounded as we are by slogans and the hard sell, it is easy to believe that only recently has communication become something to be 'skilled at'. But, as this chapter's introductory quotation confirms, Greek philosophers twenty-five centuries ago had the art of spoken persuasion down to a T. They used oratory as a vehicle to sway the moods, opinions and decisions of their listeners with an effectiveness contemporary politicians might envy. And like the know-alls they've turned out to be, the Greeks had a word for it – rhetoric.

Aristotle, who was Plato's trainee, conceived and practised rhetoric as a set of techniques whereby a man of supposedly impeccable moral soundness might intentionally alter the attitudes and beliefs of his audience. Antiphon of Athens in the 5th century BC invented an 'art of solace'; he encouraged people in distress to talk about their suffering and so change their perception of it. Antiphon, the original counsellor, was given an office in Corinth, where he put up a sign to the effect that he was 'able to heal by words those who were sick.' Six centuries later, a Roman rhetorician called Quintilian wrote a training manual (*Institutio Oratoria*) which describes body language, non-verbal communication, and different styles of vocal delivery. "For my own part," he wrote, "I would not hesitate to assert that a mediocre speech supported by all the power of delivery will be more impressive than the best speech unsupported by such power."

The aim of this chapter is to equip you to reach the 'HANDOVER' checkpoint. First of all, would you please check that you can still visualize the word 'HANDOVER' on your left ring finger? Give that finger an alerting tap now, and at other times during the next few sections when you read anything that strikes you as worth remembering.

I'ld like to continue with the 'pharmacist handing over a recommended bottle of medicine' analogy. The 'bottle' is whatever management plan you have devised by your clinical decision-making process. Remember that your management plan, however complete and efficacious, is useless unless the patient understands it, welcomes it, and complies with it. So when it becomes clear to you what course of action you in your professional judgement want to propose, your unashamed intention must next be to try and sell it. In some cases, your management plan may need to be modified during your sales pitch, if the patient for instance has already tried your remedy, or has a strong aversion to it. But nevertheless, whatever final plan you agree upon, you have to sell it, so that the patient leaves your room committed to trying out your proposal.

At best the patient can only be as clear in his mind about your management plan as you are yourself. (Often he will be less clear; that need not matter as long as he is clear enough to implement its key features.) So an essential prerequisite for handing over your plan to the patient is for you to be quite clear in your own mind what you are proposing. Make sure you know exactly what you want to achieve in the remainder of the present consultation. And make sure also that you are clear about what you want the patient to do after he leaves. The key word is 'do'. It is not enough for you to know what you want the patient to think, or to hope, or to intend. Unless you could close your eyes and imagine a movie of the patient *doing* what you suggest, your plan isn't clear enough. An effective management plan is one formulated in terms of specific, detailed, recordable-on-video-tape behaviour. Your management plan might be something practical like contrast bathing a sprained ankle every three hours and taking a tablet every six; or it might be advice to change the bedtime routine of a child who doesn't sleep; or it might be making a 'decision not to decide right now'. Whatever your plan is, you should be able to describe it precisely.

Admirers of Milton Erickson, who include me, are wont to say, "the meaning of any communication is the effect it produces." You judge whether your message has been clearly expressed by observing its effect on the recipient. If you deliver what to you seems a cogent explanation of why you're withholding antibiotics from someone with a cold, and the patient says, "Well if that's your attitude I'll see another doctor," then whatever you *thought* you meant, the meaning that came over to the patient was a snub. It's tempting but wrong to blame poor compliance or misunderstanding on the patient. It is the doctor's responsibility to make sure that his plan is accurately conveyed to the patient. All professionals regale each other off duty with tales of the apparent idiocies of their clients. But all human behaviour is understandable to the person doing it. If the patient, who after all came to you in good faith seeking help, doesn't carry out your reasonable plan of management, it is for one of two reasons. Either you didn't get the patient to see things your way, or you didn't see things her way.

In this chapter I shall be outlining a range of ways to hand over your management plan in ways acceptable to the patient. I think you may feel more positive towards them if we clear up some possible attitudinal difficulties first.

A TUTORIAL

Chris: This idea of the consultation as a journey: I've found that helpful, because it gives me an order to do things in; connecting first, then being in a position to summarize, and so on. But although it seems logical that making a management plan should come next – that's where I'ld put it if I was designing a computer programme – in fact it doesn't work like that. I find that I get my ideas of how to tackle a particular problem at all sorts of odd times during the consultation. Sometimes I've decided almost before the patient has sat down, if it's one of those problems you recognize at a glance. Other times, I seem to have elicited everything I can think of and still I'm not clear what to do. Doesn't that get in the way of an ordered progression to the HANDOVER checkpoint?

Me: It needn't. First let me say you're perfectly right – management plans do have a habit of forming themselves in your mind when *they* choose, not when a theoretical scheme calls for them. In fact, doctors quite often get their initial "Aha, I know what to do about this" feeling within the first two or three minutes of most consultations, sometimes before the patient has finished describing the problem, and usually well before they've completed any examination. But you have to hang on to your management plan and keep it to yourself until the consultation reaches the handing-over stage, and only 'go public' with it then. You've probably met used car salesmen who weigh in with answers before you've finished asking your question, and been put off by them. I imagine a pharmacist who thought he knew his customers so well that he tossed them a bottle of 'their usual' before they had a chance to open their mouths would soon go out of business. Anyway, not every first draft of a management plan becomes the final version.

Chris: Fair enough. On a different tack: I started to get a bit suspicious when at the start of this session you used words like 'persuade', and 'sway', and 'rhetoric'. It sounds as if the handing-over process might be rather manipulative and underhand.

Me: Many people have that response when it is suggested that they use language in a calculating fashion in order to change the way someone else thinks. The word 'manipulate' has overtones of exploitation, domination and coercion, activities we'd as soon not soil our hands with. And yet it's only the other side of the same coin that enables us to try to understand our patients as fully as possible. Do you think you might look at it this way? The strategies for building rapport and eliciting which we've already thought about have been based on the idea that paying very close attention to verbal and non-verbal cues is the best way a doctor can fulfil the patient's need to be understood. When the emphasis of the consultation shifts, as it must, to considering how to solve the problem, the patient will gain most benefit from your expertise if your suggestions are made with maximum effectiveness. The same knowledge of minimal cues that enabled you to understand the patient also serves the patient's interests now that it's your turn to be understood. No-one would thank you for being careless in your use of a speculum; why not try to use your language with equal skill?

You can't not influence somebody. You can't not communicate. Everything you say, every non-verbal cue that leaks out is likely to have an effect on what the patient thinks and feels. The only question is whether that effect is for good or harm. And by knowing about communication skills you have the choice. As long as you can be reasonably sure of your basic integrity and benevolence, a conscious decision to influence your patients is your duty, not a danger.

Can I quote one more piece of Plato at you?

> (Rhetoric) should be used like any other competitive art – the rhetorician ought not to abuse his strength any more than a pugilist or pancratiast or other master of fence; because he has powers which are more than a match either for friend or enemy, he ought not therefore to strike, stab, or slay his friends. Suppose a man to have been trained in the palestra and to be a skilful boxer – he in the fulness of his strength goes and strikes his father or his mother or one of his familiars or friends; but this is no reason why the trainers or fencing-masters should be held in detestation or banished from the city – surely not ... Not on this account are the teachers bad, neither is the art in fault, or bad in itself; I should rather say that those who make bad use of the art are to blame. And the same argument holds good of rhetoric. [1]

Chris: I have the feeling –
Me: There, you're doing it now.

Chris: I have the feeling that what you call 'communication skills' are going to turn out to be rather gimmicky.

Me: It depends how you choose to look at them. You could say that communication techniques are 'tricks up your sleeve', or 'cards in your hand', or 'tools at your disposal'. Yes, I'm going to review some methods of making patients do what you want them to, and encourage you to use them. Like the other techniques I've described, you're probably familiar with many of them already in other contexts. All they are are options: some possible ways of putting points over so as to enhance the likelihood that they will be taken up. Having lots of options gives you flexibility. If you only know the dose of two drugs, you're limited in the number of diseases you can treat. If you know about lots, you can prescribe more effectively more often to more people.

GENERAL PRINCIPLES OF HANDOVER

Look at Figure B5.1. It is intended to convey the idea that HANDOVER involves interaction between the knowledge and belief systems of two people, patient and doctor. In our journey through the consultation, we have reached a stage where the patient has conveyed to the doctor a portion of her belief system which is to do with her problem and its context, and the doctor has brought to the forefront of his mind that portion of his own belief system which he thinks will benefit the patient. The object of the exercise is to bring these two 'portions' into contact and overlap, so that when the two parties separate again, each has been changed as a result of the interaction. The doctor will be changed insofar as he has learned new things about that patient. The patient, we hope, will have been changed by having her problem dealt with.

The patient's framework

Patients differ widely in their factual knowledge, in their beliefs, their attitudes, their habits, their opinions, their values, their self-images, their myths, taboos and traditions. Some of these are relatively labile and easy to change on a day-to-day basis. Others are much more firmly held and difficult to alter. Some are negotiable, others comparatively non-negotiable. The distinction is analogous to the different types of computer memory – the transient RAM (Random Access Memory), the permanent in-built ROM (Read-Only Memory), and PROM (Programmable Read-Only Memory) which can be changed, but only with an effort, and which then lasts until the next

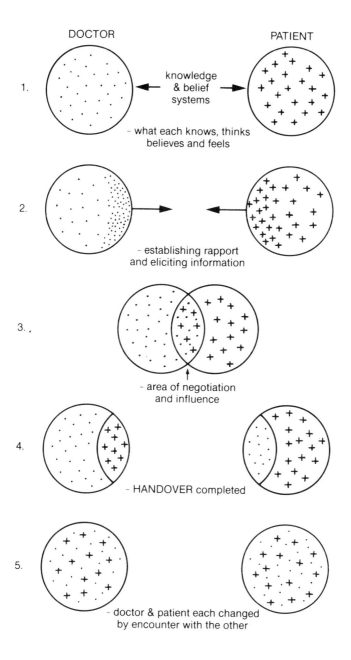

Figure B5.1 The HANDOVER process

time it is changed. Those parts of the patient's knowledge and belief system which are fixed or as good as fixed – the ROM and PROM – I call the patient's **framework**. The framework acts as a rigid mental scaffolding onto which any new experience (including the intervention of a doctor) has to be attached. In order for your management plan to be successfully handed over, it must fit with and sit comfortably on the patient's framework. Your proposed solution must be congruent with the patient's perception of herself and her problem.

Here are some examples of framework elements to which you might have to accommodate your management plan.

Knowledge: Not every patient knows what the lungs do, or how tablets 'get from the stomach to the places they're needed'.

Beliefs: Some patients believe there is a 'pill for every ill'. Others believe 'all drugs are dangerous'.

Attitude: Some patients revere the doctor as infallible and God-like; others view him as their paid employee.

Habits: "I never eat breakfast – I like to have my main meal in the evening."

Opinions: "A woman's job is looking after her family." Or, "A woman has as much right to a career as any man."

Values: "If you don't have to to work for something, it's not worth having." Or, "I'll get better treatment if I go private."

Self-image: "I'm ever so sorry to trouble you, doctor, really I am." Or, "Lord knows we've always tried to do the best for our children."

Myths: "Everyone knows you shouldn't bring a baby out with a cold!"

Taboos: "My mother never told *me* about periods, and it hasn't done me any harm." Or, about expressing feelings, "Least said, soonest mended."

Traditions: "We McGillicuddy's have always died in our own beds."

As you talk with patients, you gradually pick up a sense of the frameworks onto which you have to hang your management plan. Sometimes the indications come with an explicit 'position statement' – "What I always say is . . .", or, "I'm dead against . . ." Other times you have to do what you're getting better at all the time, i.e. read between the lines. A patient's attitude towards doctors can give a good indication: it might be one of subservience, or rivalry, gratitude, resentment, awe, sycophancy, dependency, rebelliousness, flirtation, or egalitarianism. Some other parameters against which to assess patients' frameworks are:

active or passive role in treatment
co-operative–disruptive

optimistic–pessimistic about outcome
naive–sophisticated
conservative–willing to experiment
trusting–suspicious

Each individual patient's personal framework places constraints on the overall type of solution that person will find acceptable. A course of treatment – say, taking an analgesic for a painful osteoarthritic knee joint – might be welcomed by one patient who thinks modern medicine's wonderful and the doctor knows best. Another patient would reject the same approach as being at odds with cherished beliefs about independence and the healthy life.

Accept the patient's framework, don't confront it

In the 'painful knee' example, you might be more successful at getting the second patient to take the analgesic if you advised along the lines of, "I don't think you need to get too involved with complicated treatment. Your knees are used to being active, so I'd do something simple and effective, like buy a few ordinary paracetamol, take them for a few days, and then get back to normal activity." The suggestion put this way would be more congruent with that patient's down-to-earth philosophy and reluctance to become dependent on doctors, but would have the same result as giving straight advice to the first patient.

As you prepare your handover, you are trying to get a sense of what is negotiable or non-negotiable in the patient's knowledge and beliefs. On this depends whether or not the patient finds your plan acceptable. You want to avoid provoking resistance; you want to devise a plan that stands the best chance of being accepted; and you want to couch your delivery in ways that maximize the patient's co-operation. Your skill as a doctor comes not from winning a trial of strength as to whose opinions are better, but from being able so to present your suggestions that the patient's usual habits of thought become your allies. The difference is the difference between an off-the-peg suit that might fit badly and chafe, and a comfortable made-to-measure version.

Six centuries BC a Chinese sage named Lao Tzu wrote the Tao Te Ching, an inspirational description of how to live in harmony with the flow of natural events. Here are three brief extracts, relevant at this point [2].

Not putting on a display, wise men shine forth.
Not justifying themselves, they are distinguished.

197

Not boasting, they achieve recognition.
Not bragging, they never falter.
They do not quarrel, so no one quarrels with them.
Therefore the ancients say, "Yield and overcome."
Is that an empty saying?

When men lack a sense of awe, there will be disaster.
Do not intrude in their homes. Do not harass them at work.
If you do not interfere, they will not weary of you.
Therefore the sage knows himself but makes no show,
Has self-respect but is not arrogant.
He lets go of that and chooses this.

Under heaven nothing is more soft and yielding than water.
Yet for attacking the solid and strong, nothing is better;
Under heaven everyone knows this,
Yet no one puts it into practice.

Lao Tzu would have made an excellent non-directive counsellor in the Carl Rogers mould. You might think, however, that to be an effective GP you have to temper acquiescence with judicious interference. The ideal is to be able to accept what cannot be changed about your patient and work with that, to influence what is capable of being influenced, and to be able to tell the difference.

PITSTOP

The next section gives some examples of three types of handing-over techniques. It is not exhaustive, nor meant to be. Let my suggestions be a stimulus to your own flair and creativity. As usual, if you are clear what you are trying to bring about, your unconscious recall will find the right words at the right time.

Strategies for handing-over fall into three categories, which seem to me sufficiently different to deserve their own names. The three are:

Negotiating,
Influencing,
and **Gift-wrapping.**

Negotiating is self-explanatory. It is part of Byrne and Long's Phase IV ('doctor and/or patient consider the condition'). In the Pendleton *et al.* model, negotiating is included in 'choosing appropriate action', 'achieving shared understanding' and 'involving patient in management'. (See Chapter A3 to refresh your memory if necessary.)

Influencing describes the various ways in which you can increase the patient's receptivity to your management plan.

Gift-wrapping means presenting your plan in an attractive package, personally chosen and labelled, which the patient is pleased to receive and take rejoicing away.

NEGOTIATING

The doctor goes first

Although when eliciting it's a good idea to let the patient give her ideas first, when considering management I think it makes for greater comfort all round if you make the opening move. I've not found that asking, "Well, what are we going to do about this then?" does much more than unsettle the patient and cast doubt on your competence. Unless you give at least a hint of your position, the patient will have no idea of what areas are up for negotiation.

Think aloud

Presumably your assessment, decision-making and management plan are all based on a reasonable grasp of the problem and are at least to some extent logical – so why not let the patient in on your thought processes? Be open about the steps that have led you to your conclusions. If you have some doubts, why not say so? If your thinking seems sensible to you, it probably will to the patient as well. Furthermore, you will set the patient an example of frankness and willingness to say what's in your mind, which will encourage the patient to do the same.

State your position

We discussed earlier the patient's framework of cherished knowledge and beliefs. Doctors have frameworks too. There are some things which you take for granted, some actions you simply will not take, some principles you strive to adhere to. Be explicit about them. Tell the patient what your non-negotiable areas and minimum goals are, if you have any. If you never arrange termination of pregnancy, or aren't going to give this patient tranquillizers, or very much want a consultant opinion, or are short of time – say so. Then you both know where you stand, and can concentrate on negotiating what is negotiable.

Say what you expect to happen

Describe to the patient the results you expect from your proposed course of action. Explain how you think your treatment plan will influence the patient's problem, in the immediate future, short-term and long-term. If you have reason to anticipate any negative consequences – side effects of treatment, say, or failure to respond – say so.

Fly some kites

Most problems presented to general practitioners have more than one possible solution. An ear-ache might develop into suppurative otitis media needing antibiotics, or it might settle down with analgesia and a decongestant. Antidepressants might help a patient, but so might counselling, or relaxation, or family therapy, or a psychiatric referral. Speculate out loud on some of the available options, so that the patient doesn't have to do all the searching for alternatives if she happens not to like your own favourite suggestion.

Give the patient a choice

If there seem to be several alternative solutions of genuinely equal merit, as in the examples immediately above, let the patient make the choice – a real informed choice. And be willing to abide by it.

(What do you do if you have sound reasons for thinking one option is far better than the others, but the patient chooses the 'wrong' one? I never promised you an end to moral dilemmas. You could either accept the patient's choice for the moment, and let time be the teacher; or you could use some of the more covert influencing techniques we shall be discussing shortly. Or you could ask your medical protection society. Or your priest.)

Ask what the patient thinks

As different options crop up for discussion, ask the patient what she thinks of them. How would she feel about option one? Might option two be better? Do there seem to be any snags in option three? Would she like any more information about option four?

If you don't see a 'yes', you've got a 'no'

At this point in the consultation, as at every other, you should be able to tell whether the patient feels well-disposed or doubtful about any particular topic by listening and watching for the verbal and non-verbal signals of the acceptance set.

At the negotiating stage, signs of internal search mean the patient is seriously considering your suggestions. The acceptance set is your signal to draw negotiation to a close. If you don't see the acceptance set, keep negotiating.

INFLUENCING

How about the obvious?

Quite a good way to influence patients so that they do what you want is to tell them! Although this book, this chapter and this section are about subtlety, there's nothing wrong with being straightforward and directive – if it works. Let's not make problems where none exists; in most consultations the patient is receptive to ungarnished advice or instructions. More often than not, that's what they came for. The doctor is credited with expertise, charisma and respect amounting to what Michael Balint called his 'apostolic function'. This lends 'doctor's orders' an authority which, while we may secretly consider it undeserved, we should be foolish not to use in the patient's interests.

Gregory Bateson, a noted expert on communication who proposed the 'double bind' theory of schizophrenia, and Milton Erickson (him again – a master of hypnosis and indirect suggestion) were once chatting on the telephone. When Bateson hung up, he said, "That man is going to manipulate me to come to San Francisco and have dinner with him." His companion asked, "Why? What did he say to you?" Bateson replied, "He said to me, 'Why don't you come to San Francisco and have dinner with me?'" [3]

Sometimes a piece of medical advice needs no preamble; it is acceptable because it's you who gives it. Some younger doctors feel very hesitant about throwing the weight of their professional status behind the advice they give. But diffidence, by which the doctor means to show respect for the patient's autonomy, may to the patient come across as uncertainty, and so be counterproductive. If you've got good sound advice to give, deliver it with the confidence it deserves. I once did a workshop where, in role-play, young doctors tried to tell a heavy smoker to cut down. As an exercise, they were asked to preface their advice with an emphasis-giving phrase like, "I strongly urge you to ...", or "My advice to you is ...", or "There's no doubt in my mind

201

that ..." They couldn't do it. They got the giggles, like six-year-olds when someone says "bum". Back in their consulting rooms, however, they were able to overcome their self-effacing impulses.

The 'shingles' technique

'Shingles' in this context are those rather attractive wooden roofing tiles, not herpes zoster. Shingles have one end thicker than the other, so that when they are laid overlapping on a roof they form a natural gradient down which the rain is channelled into the guttering. A line of thought can be presented as just such a pattern of overlapping ideas, where each step in the argument leads inexorably on to the next. The initial data appear to lead to only one possible conclusion, which itself in turn becomes the start of the next stage of the argument, and so on. In diagrammatic form, the shingles technique goes:

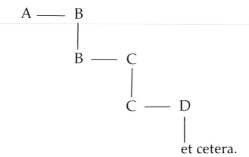

Here's an example. You're having difficulty getting an obese patient with osteoarthritis of the knees to see the need to lose weight. Note how the last word or idea of one sentence becomes the beginning of the next.

"Your knees have a problem. Their problem is, you aren't listening to what they're trying to tell you. They're trying to tell you, by hurting, that you're asking too much of them. You're asking them to carry more weight than they can stand, and they don't like it. What they would like is for you to take some of the load off them. The only way you can lessen the load is to weigh less. So in order to weigh less you're going to have to diet. Now I know you find dieting difficult; but difficulties are there to be solved..."

The shingles technique gives an argument the persuasive feel of inevitable logic leading one short step at a time to the only possible conclusion. It is a good way to counter red herrings. It is also a useful manoeuvre in response to patients who can think of a dozen reasons why anything you suggest won't work.

Don't say 'don't' (unless you mean 'do')

There you are, sitting in a railway carriage minding your own business, not a care in the world. Then a total stranger on the opposite seat sighs deeply, leans forward, and says to you, "Don't talk to *me* about traffic wardens." Well, you hadn't been going to. Nothing was further from your thoughts – until then. But from then on you can't think about anything *but* traffic wardens, and how they would have featured in the conversation you're not going to have. There is nothing more guaranteed to make me brace myself rigid in the dentist's chair than being told, "This won't hurt." Until then, I might have managed to convince myself that modern dentistry was a pleasure, and then – wham! – what's 'hurt' doing in the dentist's mind?

As we've found already, most thought is figurative rather than logical. We (or at least our right hemispheres) think in pictures, imaginery conversations, and feelings. All of these are positive experiences; how do you convey their opposites? Whereas in the logical left hemisphere realm of grammar and syntax, negation is easy – you just stick 'not' into the sentence – in figurative language, you can't see a 'not' picture, or feel a 'not' sensation. The opposite of an image or a feeling is another different one, not the absence of any image or feeling at all.

Earlier in this chapter I quoted the maxim "the meaning of any communication is the effect it produces". The right hemisphere doesn't understand negation. It responds to negatives as if they weren't there. To the right hemisphere:

> **don't** means **do,**
> **won't** means **might,**
> **can't** means **could,**
and **shouldn't** means **probably will.**

"Don't worry," means worrying is an option. "This won't hurt," means it might. "I can't get you seen any earlier," means that somebody else could. "Don't forget, you shouldn't stop the course of tablets until they've all gone," is a clear challenge.

If you want to tell someone's right hemisphere something, put it positively. Instead of these examples, you could say, "Relax". "You'll just feel me touching you." "That's the earliest appointment." "Remember to finish all the tablets."

A pub bore was telling his favourite "what I did in the war" story.

"There I was, flying over the desert, miles and miles of sand. Can you imagine, nothing but sand?" "Right, got you," said the little fellow listening to him. "No trees, nothing," the bore confirmed.

"Ah," said the little fellow, "sorry. Just give me a moment." A lone palm tree had appeared in this imaginary scene, bottom left. It wouldn't just vanish, so in his mind's eye he had two Arabs ride up on camels, discount, unpack a saw, saw down the tree, and exit stage right, dragging the tree behind them. "Okay, nothing but sand," he said. "Carry on."

"Suddenly both engines failed. We were going to have to make an emergency landing. The sand of the desert was firm and level, so I made a perfect approach and landed. But while we were still rolling, the airplane struck an obstacle, cartwheeled, and landed on her back. You'll never guess what we'd hit."

"The sawn-off stump of the only palm tree for miles," said the little fellow. Without a word, the bore turned on his heel and left.

It is possible to turn this inability to think in negatives to your advantage, and induce your patient to consider doing something out of keeping with normal habits and attitudes. By disguising your suggestion as a negative, you can 'smuggle' it in past the logically-minded sentry which is fooled by the correctness of your grammar. Imagine how patients might respond to the following examples, bearing in mind that what you are seeking is *behavioural* acceptance of your wishes. Verbal agreement or disagreement matters less than the practical outcome.

"You couldn't get your husband to come and see me, I don't suppose." (I could ask him.)

"I shouldn't think you'ld find it easy to cut down your smoking." (I'm not *that* hooked, you'll see.)

"Not everybody can understand why we are cautious about prescribing sleeping tablets." (So tell me.)

"I wasn't really thinking of asking a surgeon to see you at the moment." (When, then?)

"You don't just have to take my word for it." (No, I do believe you.)

Questions make good statements

I reminded you in Chapter B3, on eliciting skills, how statements can make good questions because they don't give too much away about the response you're hoping for, and the patient doesn't have to commit himself to a particular answer. The corollary is also true: questions can make good statements. Having to make a reply produces a commitment to the answer given. Here are some examples.

Statement:	"I think you drink too much."
'Stone-wall' response:	"No I don't."
In question form:	"Have you ever thought you might be drinking too much?"
Possible replies:	"Yes," or "No."
Your responses:	(to 'yes') "I think so too. Let's discuss that."
	(to 'no') "Well, let's see, how much are you drinking, exactly?"
Statement:	"I want you to come off your tranquillizers."
Stone-wall response:	"Oh I couldn't do without them."
In question form:	"Do you think you'll ever come off your tranquillizers?"
Possible replies:	"Yes", "no", "maybe", "not yet."
Your responses:	"Good, I'll help." "Are you really *that* pessimistic?" "Let's see if I can push you to a decision." "Would you like to set yourself a dead-line?"
Statement:	"It's quite safe to bring a child to surgery with an earache."
Stone-wall response:	"Well you would say that, wouldn't you?"
In question form:	"How do you decide whether it's safe to bring your child out when she's not well?"
Possible replies:	"Don't know", accurate knowledge, inaccurate knowledge.
Your responses:	"Let me tell you." "What were you not sure about on this occasion?" "That's not quite right; let me explain."

Reframing

> It is not the things themselves which trouble us, but the opinions we have about these things.
>
> Epictetus

> There is nothing either good or bad, but thinking makes it so.
>
> Shakespeare

When we were thinking about eliciting, we saw how the meaning and significance attached to a problem depends very much on its context. Sometimes we can help a patient by altering the physical reality that causes suffering, by intervening at a physiological or anatomical level. But such mechanistic solutions are all too rare; more often than not we have to substitute or supplement concrete relief by assisting the patient to take a different view of the situation. We may not always be able to change the hard facts of experience, but we can put them in a better light, call them something less paralysing, and nudge the patient's imagination into a different network of associations. The name given to this process, when used therapeutically, is 'reframing'.

The language is full of sayings and stories that reflect the universal nature of this phenomenon:

- the pessimist's beer glass is half-empty, but the optimist's is half-full;
- 'beauty is in the eye of the beholder';
- one's prospects can be viewed with a 'jaundiced eye', or through 'rose-tinted spectacles';
- if, as Shakespeare claimed, 'that which we call a rose by any other name would smell as sweet', why is there a rose named 'Peace' but not one called 'War', or 'negotiated settlement'?

The classic example of reframing in action is found in Mark Twain's novel, *Tom Sawyer* [4]. One Saturday afternoon Tom, as punishment for fighting, has been set to whitewash a fence.

> Thirty yards of broad fence nine feet high! It seemed to him that life was hollow, and existence but a burden. (Tom) sat down on a tree-box discouraged... At this dark and hopeless moment an inspiration burst upon him. Nothing less than a great, magnificent inspiration! He took up his brush and went tranquilly to work. Ben Rogers hove in sight presently; the very boy of all boys whose ridicule he had been dreading...
>
> Ben said: 'Hello, old chap; they got you to work, hey?'
> 'Why, it's you, Ben! I warn't noticing.'
> 'Say, I'm going in a swimming, I am. Don't you wish you could? But of course, you'd druther work, wouldn't you? Course you would!'
> Tom contemplated the boy a bit, and said:
> 'What do you call work?'
> 'Why, ain't that work?'
> Tom resumed his whitewashing, and answered carelessly:
> 'Well, maybe it is, and maybe it ain't. All I know is, it suits Tom Sawyer.'
> 'Oh, come now, you don't mean to let on that you like it?'
> The brush continued to move.
> 'Like it? Well, I don't see why I oughtn't to like it. Does a boy get a chance to whitewash a fence every day?'

That put the thing in a new light. Ben stopped nibbling his apple. Tom swept his brush daintily back and forth – stepped back to note the effect – added a touch here and there – criticized the effect again, Ben watching every move, and getting more and more interested, more and more absorbed. Presently he said:

'Say, Tom, let me whitewash a little.'

Tom yields up the brush "with reluctance in his face, but alacrity in his heart." Soon boy after boy has bribed Tom into allowing him a turn with the brush. The fence has three coats of whitewash. Mark Twain continues:

> (Tom) had discovered a great law of human action, without knowing it, namely, that, in order to make a man or a boy covet a thing, it is only necessary to make the thing difficult to attain. If he had been a great and wise philosopher, like the writer of this book, he would now have comprehended that work consists of whatever a body is obliged to do, and that play consists of whatever a body is not obliged to do.

General practice is full of people like Ben Rogers, and fences that have to be whitewashed. Tom Sawyer was able to reframe his punishment as an enviable privilege. One of the greatest kindnesses a doctor can do for a patient is reframe a distressing or painful problem as something that can after all be coped with.

Suffering is inevitable – inherent in the human condition –and it is always difficult to bear. If you call a difficulty a 'problem', you are committed to trying to find a 'solution' for it. If a solution can be found, so well and good. But if there is no solution, you are left with an 'insoluble problem', which may be worse than what you had to start with. If on the other hand you reframe the initial difficulty as an 'opportunity', it can become something to be gratefully learned from.

This idea of 'symptoms as opportunity' is potentially one of the most far-reaching shifts in medical perspective, consistent with the present widespread interest in holistic approaches to health restoration and maintenance. It is not a doctrine of laissez faire, but rather an additional dimension to your therapeutic options. Pain, while still being diagnosed and relieved, can in addition be seen as the body's way of alerting the patient to the need for corrective action. Angina can be heeded as a timely warning that a stressful and unhealthy life-style needs some reappraisal. Post-bereavement depression means that a widow has not yet fully expressed the love and sadness in her heart.

The more you think about the power of reframing, the more chances there are in practice to use it. So often the answer to a difficult question is, "ask a different question."

The behaviour of a twelve-year-old who steals from her parents might be seen as 'bad' by her father and 'mad' by her mother. If you can offer them the alternative view of their daughter as 'sad', you might manage to enlist their parental love rather than punishment or rejection.

A four-year-old starts 'wilfully' scratching the face of his new baby sister. If this is seen as 'attention-seeking' behaviour, the natural response is to impose sanctions, which usually make things worse. Call it 'attention-needing' instead, and the solution becomes obvious.

Persistent truanting can be interpreted either as the child refusing to go to school, or, often more profitably, as being afraid to be away from home.

Secondary impotence need not be the 'last straw' in an already flagging relationship, but a hint of the cure, namely a period of enforced abstinence.

We spoke earlier in this chapter of the patient's 'Framework' – the implicit skeleton of assumptions, attitudes and beliefs that shapes the outward configuration of a person's responses to new information. It should be apparent now that it is vitally important that the doctor 'frames' his management plan in terms that are congruent with the patient's belief system. A single suggestion – "Let the nurse check your blood pressure next month" – can be framed in a variety of ways, according to what will best fit in with the patient's framework. The straightforward instruction may suit a compliant patient. An apologetic patient will understand you 'delegating' his case "because, as you know, my surgeries get so busy." A third might like the explanation, "since the nurse is trained to go into greater detail about all the things you can do yourself to keep your blood pressure low." Another might prefer, "because, after all, you're not ill and needing to see a doctor."

Trying to reframe at least part of every patient's presenting complaint is one of the challenges I most enjoy about the consultation. If you are successful, the patient leaves the room feeling buoyant with the novelty of an unexpected shift of perspective. A considerable body of literature about this single concept is being built up. Books by Bandler and Grinder [5], and by Watzlawick and his colleagues at Palo Alto [6], will amply repay study.

Shepherding

I feel almost ashamed of the word I have chosen to describe a group of 'influencing' techniques, and yet no image so succinctly captures the ideas I have in mind as that of a shepherd with his dog trying to get a flock of sheep into a pen. If you can rid yourself of the invidious 'patient = sheep' associations, you will perhaps recognize the task of persuading some patients to see the merits of a particular course of action as similar to that of a shepherd with a recalcitrant flock. It is necessary sometimes to do the verbal equivalents of opening the gate of the desired pen, blocking off any alternative pens, and exerting some directional pressure as would a sheepdog. In other words, you have to make your preferred option appear to beckon enticingly, to make less acceptable alternatives look unattractive, and to provide a little gentle coaxing so that the patient stops vacillating and makes a choice.

Shepherding techniques include:

value-laden phrases,
presuppositions,
pre-empting,
and **my friend John** (again).

I'll describe each briefly, then show you how they can work in a case transcript.

Value-laden phrases

Events and sensations are intrinsically neutral and free of value judgements, but the words we use to describe them are most definitely not. By choosing language with 'good' or 'bad' overtones, you can hook into the patient's networks of associations so that one course of action is seen as worthy and another not. It makes a difference whether you describe an osteopath as a 'bone-setter chappie' or a 'colleague who's had more training in manipulation than me'. Referral to a hospital out-patient department could be presented, according to whether you were in favour of it or not, either as 'packing you off to a so-called specialist', or 'asking a Consultant to give us a second opinion'. When wondering whether or not to prescribe an anti-inflammatory, one doctor might say, "I think some mild medication would be the best course", and another, "You don't want to go dosing yourself up with drugs." When the time comes to consider admitting an old person with a chest infection to hospital, either decision can be softened by careful choice of words: the patient might be better off "here in your own home, amongst friends, without all the upheaval of going off to that hospital", or "tucked up in St Saviour's, where all the treatment you need is on hand and the nurses can look after you right round the clock."

Presuppositions

We make assumptions in almost everything we say. When someone asks you, "Tea or coffee?", it is assumed (a) that you want a drink, (b) you could have either, (c) cocoa and alcohol are not on offer, (d) you have a preference, (e) you are willing to state your preference, and (f) you'll be given your choice. A presupposition is a question or statement that makes an assumption about someone's future behaviour, and that only makes sense if the assumption is correct. The general forms of presupposition are:

(1) If you want someone to do A, suggest B, provided that B can only be done by previously doing A.

    For instance, if I want you to read this book, I could ask you to let me know what you think of it, which presupposes that you read it – otherwise you couldn't tell me your opinion.

(2) If you want to know about A, enquire about B, provided that in answering B, A is indirectly answered.

    For instance, if you want to know whether a patient is having marital difficulties, you might ask, "Which member of your family do you worry most about?", which presupposes concern about somebody.

The consultation, whether you had already realised it or not, is inevitably full of presuppositions designed to secure a particular outcome. When you give a prescription for drug A in preference to drug B, you presuppose that a prescription of some kind is called for. When you subsequently ask the patient what effects they've noticed, you presuppose that they took the tablets and the tablet did have some effect.

It is possible to develop the technique of presupposition to a quite powerful degree. If you talk to the patient *as if* your desired outcome had already been achieved, the patient in forming a reply will share your assumption, even if only for the time being. By virtue of having entertained the possibility of your outcome, in order to respond to your suggestion, the patient is more likely to accept it. Here are a few clinical examples of this process.

Desired outcome: The patient is to return next week for follow-up.
Presupposition: "Which day next week would suit you best to come again?"

Desired outcome: Get the patient to take medication regularly.
Presupposition: "I'm going to give you a tablet with a 'three-times-

a-day' dosage, as that's easier to remember to take regularly."

Desired outcome: Persuading a reluctant patient to let you take a cervical smear.

Presupposition: "Would you feel more comfortable if I asked my nurse to come in while I do your smear test?"

Desired outcome: Refer the patient to a counsellor.

Presupposition: "Now, who might be better placed to help than me? Well, let's think, there's ..."

Desired outcome: Have the patient decide to stop smoking.

Presupposition: "Do you think you'll find it easier to stop smoking all at once, or gradually cut down over a fortnight?"

Pre-empting

Suppose that of three possible management plans, X, Y, and Z, X is the one you favour. In addition, you suspect that the patient has a hankering for A or B, which even after discussion remain, in your judgement, impracticable. You can increase the patient's appreciation of the merits of plan X by making pre-empting comments about A, B, Y and Z. "We could do Y or Z," you begin, "but the snags about those are ... I don't know whether you'd even thought about A or B, but there again there are problems ..."

'My friend John'

'My friend John', if you remember, made his appearance in Chapter B 3. He is the model patient whose circumstances are strangely similar to those of the patient you are talking to, who provided an example of being willing to discuss just those topics which your patient is finding difficult to put into words. 'My friend John' can also be a useful salesman's assistant at the hand-over stage. Hearing your description of what might or did happen to a third party in like circumstances, your patient can rehearse and anticipate his own reactions to your proposed management plan without yet being committed to it. 'My friend John' is a way of smuggling a possibility into the patient's imagination. Once a possibility is known to exist, it can never again not exist, and can perhaps be nurtured into fruition.

Here are some examples of 'my friend John' working as a shepherd.

211

"Let me tell you the last time I had a patient who ..."

"I remember someone else in this situation who found out the hard way ..."

"A lot of people these days are coming round to thinking..."

"Someone less sensible than yourself might easily have been tempted to ..."

"I can understand how someone might wonder ..."

"Did you see that article in the paper about problems like yours? What it said was ..."

Case illustration

I'm aware how manipulative some of these techniques can appear at first sight (presupposition – when you take a second look you'll see that they aren't!). There is obviously a line to be drawn between coercing an ill-informed patient into a course of action not freely chosen, and your professional obligation to help your patients overcome the limitations of their previously attempted solutions. Make sure that you are certain whose needs you are satisfying. I hope you'll agree that, in the following example, this line is not overstepped.

In this transcript, the patient is a beautician aged 32, married for ten years but childless. She has a six year history of a succession of multiple bizarre symptoms, not found to have any organic basis despite innumerable investigations and referrals, NHS and private, orthodox and alternative. The doctor considers her to be a 'somatizer' – someone who learned in childhood that only physical complaints get taken any notice of. He suspects there may be a deep-seated marital conflict, but this is denied. The doctor's desired outcome is to arrange a joint interview with her and her husband, something she has so far resisted. Ideally, he would like it to be the patient who conveys the request to her husband, so that they discuss it at home first.

Value-laden phrases are indicated (VP), presuppositions (PS), pre-empting (PE), 'my friend John' (MFJ), and reframing (RF).

Mrs Silver: So I want you to refer me to a different gastroenterologist, privately this time.

Doctor: Yes, I was afraid you were going to say that (VP). That would be so easy, but I'ld feel I was letting you down if I did (VP, RF). Anyone who's had as much pain as you have (MFJ) could be forgiven for thinking there must be something that the other doctors had missed (PE). I've known people (MFJ) spend a lifetime chasing after mirages (VP), spending an absolute fortune on Harley Street specialists, acupuncture, herbalism, yoga, unnecessary operations sometimes even, and all to no avail (PE). I mean, look how thick your notes are, with all the various specialists you've seen, and yet you're still in pain (PE). So I don't think that referring you again is the best move we could make (PS). I think that the fact you're still in pain means that your body is drawing our attention to something (RF). I think your body (MFJ) is telling us that it's tired of showing its pain to doctor after doctor, and wants to tell someone else instead (RF). Wouldn't it be marvellous (VP) if we could find out who (PS)?

Mrs Silver: Well yes, but who do you have in mind?

Doctor: I have a hunch your husband will be able to help us initially (PS). In my experience, people (MFJ) are understandably a bit hesitant to discuss this sort of problem as a couple – they can't at first (PS) see the point of it (PE). But the things that look the unlikeliest are often what are most worth doing (VP, RF).

Mrs Silver: Michael won't come, I know he won't.

Doctor: Which of us is going to ask him (PS)?

Mrs Silver: It's no use me.

Doctor: Okay, I will.

Mrs Silver: I don't want you ringing up at home. And he's out of the office a good deal (PE!).

Doctor: Yes you're right, a letter would be much better (VP). Tell you what, I'll write out a letter now, asking Michael to make an appointment at the most convenient time (PS), and I'll give it to you and ask you to deliver it. You wouldn't mind being postman, would you, save us the cost of the stamp? That's kind, thanks (VP). And perhaps you could tell me his office phone number, so that if I haven't heard from him say by next Thursday (PS) I can give him a ring and sort something out (PE).

PITSTOP

How does your own attitude stand at the moment towards the more indirect influencing techniques? Which do you use already? Can you imagine yourself using others? Which of any unfamiliar ones do you think you might feel relatively comfortable with? Or do you feel, perhaps, that what can't be done overtly shouldn't be done at all?

GIFT-WRAPPING

In this the final set of HAND-OVER skills, we move on from the selection of an appropriate management plan, whether agreed overtly by NEGOTIATING or more indirectly by INFLUENCING. That decision is made; GIFT-WRAPPING refers to the art of handing over the management plan to the patient in such a way that it is understandable, acceptable, personalized, desirable, sensitively and compassionately presented.

Just to give you the general idea, here are some examples of good and bad gift-wrapping.

Bad: "Now Janice, we don't want your mother in here do we? Please leave the room, Mrs Pry."

Better: "Mrs Pry, sooner or later your daughter will be old enough to talk to me by herself, and I think that time might be now. Would you mind waiting for her in the waiting room?"

Bad: "Goupthechemistsgetthisprescription,
        twotabletstwiceadayforthenextsevendaysbeforemeals,
        gotothenursegetamidstreamspecimenofurinecollected,
        takeitdowntothehospitalpathlabbeforemiddaytoday,
        phoneonMondayandaskfortheresults,
        makeanappointmenttoseemeagainnextweeknotonTuesday
        thoughI'monholiday. Any questions?"

Better: Work it out!

Bad: "Now psoriasis, Darren, is an essential dysfunction of the
        pilo-sebaceous apparatus of the rete peg, and as such, your
        prognosis vis-à-vis a permanent clearing is – what do you
        young people say? – a bit iffy. But you can rub in this
        emollient-based fluorinated topical steroid preparation ..."

Better: "We can't cure your skin permanently I'm afraid, Darren, but
        we can get it looking better if I prescribe some cream for you
        to use."

Cellophane

The best thing for a management plan to be wrapped in is Cellophane.
It's transparent, you can see what's inside it, so that you can tell
whether it's what you want or not, it doesn't raise false expectations
or conceal unexpected disappointments. Cellophane is honest and
open, straightforward and above board.

Delivery

By 'delivery', an actor means the vocal techniques for converting a
written text into a live performance, with the voice being used for
maximum effect and impact on the audience. Delivery is 'how' things
are spoken, not 'what'.

Timing

The presentation of your management plan needs to be timed for
when the patient is most ready for it, which may not coincide with the
precise moment it forms in your mind. States of readiness are usually
no more simultaneous than orgasms. You may have to hold on
patiently to your plan for a while until the patient is at maximum

expectancy. Sometimes you can focus the patient's attention by saying, "I'ld like to move on now to think what we're going to do about this," or, "Would you like me to tell you now what I think we should do?"

'Chunking'

Large amounts of information need to be broken down into bite-sized chunks in order to be digestible. The size of the chunk depends on how familiar the patient is with the gist of what you are saying. To a patient on warfarin, used to regular venepunctures, the single instruction, "Get a blood test tomorrow," is a handleable chunk. For another patient who had never had a blood test before, you might need to break this down into smaller chunks and say, "Tomorrow morning, before ten o'clock, come back to the surgery. Ask to see the nurse and give her this form. She'll take a blood sample from you. What she'll do is . . ."

As you speak, watch the patient for signs of impatience or incomprehension as an indication of whether your chunks are the right size.

Pausing

As you present each significant chunk of information, it is a good idea to pause and see whether what you have said has been understood. We all need time to process new information, to check that we understand it, and think about some of its implications. Again, the patient's minimal cues will indicate the degree of understanding and acceptance, if you pay attention to them. Particularly at the most important points in your delivery, pause and check that you still have the patient's agreement. If you don't get a 'Yes', you've got a 'No'.

Pace

The speed of delivery is important. You should aim to match the overall pace of your words to the patient's rate of speech, speaking perhaps unnaturally slowly to someone whose own speech is leisurely.

Variation in pace can be used to provide a means of emphasis. You can slow the pace for the parts that, if you were to write them down, you might underline or put in capital letters, and speed up for the less important 'small print'.

Eye contact

Establishing eye contact as you begin your delivery is a signal to both of you that the lines of communication are open. Although you need not of course prolong the contact till it seems you are trying to stare each other out, nevertheless keeping a degree of eye contact is a good way of getting and maintaining attention.

Watch the minimal cues

As you speak, awareness of the patient's minimal cues helps you keep in rapport, and gives you the feedback you need to know about whether the patient is taking in what you are saying. Minimal cues will show you resistance, or doubt, or relief, or incomprehension. Rapid eye movement 'accessing cues' will indicate that the patient is processing what you are saying, and perhaps anticipating its effects. Internal search, as always means something important is going on; you should pause in your delivery at the nearest convenient spot, wait till the search is ended, then check what the patient had been thinking before you continue. You are hoping, of course, to see the acceptance set which shows that what you are saying is going down well. Again, if you don't see a 'Yes', you've got a 'No'.

How to give instructions

Presenting your management plan often involves giving detailed instructions about something you want the patient to do; a course of treatment, or a plan of action. Here are some useful rules of thumb.

(1) The rule of three:
   Say what you're going to say, say it, then say what you've said.
(2) Preface:
   Give your instructions a title and paragraph headings, such as, "Now I'll tell you what I think is wrong, then what treatment I suggest. First, what you've got is ..."
(3) Short words and sentences:
   are better than long ones.
(4) Jargon:
   Avoid it. Use the patient's everyday vocabulary.

(5) 'Shingles' technique (see under INFLUENCING):

Overlapping your instructions makes them easier to re-member. "Do A, then B. When you've done B, do C. After C comes D."

(6) Order:

In a list of items, the ones which are best remembered are the first and last. Make your most significant points at the beginning or the end.

(7) Write things down:

Summarize your main points or instructions on a piece of paper for the patient to take away as an aide-memoire. Or give a leaflet. Although it's technically naughty, I often use a blank prescription form; after all, advice is a prescription, too.

(8) Be specific:

Vague instructions are hard to remember, let alone carry out. Be specific about what the patient is supposed to do. Saying, "Let me know how things go," is not as effective as, "Make an appointment to see me in a month's time and tell me then whether these tablets have improved your ulcer pain."

(9) Give illustrations:

Reinforce your advice or explanation pictorially with a diagram, or in a metaphor or analogy.

Politeness

Your management plan should be handed over with courtesy, not tossed across with a 'take it or leave it' attitude, nor tantalizingly dangled just out of reach, so that the patient has to beg for it. Imagine how the patient might feel in the following exchange.

Doctor: I suppose you'd like to know what I think the problem is. *(pause)*

Patient: Well yes.

Doctor: It's complicated.

Patient: Oh.

Doctor: Well not so much complicated as – well yes, complicated. *(pause)* There's good news and bad news.

Patient: Oh.

Doctor: Which do you want first?

Patient: The bad, tell me the bad news.

Doctor: The bad news is – no, I think I'd rather give you the good news first. It's not as bad as it might have been.

Patient (at screaming pitch): WHAT'S NOT?

In Vietnam, prisoners for interrogation were blindfolded, flown around in a helicopter, then pushed out of the aircraft door. Because the helicopter was in fact hovering only a few feet above the ground, the fall was nothing at all. But the suspense and the anticipation were torture.

Respect the patient's self-esteem

Almost by definition, anyone who comes to a doctor with a problem is in a 'one down' position, worried, vulnerable, forced to acknowledge that a problem exists which cannot be coped with unaided. This is a threat to self-esteem. The problem and (more importantly) its management may not fit in with the patient's self-image, the framework of attitudes and beliefs. It is important to try to couch the explanation of your management plan in terms which are congruent with the patient's self-image, and which do no further damage to an already precarious self-esteem. The patient should definitely not leave your room 'two down', and preferably not even 'one down' any longer.

A business executive develops an inguinal hernia which hurts and slows him down. This is out of keeping with his ideal of himself as an active go-getting youngster. He needs surgery. To him, surgery might threaten to make him even less indestructible, even more emasculated. If you preface your advice by saying, "There we are then, all flesh is as grass, no more squash for you for a bit, ha ha," he will feel at an even lower ebb. The same recommendation could be made much more acceptable if framed as, "Being a businessman, you'll want to solve this problem quickly and efficiently, so that you're back on top as soon as possible, even if it means a temporary set-back."

When something happens to us which doesn't fit in with the way we like to think of ourselves, an uncomfortable, uneasy feeling results to which the name 'cognitive dissonance' is usually given. Guilt, shame, embarrassment, frustration, resentment are all examples of cognitive dissonance. Our impulse is to do something – anything – to reduce the sense of discrepancy between real and ideal. If we can't change the facts, we change the way we think about them; in other words, we reframe our perception of the experience and reinterpret it, so that it can after all be made to fit comfortably into our existing framework. In the example I just gave, the first way of introducing the prospect of surgery would have increased the patient's cognitive dissonance. It is quite likely that, in order to restore his self-esteem, the patient would have decided the doctor was talking through his hat and requested a second opinion. In the second case, surgery was presented as the option most in keeping with that particular patient's framework, and would probably have been gratefully accepted.

By gift-wrapping your advice in language that blends with the patient's framework, self-esteem and compliance can be enhanced. It may not always be possible to frame your advice so that the patient feels a million dollars, but it's worth a try!

Match the patient's language of self-expression

As well as suiting the overall style of your hand-over to the patient's pre-existing framework, you can also match your sentence-by-sentence choice of words to the patient's language of self-expression. If you have noticed that the patient has a strong preference for Visual, Auditory or Kinaesthetic language and descriptions, try using that representational system yourself. You will also have formed an impression of the patient's natural vocabulary and degree of understanding of human biology; stay within these limits when you are explaining your management plan.

A TUTORIAL CONCLUDED

Chris: Phew! That was a long session.

Me: I think we both felt that. If it's any consolation, you have now finished the hard slog of skill-building. It's downhill all the way now to the last two checkpoints; and I think you might positively enjoy the 'Inner Consultation' techniques which will help all of this become internalized and automatic. Do you think you can now recognize the HANDOVER checkpoint when you reach it?

Chris: I think so.

Me: For the benefit of our eavesdroppers, I'll nevertheless make sure. First of all –

Chris: I know; make sure I can imagine 'HANDOVER' written on my left ring finger.

Me: Right. Do you understand why I ask you to do that?

Chris: It seems to have a kind of 'imprinting' effect, so that when I catch sight of my hand during consultations, there's a ready-made reminder about the checkpoints.

Me: Yes. Also, by setting up the finger mnemonics at a time when you're reasonably clear what each checkpoint represents, I'm (I hope) calibrating the fingers with an accurate representation of what to aim for and how to achieve it. Why the left hand, incidentally?

Chris: Because I'm right-handed, so that the left hand is the one linked to my perceptive non-dominant hemisphere. If I'd been left-handed, should it have been my right hand we used?

Me: Most probably not. Most left-handed people still have the right hemisphere as their intuitive one. Got your left ring finger poised?

How to recognize the HANDOVER checkpoint

(1)   Ask. Ask the patient whether she has understood what you've suggested; whether she's happy about it; whether there is anything she would like to go over again; whether what you've agreed does in fact seem likely to help.

(2)   Look and listen. Watch her minimal cues – her expression, and head movements; listen for the 'Mmm, yes,'noises her eye and that indicate the acceptance set.

(3)   Reverse summarize. Ask the patient to summarize back to you the essential points in the management plan. This can be a chastening experience, because it shows you what the patient takes to be the salient features of the consultation, and how much (or little) of what you said has actually registered.

(4)   See what happens when you try to move on. The fourth checkpoint, SAFETY-NETTING, is a form of presupposition, when you make some contingency plans based on the assumption that the patient has accepted your management plan. If you are mistaken, and she still has some reservations, you will pick up signs of resistance when you try to move the consultation on towards a conclusion. If you don't get a 'Yes' –

Chris: – you've got a 'No'.

Me: Okay, smart-alec; how do you fancy some practice?

EXERCISES

Discriminating

Look at the final stages of a few video-taped consultations, your own for preference. See if you can distinguish between NEGOTIATING sections, where management is being jointly decided openly and with all cards on the table; INFLUENCING sections, where you can tell that the doctor is trying to bring the patient round to a particular course of action; and GIFT-WRAPPING sections, where it is apparent that the management plan has already been agreed, and the doctor is merely explaining it.

Influencing

Prepare another pack of instruction cards, this time saying:

Shingles
Put things positively
'Don't' means 'do'
Questions make good statements
Reframing
My friend John
Presupposition
and Pre-empting.

Re-read the appropriate sections if necessary. Introduce an example of each in turn into a series of consultations, in random order as given by turning one of the pack over just before the consultation begins.

Gift-wrapping (1)

Look at some video consultations. For each patient, devise two ways of presenting the management plan that the doctor proposed: the first, as congruent as you can make it with the patient's framework; and the second, as much at odds with it as possible.

Gift-wrapping (2)

– another 'playing card' exercise. The cards read:

Rule of three
Preface
Shingles
Write it down
and Reverse summarize.

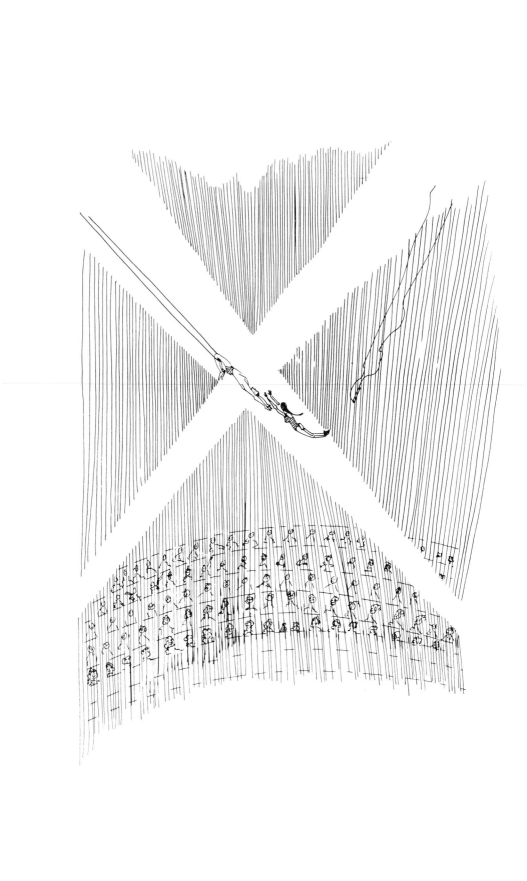

B6
Checkpoint 4 (Safety-Netting) – predicting skills

Without prognosis, diagnosis is just Godknowsis.

Anon.

Doctor Ecks gives you that much reassurance, it makes you nervous.

A patient

Circus! The lights go down. The band begins to play danger music. From the big top, at first almost indistinguishable amongst struts and guy-ropes, then picked out with a single spotlight, the trapeze is lowered. Necks crane. Chocolates hesitate. The clowns aren't funny any more. A fanfare. Into a second spot steps the lovely Samantha. Heads turn. As she walks, her vibrant body quivers against the restraining lurex and fish-net. Lips are fixed and dilated. Fanfare again. The ring-master announces, points, eyes follow – how did he get up there? – "Doctor Wonderful!"

A roll of drums. A dangling rope. She climbs, reaches the bar, strikes a pose, begins to swing, wider and wider. Across the abyss Doctor Wonderful nonchalantly casts off, hangs from his knees, outstretched arms approach, recede, approach, recede. A triple somersault is contemplated. Not yet, not yet, not synchronized. Saliva dries, breath freezes. She leaps. He reaches. An eternity. A fumble. And then? Applause? Headlines? ...

... Back in the surgery, Doctor Wonderful continues to make most of his diagnoses by hypothesis testing. In fact, it's largely because he makes his diagnoses this way, checking out his hunches, that his patients do think he's wonderful. They tell him what's bothering them, he asks a few well-chosen questions, seems to read their minds sometimes, examines them when he has to, but not too often, then comes up with good advice and good treatment. He doesn't mess you about, doesn't Doctor Wonderful. You're in and out and satisfied. It's not like the hospital, where they take all day, ask you a lot of tom-fool irrelevant details, keep you shivering while they poke and prod, where you can never get a straight answer out of them. At the hospital, it's always, "We'll do some more tests – come back in a month." No, they go for Doctor Wonderful; he's seen it all before, and knows what's best. They all say that.

Well, nearly all of them say that. The occasional dead patient doesn't, nor a tiny minority who swear he nearly killed them once, by missing something serious, and who wouldn't see him again, not if he was the last doctor on earth. Nor a larger minority whom at various times he has misdiagnosed and mismanaged, but not too badly. Of course, they wouldn't tell him to his face. So of course, he never knows. He just swings on, backwards and forwards, arms outstretched, getting it right, catching the lovely Samantha, time after time, until ... A fumble! And then? Embarrassment? Guilt? Criticism? Explanations? Headlines? Inquests? Litigation? Not usually. Usually just a wry shake of the head, a "Well, there we are then", a chalking up to experience, a few musings on the uncertainty of general practice.

In general practice we make our differential diagnosis by knowing what's most likely, and our working diagnosis by deciding what the positive clinical signs are most typical of. (And we choose our treatments by remembering what has usually worked in the past.) This process serves very well most of the time, but it has an inherent weakness that can be summed up in the two words, "What if?" What if this crying baby should turn out to be the next cot death, even though teething or a cold is much more likely? What if the rash that looks for all the world like the start of rubella is in fact meningococcal septicaemia. What if this morning's depressed patient whom we spent ten minutes with and told to come back tomorrow is found hanging tonight? When the world's best laxative, the defence society's annual report, comes through the letter-box and for once the subscription seems cheap at the price, we all feel a frisson of the GOGGI phenomenon (there but for the Grace of God Go I.)

The only possible precaution we can take – and it *is* only a precaution, because general practice *is* the art of managing uncertainty – is to build into our hypothesis-testing a back-up process for detecting those occasions when we have got it wrong. Every time we make a working diagnosis and draft a provisional management plan, we should at the same time attempt to make some predictions, and ask ourselves three questions:

(1) If I'm right, what do I expect to happen?
(2) How will I know if I'm wrong?
and (3) What would I do then?

These three questions form general practice's SAFETY-NET. No patient is safe in our care unless the consultation includes them. When the answers to these questions are in place, you are at the SAFETY-NETTING checkpoint.

The idea of SAFETY-NETTING is easy to understand, and needs no clinical or consulting skills that you don't already possess. The reason for making a checkpoint of SAFETY-NETTING is to help with remembering to do it. Personally, I find it easy to assume that this ordinary-looking case *seems* straightforward because it *is* straight-forward. I tend to take the safety net for granted, inevitably to find on occasion that it wasn't there, and I have a clinical misjudgement to try and retrieve.

If I'm right, what do I expect to happen?

– What do I know of the natural history of the disease? What does experience suggest will be the likely evolution of the problem?

– How certain am I that I know what's going on? How reliable is my assessment?

– On what time-scale can I make predictions – today? tomorrow? next week? next year?

– Would any intervention by me make any difference?

– Can I reasonably foresee the clinical course both with and without my proposed intervention?

– Are any complications likely, or possible? How serious would they be? Is anything I do now likely to affect them?

– What are the beneficial consequences of intervention? And what ill-effects, if any, are probable, or possible, in the immediate and long-term future?

How will I know if I'm wrong?

– Does it matter if my prediction is wrong? What risks could the patient unwittingly run? What is the worst possible outcome I think it's worth making contingency plans for?

– Is it enough to leave it to the patient's common sense to report if the unexpected happens? Or should I take the initiative in arranging follow-up?

–If I want the patient to come back for review, am I clear about the reasons? Is follow-up obligatory, or are there conditions?

– Shall I ask the patient to come back *IN* (a specified time interval), or come back *WHEN* (something else has happened),

or come back *UNLESS* (the problem vanishes meanwhile),
or come back *IF* (some fresh development occurs),
or come back *BUT* (with different arrangements next time)?

– What will I do if the patient defaults on intended follow-up? Am I content to let things go, or need I take further steps, such as telephoning, writing a letter, visiting, or asking a colleague to make contact?

What would I do then?

– If events prove my initial assessment to have been mistaken, and my management plan inappropriate, what would I need to do next?

– Would I need more information? If so, would I need to review the history, or repeat the examination, or arrange investigations? If so, which investigations?

– Am I confident that my diagnostic methods and knowledge are sufficiently rigorous and extensive to produce a better assessment? Or would I need to turn elsewhere for help? If so, where should I go for it?

– If my assessment is sound but my management plan isn't working, what would I need to do? Would it be case of adjusting the present plan, or trying a different approach? If the latter, what alternative options do I have?

– What would be the next decision I would have to make? Even though I may not know the answer, can I at this stage predict the next question? Would I have to make a decision about investigating? Or about making a referral? Or about admitting the patient to hospital?

– How much time can safely elapse before a definitive decision must be taken?

A useful opportunity to test your arrival at the SAFETY-NETTING checkpoint presents itself when you come to make an entry in the patient's clinical case-notes. At this point you have to condense the subtleties and complexities of the consultation into a few lines of writing intended to alert you (or more importantly, anyone else the patient might consult) to the essential features of your assessment and management plan. Most general practice notes contain entries structured, if they have any structure at all, on the traditional medical school rubrics of C/O (complains of), O/E (on examination), diagnosis and Rx (treatment). A typical entry displays a greater mastery of compression than of comprehensiveness. The following is fairly representative; an unwell child has been brought with a rash:

C/O – off colour 2/7. Rash today.
O/E – T 39°C, morbilliform rash. No Koplik's.
D   – viral, ? measles
Rx   – symptomatic

Something even more stark would not be unusual:

? Measles – advice.

SOAP

'SOAP' is an alternative basis for recording clinical information which has become deservedly popular in general practice. It stands for

SUBJECTIVE (what the patient tells you)
OBJECTIVE (your objectively-verifiable findings)
ASSESSMENT
PLAN.

ASSESSMENT, while it might contain a diagnosis if you have made one, could also include your hunches, alternative diagnoses, gut feelings, aggravating factors, and some of the patient's concerns which your eliciting had revealed.

PLAN includes not only your advice, treatment and medication, but also your safety-net: the measures you might take if the problem persists. In the example just given, a SOAPed entry might run:

S – off colour 2/7. Rash today.
O –T 39°C, morbilliform rash. No Koplik's.
    No neck stiffness.
A – viral, ? measles
    But no known contact.
    ?? rubella, ??? meningococcal meningitis.
P – symptomatic, tepid sponge.
    Mother to telephone if rash alters, or if child appears to worsen.
    Warn duty doctor,? need to admit.

By structuring the entry in the notes in SOAP format, the doctor has been prompted to ask some of the 'What if?' safety-netting questions we considered under the three headings given above. By entering an assessment rather than a diagnosis, this doctor has given some thought to other possible explanations, of which the most serious is meningitis. This reminded him to look for signs of neck stiffness, and to remember that the absence of this sign does not exclude that diagnosis. Accordingly his plan contains some explicit safety-net measures. The child's mother has been told what developments to look out for, and what to do if they occur, and the duty doctor she may contact has been informed.

WHAT TO SAY TO THE PATIENT

The foregoing sections have dwelt on what you might think of in preparing your safety-net. A more difficult dilemma arises as to how much of your safety-netting thought processes to share explicitly with the patient. By its nature, safety-netting requires you to think ahead to the worst possible outcome; where is the boundary between being frank and being alarmist?

In my garden at home is a shed containing some heavy electrical plant, which developed a fault and brought the installation to a standstill. I arranged a house call from the engineer, who unscrewed things and plied his test meter, and then treated me to one of those long slow inspirations through pursed lips that garage mechanics do so well and that spells trouble, as in TROU – BLE. I'm squeamish about machinery, especially when it goes wrong. "I'll leave it to you," I told him, wanting to be spared the gory details, "please just get it going again." "Okay," he said, and set to work. Ten minutes later he emerged. "There you go," he said. "You need a new cormthruster, but that'll see you through till I can get hold of one."

One of my professed values is to be open and honest with patients, to tell them the full facts as I see them, so that they can play a fully autonomous role in deciding on the management of their problems. I think that's good for human dignity, theirs and mine, and good for compliance. I advocate being explicit about what I think the problem is, what else it might be, what we might have to think of doing if the worst comes to the worst.

But we also know that the right hemisphere doesn't understand negatives. Being told you have got 'not cancer', or you have symptoms of 'not multiple sclerosis', if neither had entered your head, is almost as worrying as their opposites. If you warn someone that reported side-effects of your treatment include nausea and green spots behind the knees, even if you stress in all honesty that these are rare, you may significantly increase the likelihood of the patient reporting them. I don't know of any research into this 'negative placebo effect' that can turn well-intentioned frankness into self-fulfilling anxiety. Until then, we shall just have to face the dilemma.

Back to the saga of me and the electrician; when he left, the equipment seemed to be working. Feeling I'd escaped lightly, I pressed the switch to engage an auxiliary appliance. Nothing happened. Moreover, various lights and dials were doing things I didn't recall them doing before. Relief turned to outrage. An aggrieved telephone call, and the engineer returned, reminding me what the minimum call-out fee was. I pointed out that although this was working, that wasn't, and that light shouldn't be on, and that dial shouldn't be doing that. "Well it's bound to, isn't it?" he said, with elaborate patience. "You haven't got your cormthruster. I'ld have thought you'ld have known that. Not that it matters; it's perfectly safe as it is." And he left. I like to think that when we parted we were both sadder and wiser men.

Patients differ in the degree of explicitness they like about the extent and nature of your safety-netting. Only experience can determine where the balance is struck in the individual case. But I think it is possible always to indicate the *fact* that you are thinking ahead, even if you don't necessarily specify the details. It is possible to leave an invitation hanging in the air, such as, "I'm *fairly* sure that's the problem ... we can think always think again if we need to ... would you like me to elaborate on anything?" Some patients will reply that they're happy to leave decisions to you, while others will tell you they want to know exactly where they stand.

NOW CALIBRATE YOUR LEFT LITTLE FINGER

Don't waste your thoughts about safety-netting. Turn back for a moment to the sections giving examples of the three SAFETY-NETTING questions:

If I'm right, what do I expect to happen?
How will I know if I'm wrong?
What would I do then?

When you have got whatever you want from them, visualize the words SAFETY-NET on your left little finger. Repeat the three questions – out loud and in private is best – and tap the finger gently with your right index finger to imprint the message. Your little finger may be small, but it's nevertheless the one that provides the bass in piano chords.

EXERCISE

Write on a single card:

> If I'm right, what do I expect to happen?
> How will I know if I'm wrong?
> What would I do then?

Place it on your desk in a position where you catch sight of it as you reach for each patient's set of notes. For at least one surgery, use the SOAP format for making your entries (or at least the ASSESSMENT and PLAN parts). Include in the written record some indications of your safety-netting.

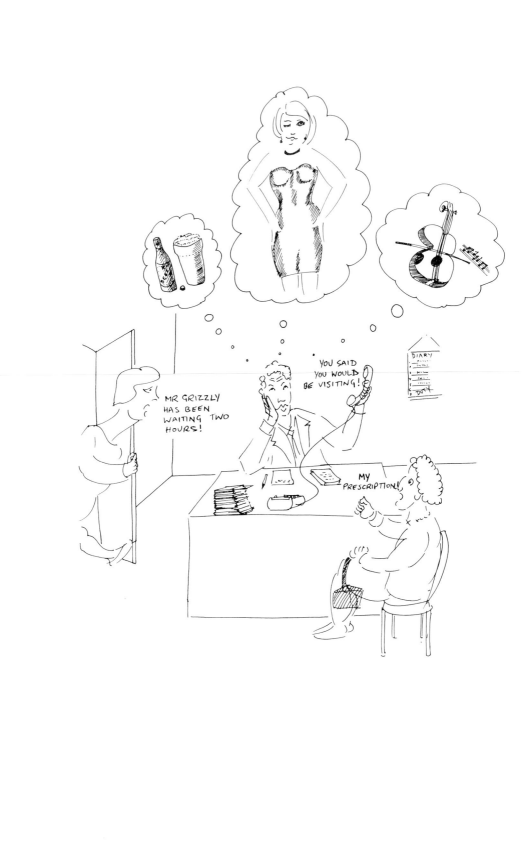

B7
Checkpoint 5 (Housekeeping) – taking care of yourself

When men are easy in themselves, they let others remain so.
Lord Shaftesbury

The thesis of this chapter is simple: seeing patients is a stressful business; too much job stress is bad for the doctor, and hence for his patients; so a competent doctor recognizes his own mounting stress-level, and does something constructive about it. He looks after his own state of mind, his own needs and feelings, no less assiduously than those of his patients, for his own sake and for theirs. Prevention is better than cure; the HOUSEKEEPING checkpoint is concerned with stress prevention.

Put as baldly as that, it sounds obvious enough. Yet it seems to me that surprisingly few doctors deal with their own stresses as competently as we advise our ulcer- and coronary-prone patients to do.

If you ask a group of doctors whether they find the job stressful, the usual reply is, "Yes, but it's worth it." If you persist, and ask what exactly it is they find stressful, doctors cite long hours, irregular meals, disturbed nights, or interrupted evenings and week-ends – things which try the tolerance of any mortal. Doctors tend to mention these sources of stress rather coyly, as if they ought to be able to, and for the most part can, take them in their stride. Only if pressed will some doctors admit to being affected by aspects of the job which call into question their own inner needs and attitudes. "Sometimes the responsibility gets to me," someone might allow. "I become too wound up by demanding patients," says another. "Me, I tend to get over-involved, and take the patients' worries home with me," confesses a third. If you then ask these refreshingly honest doctors what they do to offset such pressures, they will mention the stiff upper lip, a cup of coffee, 'letting off steam' to the receptionists,

235

discussing the day with their spouse over a drink or three in the evenings, having regular holidays, kicking the cat – again, nothing special.

But try to get more specific answers, ask precisely what feelings surface during a series of consultations, enquire exactly what irrational and exaggerated reactions are provoked by which particular patients and situations – and unless the setting is very safe indeed, most doctors will clam up tight. It seems to be 'not quite nice' to go into much detail about how the job affects us.

It's as if there was some part of our make-up that we felt ashamed of and had to keep hidden, like a Victorian family would keep a mentally handicapped child locked in its bedroom in case the neighbours caught an unexpected glimpse. The part of us which we feel shouldn't be seen in consulting room, let alone heard, is the part where we keep our private fantasies, our personal prejudices, our needs and hopes and wants and fears. We feel that such thoughts, were the patient to know about them, would detract from our professional standing and reduce us to – reduce us to what? Yes, to the same level as the patient; human, fallible and vulnerable. For this is exactly the same world of inner experience which, in the patient, we try to explore and give attention to during the consultation. Indeed, the earlier chapters of this book have been intended to improve the keeness of our eyes and ears in perceiving in patients the tell-tale signs of these often-suppressed thoughts and feelings.

We are in danger of applying a double standard here: it's all right for the patient's camouflaged needs to be revealed and catered for, but not our own. And indeed, no one would argue that the consultation should be exploited as an opportunity for doctors to gratify their own needs or to off-load their own bad feelings onto unsuspecting patients. But the truth is, even though our understanding of the Freudian unconscious mind is as old as the century, we remain suspicious of it. As the French poet Paul Valéry observed, "a man who is 'of sound mind' is one who keeps the inner madman under lock and key." We don't mind patients and psychoanalysts having unconscious needs, but not us, thank you very much.

Unfortunately, whether we like it or not, doctors are as human as the next person. We are as much subject to the irrational demands of our emotions as any one else. Our reactions to the job won't just go away; we have to do something about them. I want to suggest that it is not enough just to grin and bear them, or save up our unwinding for evenings, weekends and holidays. In addition, we should know how to handle our feelings on a minute-by-minute, patient-by-patient basis as well. It's like housework. All houses gather dust, and every so often we have a blitz and do some serious spring-cleaning. But we also carry out day-by-day dusting. The regular and frequent dusting of the doctor's emotional state, so that stress doesn't settle on his equanimity, is so important in the consultation that it merits a final checkpoint of its own, which I call HOUSEKEEPING. If dusting is grime prevention, HOUSEKEEPING is stress prevention.

Here is a story told by a Chinese Taoist philosopher Chuang Tsu, who lived four centuries B.C. and who knew all about housekeeping [1]. This story is a useful metaphor for two important ideas.

> Yen Ho was about to become tutor to the Crown Prince, the son of Duke Ling of the state of Wei. He went to consult Chu Po Yu, saying, "Here is someone who is naturally violent. If I let him remain undisciplined, the state will be in danger. If I try to correct him, I shall endanger myself. He knows enough to see the faults of others, but not to see his own. Under these circumstances, what shall I do?"
>
> Chu Po Yu replied, "That is a good question! Be on guard, be careful, and be sure you are acting appropriately. Appear to be flexible but maintain harmony within. However, there is a danger in doing these two things. While being flexible, be sure to remain centred. While maintaining harmony within, do not display it openly. If you are too flexible and lose your centre, then you will be overcome and destroyed, and you will collapse. If you try to demonstrate your composure, you will be criticized and slandered, called a devil and a son of a bitch. If he wants to be a child, be a child with him. If he wants to act strangely, act strangely with him. If want to be reckless, be reckless with him. Then you can reach him and bring him back to his senses."

The first useful analogy emerges if you equate the Crown Prince with a psychologically naïve doctor. Some doctors are 'naturally violent', in the sense that they like to dominate and control, to ride rough-shod over their patients and to assert their own point of view, so that if they 'remain undisciplined' the patient is in danger. They know enough to tackle the needs of their patients, but not to see their own. (And I share Yen Ho's trepidation at the prospect of trying to correct such a one, for if he reads this chapter, I shall be criticized and slandered!)

Secondly, put yourself in the place of Doctor Yen Ho the tutor, and listen to Chu Po Yu's advice about the need for 'flexibility' and 'composure'. Our journey through the consultation to date has called for just such flexibility. When Chu Po Yu advises acting in the same way as the pupil, initially matching his child-like or reckless whims in order to 'reach him and bring him back to his senses', he is exactly anticipating what I have suggested is the way to establish rapport and exert benign influence on your patients. Chu Po Yu knows how demanding this can be, and how important it is to work at preserving your equanimity: 'While being flexibile, be sure to remain centred.'

When he speaks of 'losing your centre', and being 'overcome and destroyed', he is referring to how stress can overwhelm peace of mind, and diminish your effectiveness as a helper.

An essential step in dealing with any danger is to discover its origin and nature. Let's consider now where our job stress comes from, and what causes it. I hope you'll forgive me if I coin two more phrases. The intrusive reactions that unsettle us are caused by three varieties of 'Time-stress', and come from the 'red light quarter' of the mind.

'Time-stress'

I find it helpful to classify job stress into the three natural divisions of time – past, present and future. They have different causes, and call for different remedies.

'Present' stress describes any unpleasant thoughts and feelings that arise during the course of the consultation, while the patient is actually in the room and expecting our full attention. Some present stress is of our own making, such as being hungry or having a full bladder. Other causes are to do with the particular patient and our reaction to him or her. To paraphrase Dean Howells, 'some patients can stay longer in five minutes than all the others in a two-hour surgery put together.' The patient may need what we are not of a mind to give, or may unwittingly stimulate, by word or deed or sheer existence, our own prejudices and dislikes. In principle, the remedy for present stress is the ability, which can be readily acquired, to free the present moment from its unpleasant associations by focusing non-judgemental attention in the experience of the 'here and now'.

'Past' and 'future' stress is felt most acutely not when the patient is in the room with us, but when we are alone between patients. It is caused through contamination of the present moment by memory and imagination. We have regrets and second thoughts about whatever has just happened, and we are anxious about what may happen next. As one patient leaves, we are prey to a variety of 'if only' thoughts – 'if only' I had handled that differently; 'if only' that patient hadn't come with that problem at that time. And in an attempt to rectify a situation we are unhappy with, we further torment ourselves with 'what if' thoughts about the next patient – 'what if' the next consultation takes a long time; 'what if' I can't cope with it. There are various techniques which help dispel past and future stress which I'll describe later in this chapter.

The 'red light' quarter

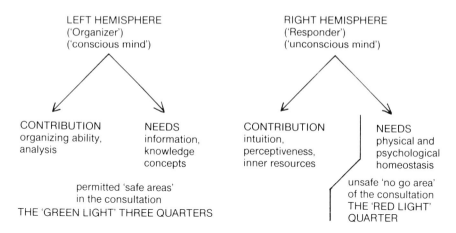

Figure B7.1 The 'red light' quarter

The brain has left and right hemispheres, which function synergistically but in sufficiently different ways to justify thinking of them separately. In this book, I've used the imagery of 'Organizer' and 'Responder', and of 'conscious' and 'unconscious' minds. Although this is an over-simplification, it is adequate for working and descriptive purposes.

Think of each – Organizer and Responder – as making its own separate contribution to the consultation (as described in Chapter A4), and having its own separate needs in order to make that contribution. The left hemisphere Organizer contributes intellectual understanding and logical analysis; in order to do this, it needs to have been primed with information, knowledge and concepts. The right hemisphere Responder contributes its ability to notice non-judgementally, and react intuitively to, the stream of information coming from the patient. The Responder also contributes the thoughts and feelings which arise internally within the doctor. Many of these are helpful; they are the source of intuition, the unconscious process that accesses your resource store unerringly and unbidden. But some are signals of the doctor's own physical and psychological needs. Although these are homeostatic, warning the doctor that he is under stress and needs to take corrective measures to maintain his physical and mental well-being, they nevertheless compete for his attention and are potentially distracting to the avowed purpose of the consultation.

The first three quarters – Organizer's contribution and needs, and Responder's contribution – are all immediately welcome in the consultation. They are safe 'green light' areas. The remaining quarter, the Responder's awareness of the doctor's own needs, is usually deemed a 'no go' area in the consultation – the 'red light' quarter.

We'll look next at some of the sources of consultation stress in more detail. The point I want to make at the moment is that what at first seem like unwelcome and unpleasant signs of stress are in reality the doctor's unconscious mind telling him, in the only way it can, that he has some pressing personal agenda of his own that needs his attention.

Job stress as doctors' frustrated needs

In Chapter B3 and Figure B3.3, when we were thinking about the various types of motivational need a patient might experience in connection with her symptoms, I drew on Maslow's 'Hierarchy of Needs' as a framework. Since stress is what we feel when a need is frustrated, and human needs are universal, this same hierarchy is useful to focus our attention on the various forms of professional stress experienced by doctors. Turn back to Chapter B3 to refresh your memory if necessary. In summary, Maslow's hierarchy arranges needs like a multi-decker sandwich, with the most basic and pressing needs at the bottom and the rest superimposed in ever-more-optional layers on top. (See Figure B7.2)

SELF-ACTUALIZATION NEEDS

SELF-ESTEEM NEEDS

ESTEEM NEEDS

BELONGINGNESS NEEDS

SAFETY NEEDS

PHYSIOLOGICAL NEEDS

Figure B7.2 Summary of Maslow's 'Hierarchy of Human Needs'

During the course of a working day, the doctor's contacts with patients produce endless opportunities for these needs to be either gratified or frustrated. It is largely because of the richness of such opportunities for feeling loved, needed and admired that people are drawn to enter the helping professions in the first place. If through the practice of medicine, patients' needs can be met and at the same time the doctor's own personal potential be fulfilled, so much the better. But inevitably clashes of interest arise, when the doctor has to suppress or postpone his own needs in favour of the patient's; at such times, we become aware of job stress in its various guises. I'll say a little about each level in the hierarchy as it applies to the doctor, in order to produce a kind of 'checklist' of potential stresses; see which you recognize as applying to yourself.

Physiological needs

Doctors' incomes are sufficient to free them from the worry of having enough food, drink and creature comforts. On the other hand, we frequently have to work despite missing meals, being short of sleep, or suffering from minor illness.

Safety needs

We need a sense of security and stability as far as the practice organization – partners, staff, premises – is concerned. Without it, it is hard to give attention to the needs of patients.

We also need to feel that our level of clinical knowledge and technical competence is adequate for the type of problem we encounter. It is difficult to work wholeheartedly to get to the bottom of someone's problem if we fear that when we do, and have to diagnose or manage it, we shall be found wanting. This 'safety need' is felt particularly acutely by young or inexperienced doctors, but reappears every time we or our partners have to deal unexpectedly with a life-threatening crisis.

General practice is by its nature unpredictable. Long periods elapse when we seem to see 'the same old things', and complain of boredom. Then unexpectedly we are thrown out of normal routine by an urgent problem, or have to reschedule the day's arrangements, and as a result run round in circles protesting, "Am I the only one who ever does any work around here?" The maxim 'if you don't think you're doing more than your partners, you're not doing as much' was coined to reassure us that we all have to contend with fluctuating work-loads. The trouble is, our own periods of unexpected busyness don't usually coincide with those of our colleagues; if they did, we'ld have a crisis on our hands we could all be good in! Even the unpredictable is unpredictable.

Another form of unpredictability is the rapid changes of mood and pace that occur as patients bring problems of varying severity in quick succession. We may have to switch in the space of a minute from sharing a widow's grief to a new mother's joy, from diagnosing cancer one moment to a verruca the next. A lengthy marital discussion is followed by a quick ear-ache. Depression, elation, profundity, triviality, boredom, terror – no wonder at the end of a surgery session we sometimes feel we've been on a roller-coaster ride.

Belongingness needs

The relationship between doctor and patient is a curious 'symbiosis of denial'. Each needs the other, but doesn't like to admit it. Most doctors, at least the ones who meet conscious patients face to face, like people. The nature of the job throws doctor and patient together in situations where the exchange of confidences, physical contact, liking and being liked, create an ambience akin to intimacy. But it is an uneven and spurious intimacy: uneven because the patient offers more self-disclosure than the doctor; and spurious because legal, ethical and emotional sanctions set limits to it. Even if the legal and ethical sanctions were not there, it is likely that the doctor's own internal motives would in most instances provide an adequate safeguard. Medicine is like love at arm's length.

Some people think doctors are ambivalent about their own needs for intimacy; they simultaneously crave it and fear it. The professional setting of caring and involvement affords an ideal compromise. We use our professional role both as a passport into the lives of other people, and as a defence against our own boundaries being encroached. We say, without any apparent sense of inconsistency, "I'm a doctor – tell me everything about yourself," and, "I'm a doctor – my private life is my own."

Esteem needs

Medicine is a high-status job, though this seems to be a primary motivating factor for relatively few doctors. However, it cannot be denied that we enjoy the respect and esteem of our patients. Indeed, the doctor's 'apostolic function', as described by Balint [2], is a powerful therapeutic tool in its own right. Recent critics such as Illich [3] and Kennedy [4] have accused the medical profession of conspiring to subjugate the sick, and of exploiting the public interest in order to feather their own nests. They forget it takes two to tango. Patients need us to be estimable. It is a natural response for someone in adversity to turn to another person – mother, priest, doctor – for succour, and to credit that person with whatever skill, power or status is necessary. Nevertheless, we should concede that a medical career is not short of opportunities for self-aggrandisement. The ugly signs of power struggle and status hunger appear when doctors argue the supposed superiority of one speciality over another, or hospital medicine over general practice, or private over publicly-funded health care.

In the consulting room, too, the doctor has ample opportunities to enhance his sense of importance. Traces of self-assertiveness are revealed in the ease with which we might dismiss some patients' requests as 'minor', 'trivial', 'footling', 'unnecessary', 'inappropriate' – not worthy of our attention. I doubt I am the only doctor in the world who, when a patient arrives late for an appointment, has been known to tell the receptionist to 'keep them waiting' until I've had enough revenge?

Self-actualization needs

Every extreme contains the seeds of its opposite. Fires burn themselves out; calm succeeds storm; wild horses tire. The doctor who is aware of all these needs and forces at work in him finds that knowledge of his own human frailty brings with it a deepening humility and compassion. He begins to feel safe without barriers. He finds his curiosity to understand the lives and minds of other people enriches his own. By knowing what passions govern him, yet remaining unafraid of them, they are subdued. Who are the doctors of your own acquaintance whom you recognize as having this quality of self-acceptance?

If you'll try the following 'thought experiment' I'll show you what I mean. The experiment is in three stages, taking about 10 minutes in all. Read the instructions over a few times until you are perfectly clear what to do, then go somewhere private and try them out. This exercise will form a good bridge to the remainder of this chapter, when we'll consider ways of dealing with job stress.

THOUGHT EXPERIMENT

Stage 1

It is likely that reading the previous sections has jogged your memory of various situations you yourself have been in where you have experienced negative reactions of one kind or another to patients. Think of several such situations, then select one example to work with. It might be the most recent, or the most intense, or one example of a situation that crops up frequently.

Sit in a neutral relaxed position, close your eyes, and recall that stressful scene in as much detail as you can, as if replaying a video of it in your mind's eye. Remember how it looked, and what was said. In particular, notice how you feel as the memory surfaces: notice the places in your body where tension seems to be located – hands, neck, shoulders, abdomen and jaw are the common ones. Notice the thoughts that form which would express the way you feel, the things you would like to say but which you bit back. Turn up the intensity on this memory until it is as vivid as you can get it. Then open your eyes, get up, and move about for a few moments to break up the pattern.

Stage 2

Next, give some thought to a quality or attitude which, had you possessed it in the Stage 1 situation, would have enabled you to cope with it better. Try to narrow down your choice of 'resource quality' to a single one, and be as specific as you can. I have in mind qualities like patience, tolerance, clinical competence, good-humour, the ability to relax, politeness, calmness, humility, friendliness – that sort of thing. When you have decided on the personal attribute you would like to have displayed under stress, resume your seat and again close your eyes.

From your memory, resurrect an actual occasion from your life's experience when you displayed just the quality you have selected. This need not be a clinical example; it might be the tolerance you show when a friend's appalling children clamber all over you, or the relaxation you feel on the first day of a holiday with your favourite person, or the humility with which you witnessed your first child-birth. As with the first stressful memory, retrieve as much detail of that good memory as you can – where you were, who was there, what was said, and particularly the way you felt. You should find that you can recapture the feeling of that experience as you turn up the intensity on this memory also. When you have got the 'resource quality' memory as vivid as possible, take firm hold of your left thumb in your right hand, grasping it firmly in your fist. Hold it for a few moments, then release the grip on the left thumb and open your eyes.

Stage 3

The sensation of gripping your left thumb has now been linked with the memory of the resource quality. You can reactivate the resource by repeating the thumb stimulus, and so transfer the desired quality into another situation where it is needed.

Close your eyes once more, and call up the first stressful memory. It will appear quite readily. Now do two things simultaneously. Repeat the grip of your left thumb with the right hand. And allow your imagination to develop the previously stressful situation in a fantasy or day-dream, this time rewriting history, so that instead of what actually happened, you imagine yourself behaving as if you possessed the extra resources that will bring about a more satisfactory conclusion. You will find the pressure on the left thumb makes this easy. Allow the injection of your chosen additional quality to suggest alternative ways in which you might handle the stressful situation. Follow the new fictional scenario to its conclusion; this usually takes two or three minutes. Then open your eyes.

This exercise should confirm for you that it is possible to change one's behaviour under stress. It is a technique called 'anchoring', one of a number of visualization exercises developed in Neuro-Linguistic Programming. An excellent account of this and other techniques, useful in the surgery for helping patients overcome mental blocks, is given in *Practical Magic*, by Stephen Lankton [5].

WHAT TO DO ABOUT JOB STRESS

As with other 'Skill-Building' chapters, what follows is not a pre-scription but a menu of options. Some will be familiar to you, others may not; some can be used quickly in the heat of the moment, others operate on a longer time-scale, or need some planning in advance. They all share the aim of preventing stress from building up too much, so that you can keep yourself in the best possible state of alertness for each successive patient.

The one thing you shouldn't do about job stress is suppress it and deny that you are prone to it. A problem denied is a problem doubled. Keeping tension bottled up compels it to find other means of expression, such as attacking your temper or your marriage or your gastric mucosa. In this context, I enjoy the anonymous quip:

> There is something about a cupboard that makes a skeleton terribly restless.

For the purposes of presenting them, I've grouped my suggestions into three sections:

During the consultation,
Between patients,
and **Long-term.**

Long-term stress control methods

Leisure

To be a good doctor you have to be able to stop. Time off, time to relax with the family, hobbies (especially non-medical ones, creative ones, and ones involving physical activity), sport, holidays are both fun and necessary. The puritan work ethic still persists; some people think that a 'good' doctor is one who works day and night, week in week out, and who has no sacrosanct periods where his private and family life come first. With the exception of the occasional saint, I think that when caring for patients becomes an addiction, there are real risks to both parties.

Discussion

Confiding in another person, and experiencing the support and concern of someone who cares about us, is the nearest thing on the planet to a panacea. The obvious candidate is a spouse or close friend, but there are two caveats: first, confidentiality can be a problem; and second, we may feel constrained to hold back or censor what we tell loved ones in order to protect them or what they think of us.

These last problems can be overcome by discussing problems in groups of colleagues, with or without an outside facilitator, where the ground-rules allow total frankness within guaranteed confidentiality. Such groups include:

> partnership meetings,
> practice staff meetings,
> trainee and trainer groups,
> young principals groups,
> case-discussion groups ('Balint' seminars).

Details of local groups can be obtained from local postgraduate medical centres, or from your local Faculty of the Royal College of General Practitioners.

Stress-control techniques

Doctors in increasing numbers find benefit from learning specific techniques such as:

> relaxation,
> yoga,
> Alexander technique,
> self-hypnosis,
> Autogenic Training,
> meditation.

Details of these may be available from public libraries, or through the British Holistic Medical Association, 179 Gloucester Place, London NW1 6DX.

Ways to unwind between patients

Diversionary rituals

It helps dispel tension to use other muscles and think other thoughts. A straw poll revealed that most doctors have their own little rituals which help them clear their minds of the after-effects of a stressful consultation. They included:

making a cup of coffee,
going for a short walk,
making a phone call,
reading a book for a few minutes,
checking their in-tray for mail that might have arrived in the last ten minutes.

Talk to someone

Partners, colleagues and staff will all lend a listening ear if necessary. (And even if you don't tell them, most will notice if you are up-tight, and want to ask.)

Introduce variety

Break up the working day into periods of contrasting activity. Intersperse long surgeries with doing some visits, or catching up with correspondence. You will know what is the longest your consulting sessions can be before you begin to lose concentration. Doctors differ in their concentration span; make sure that, whatever yours is, you don't regularly exceed it without doing something different.

Icons

It is a good plan to have in your consulting room an 'icon' – some object on your desk or within view that for you has personal associations of peace and well-being. Common examples of such objects include:

photographs of loved ones or of favourite scenes,
pictures,
flowers,
plants,
souvenirs,
devotional objects or texts.

You can greatly enhance the stress-reducing power of these icons by an anchoring technique similar to the one in the last exercise. I'll explain this at the end of the chapter.

Ways of dealing with stress during the consultation

Sometimes the inner voice of your Responder sets up such an insistent clamour that it interferes with your ability to pay attention to the patient. When for instance a patient's tone of voice sets my teeth on edge for a reason I can't pin down; or I can't get out of my mind the plight of a previous unemployed patient compared with this patient's affluence; or the third person in a row begins by telling me he feels tired all the time; at times like this the quality of my mercy gets distinctly strained. It is useful to know some ways to calm the inner turmoil and be able to clear your mind of competing distractions.

Extraneous stresses

Some factors that stress the doctor during a consultation might be described as 'extraneous', i.e. the result of events not connected with the particular patient you are seeing. Examples might be telephone calls and other interruptions, unexpected problems requiring your urgent attention, or if you are running late, or have a deadline to meet, or feel tired, or unwell, or preoccupied. If the effect of these factors is seriously to impair your concentration, I think it is best to be frank with the patient, explain that for one reason or another you are not giving of your best, and then attend to the problem that you feel has greater priority. Most patients are understanding about such circumstances, and might prefer to see you on another occasion when you are under less stress.

Other stress factors are 'intrinsic' to the consultation, i.e. they arise as a result of your reactions, often irrational, to the particular patient who has inadvertently rubbed you up the wrong way or touched a raw nerve. The next sections suggest some ways of dealing with intrinsic consultation stress.

Getting rid of projections

Some patients fortuitously resemble, in looks, mannerisms, speech or personality, other people in the doctor's life whom he dislikes, such as certain social acquaintances, authority figures, family members, or other patients. The doctor may find himself experiencing negative feelings triggered by the resemblance, and mistakenly attach or 'project' them onto the unsuspecting patients before him. Or some aspect of the doctor–patient relationship might be sufficiently similar to others in the doctor's life so as to evoke inappropriate feelings of antagonism, irritation, anxiety, inferiority or frustration. The doctor's emotional reaction is 'as if' the patient were somebody else, and is an irrational over-reaction to the reality of the actual situation – "'A' looks like 'B'; I don't like 'B', therefore I don't like 'A'".

In these cases the Responder has jumped to the wrong conclusion, resulting in 'mistaken identity'. The way to deal with it is consciously to correct the misidentification, by asking yourself, "Who does this patient remind me of so strongly? When else have I felt like this?" Quite often it is possible to recognize a particular name or event. Usually spotting the source of the error is enough to rectify it. If your misplaced reaction persists in spite of knowing the reason for it, try this: look quite closely at the real patient in front of you, and note a few specific features in which he or she is *dissimilar* to the doppelganger that triggered your reaction.

De-stereotyping

Another type of misplaced reaction can arise if we are too quick to assign a patient to a particular stereotyped group about which we have a strongly-held attitude. Stereotyping is a kind of over-simplification, of the form "'A' is probably a 'B'; I feel a certain way about 'B's, therefore I feel the same way about 'A'". Our stereotype categories tend to reflect prejudices which have no place in the consulting room but which nevertheless exist. So some patients will get raw deals from doctors not necessarily because they are, but just because they look as if they might be, members of particular social, educational, occupational, political, cultural or sexual groups.

As with projections, the way to deal with stereotyping is firstly to identify that it is happening. Then, if necessary, look for and identify a few features about the person in front of you that *don't* fit in with your stereotype. Maybe the inarticulate lorry driver whom you resent 'because lorry drivers think they own the road' has surprisingly clean finger-nails. A small piece of de-stereotyping like that is usually enough for you to see through your stereotype to the real human being underneath.

I was consulted once by a young woman whose appearance, speech and expectations I associated with aggressive feminism. "I've got vaginal thrush," she announced. "I've had it for two weeks, and why you won't let women just buy nystatin pessaries over the counter I'll never understand."

I asked what she had been doing about it for the last two weeks.

"I was on holiday in Majorca," she told me, "and I didn't trust their doctors, so I went to the supermarket to get some yoghurt to treat myself with."

Typical, I thought, and still she ends up needing proper treatment.

"Anyway", she continued, "they'd only got strawberry." I blenched. She paused, then wailed, "and my husband doesn't like strawberry!"

'Here and now' awareness

As I mentioned earlier, memories of the past and anticipation of the future can contaminate our full awareness of the present moment. Much stress can be quickly relieved by knowing how to expand your non-judgemental appreciation of the 'here and now' so that it crowds out unpleasant associations and replaces them with full awareness of the way things are right here, right now.

The simplest way of doing this is to focus your attention on the sensations of breathing. For a few moments, notice how your chest feels as it rises and falls; how your nostrils flare slightly and your nose feels the temperature of the air as you breathe in; and how your upper lip is warmed as you breathe out; notice how your abdomen shifts backwards and forwards; and how some breaths are shallow; and some deep; and some breaths are so deep as to be almost sighs; how sometimes you cease breathing for a while; then resume. By the time you have dwelt on these sensations for a few breaths, you will find striking changes in your tension level. And you won't have missed much of what was going on – you hadn't been paying full attention anyway.

This 'mindfulness of breathing' in a more developed form is the basis of a meditation technique called Satipatthana, but don't let that put you off. All it means is that if you concentrate on something neutral in the here and now, and figuratively plant your feet on the ground, your head comes down out of the clouds.

Adjust your muscle tone

Laughter is a sign of pleasure. A tight jaw is a sign of tension. Every mental experience of emotion has corresponding physical con-comitants. Physiologists argue over cause and effect – does sadness cause tears, or does weeping cause the feeling of sadness, or does something else cause both? In practical terms, experience shows that it is possible to change one's emotional state by 'acting' a different one.

Suppose for some reason you begin to feel tense during a consultation. That tension might show itself as a clenched jaw, hunched shoulders, closed fists, fidgety legs – you know your own signs best. If you now intentionally alter the muscle tone in these areas, the mental feeling of tension will also abate. You can either intentionally relax the jaw and shoulders, open your hands and still your legs – or the opposite. Paradoxically, if for a few moments you isometrically increase the tension in those muscle groups, and then 'let go', you become physically and mentally more relaxed than before. This is the basis of most systematic methods for achieving bodily relaxation, but it works quickly, easily and invisibly during the consultation too.

Tell the patient how you're feeling?

This option can be helpful if the stress you are feeling is 'extraneous', but in the case of 'intrinsic stress' caution is required. There are circumstances where to tell a patient that he or she is 'making' you feel irritated, or bored, or frustrated can be the prelude to a useful and therapeutic discussion. Indeed, the potential use of the doctor's feelings as a diagnostic and therapeutic tool was a major theme of Michael Balint's training seminars. However, to do this skilfully and sensitively requires personal experience and training in psycho-therapy techniques, and is outside the scope of this book.

REACHING THE HOUSEKEEPING CHECKPOINT

You reach the HOUSEKEEPING checkpoint after one patient has left your room and before the next comes in. In this respect it is rather like taking your car in for its regular 6000 mile service – an opportunity to check for and rectify the inevitable wear and tear arising from continuous use. But the wise motorist doesn't rely solely on planned servicing. He also does his own more frequent routine maintenance; he checks the fuel level and the oil and tyre pressures, and periodically glances down while driving to see if any warning lights have come on. By the same token, the competent doctor keeps half an eye on his own internal state, ready to spot the early warning signs of developing stress.

The equivalent of the driver's warning lights are the doctor's own minimal cues that indicate mounting stress levels. You know yourself well enough to recognize your own personal signs: the feelings and muscle tensions; the old familiar grumbles complaining that the universe doesn't understand; the little behaviour rituals we engage in when we are cross or worried. Unlike mechanical faults, however, many human stresses are self-correcting once consciously noticed.

In the 'left hand checkpoint reminder' system I have been using, the HOUSEKEEPING checkpoint is associated with the left thumb. There is some useful symbolism in this. The thumb, an important and flexible digit in its own right, is doubly useful because of its ability to make contact with all of the four fingers. HOUSEKEEPING is a definite checkpoint on its own, and also an attitude of concern for one's own balance that touches all the other stages of the consultation. Respect for one's self is not self-indulgence. A dirty mirror is useless, no matter how humble its owner.

In order to establish the right associations and calibrate the left thumb mnemonic, please now ensure that you can visualize the word HOUSEKEEPING on it. This time, while you read the next section, grasp the thumb firmly in your right hand, as you will have done if you tried the three-stage 'thought experiment' described earlier. (If you didn't do the experiment, never mind. At the end of the chapter will do instead.)

The key HOUSEKEEPING questions

A consultation is not over until you are ready for the next one. So between patients, ask yourself:

Am I in good condition for the next patient? What, if anything, do I need to do to prepare myself?

Then, now that you know, do whatever it takes.

During the consultation, if you begin to be aware of your personal early warning signs, ask yourself:

What emotion is beginning to arise? What if anything do I need to do about it?

Then consider using one of the quick centring techniques described earlier.

Ebbing and flowing

Although the consultation has an overall sense of movement in a known direction, taking in the five checkpoints along the way, the movement is seldom smooth. If it were a river, the consultation's flow would not be streamlined; there are areas of turbulence and 'white water'. There is also a more gentle oscillation, a lapping and rippling, with doctor and patient alternately leading and being led, influencing and being influenced, contributing and taking in. The simultaneous presence within an overall unity of complementary active and passive elements is represented in the well-known Taoist symbol of Yin and Yang, the two snakes seizing each other's tail, each seeing its own reflection in the eye of the other (Figure B7.3).

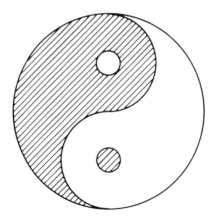

Figure B7.3 Yin and Yang

Yang, the strong 'male' assertive power, alternates with Yin, its yielding 'female' gestational opposite. Yin and Yang are the extremes between which a living, changing system is in endless alternation:

the yang having reached its climax retreats in favour of the yin; the yin having reached its climax retreats in favour of the yang.

253

A similar 'to and fro' movement takes place in the doctor's attention. Sometimes his attention is directed outwards, and he concentrates wholly on the patient. At other times, he is more aware of his own thoughts and sensations; his attention is directed inwards. The doctor alternates between caring for others and caring for himself, between being available and needing to withdraw. That people caught up in the hectic business of caring for each other need periodically to withdraw and regenerate themselves is wonderfully described in another of Lao Tsu's chapters in the *Tao Te Ching* [6]. In it, 'man' and 'woman', 'white' and 'black', refer to Yang and Yin's activity and passivity. The last line of each verse is an image of rejuvenation, of restoring the potential for events to mould as they will.

> Know the strength of man, but keep a woman's care!
> Be the stream of the universe!
> Being the stream of the universe, ever true and unswerving,
> Become as a little child once more.
>
> Know the white, but keep the black!
> Be an example to the world!
> Being an example to the world, ever true and unwavering,
> Return to the infinite.
>
> Know honour, yet keep humility.
> Be the valley of the universe!
> Being the valley of the universe, ever true and resourceful,
> Return to the state of the uncarved block.
>
> When the block is carved, it becomes useful.

In the seven chapters of Section B (SKILL-BUILDING), I have tried to make sure you have in your resource store the knowledge and skills you need to pass successfully from checkpoint to checkpoint, so that you can look back on a skilled and satisfying consultation. Section C (GETTING IT TOGETHER), which is much shorter, shows you how to put this potential skill into practice. We shall need to overcome the paradox that trying too hard can hinder success. The chapter on 'The Inner Consultation' will show you how this can be done quite easily. The final chapter might give you a sense of how skilled consulting could prove personally fulfilling in unexpected ways.

EXERCISES

'Thought experiment'

If you didn't get round to doing the three-stage thought experiment on anchoring positive resources, please do it now. (The more important exercise on 'increasing the value of your icon' depends on it.)

Recognizing your stress early warning signs

Sit down with a pencil and paper. Think about, and then jot down, the things you tend to think, feel and do when you are under various forms of job stress. Do you tend to get angry, or frustrated, or flustered, or what? Where in your body do you start to feel these various emotions? How do you usually behave when under stress? Do you go quiet, or swear, or pick fault, or slam doors, or what?

By raising your consciousness of these signals, so that you notice them readily in the consultation, you are more likely to recognize them in good time and deal with them before they build up too much.

Awareness of breathing

Re-read the paragraph on 'here and now' awareness (page 250). Try for a few minutes to become as fully aware as you can of the sensations of breathing. Do not try to alter your natural breathing, or turn it into what you imagine relaxed breathing to be. Just notice the way it is.

Increase the value of your 'icon'

You'll remember I used the word 'icon' to refer to anything – picture, plant, object – which you might keep in your consulting room because it has pleasant and reassuring associations for you. You can increase the calming effect of your icon as follows. I have to assume that you have done the earlier thought experiment.

Go into your consulting room and make sure you will not be disturbed for 10 minutes. Sit in your usual working chair, with your chosen icon easily visible.

Close your eyes, and call up from your memory a vivid impression of a time in your life when you felt as relaxed and contented as ever you remember. Choose a specific occasion or situation. Fill in as much detail as you can: where you were, who else was there and the way they looked, the weather, the colours, the scenery, what was said, any other sounds in the memory, the way you felt, the sensations in your skin, the way your body felt. As you turn up the intensity on the memory, let yourself feel again the sense of pleasure it evokes. Some people at this stage in the exercise smile and relax, and breathe a little slower.

When you have allowed this memory to develop its maximum relaxing effect, open your eyes. Fix your gaze upon your icon, and at the same time, take your left thumb in the firm grasp of your right hand. Hold the grip and the gaze for 10 to 15 seconds. Then get up and move around.

Reinforce the anchoring process once or twice within the next few minutes by sitting down again, looking at your icon, and repeating the grip on the left thumb. Most people find that the physical stimuli of sight and feel are enough to re-evoke the sense of calm. You can now use either the icon or the grip of the thumb during consultations whenever you need an infusion of tranquillity.

Section C
Getting it together

C1
On having only one head

You can do a thing thoughtlessly, or you can do it without a second thought. The difference is, an awful lot of thinking goes on in between.

_____

If you've read this far, you've been exposed to a considerable amount of information about consulting skills. Some of it was previously familiar to you; some of it perhaps not. Some of it you can recall consciously at the moment; some will have been absorbed unconsciously, in passing. Some of you will have carried out all or some of the training exercises; for others, any changes in your consulting style are still latent in your imagination. It is certainly possible for you to choose to take your curiosity no further. But that would be a shame, because it only needs a single additional step at this stage to make a noticeable improvement in your consulting proficiency. A journey of a thousand miles, we are told, begins with a single step; it also ends with one.

The final step towards improving your consultations consists not of acquiring more information or additional skills, but rather of using the knowledge you already possess in a different way. As we discussed in Chapter A2 (How have you been taught previously?), the usual thing expected of you at this stage is to go away and _try_ to apply the theoretical knowledge you have been given. By contrast, the information this book has presented is in such a form that what is needed now is not effort, but merely that you _allow_ what you already know to operate unhindered. We are all used to 'improving by trying'. 'Improving by allowing' is an unfamiliar idea, so I'm taking a whole chapter – this one – to put it over.

The first thing you need in order to 'improve by allowing' is to have the necessary component skills already in place and available. These you now have. (Even if you haven't done all the training exercises, you will have absorbed sufficient of the ideas to benefit from what follows. An integrated training schedule to reinforce them is given in Appendix 1.) The second thing you need is to know how to set up the conditions under which what you already know can be effortlessly expressed. The next chapter, 'The Inner Consultation', will tell you exactly how to arrange these ideal conditions. In essence, you have to develop the ability to keep your attention focused on and confined to the immediate 'here and now' as much as possible: you have to cultivate 'nowness'.

Staying in the 'here and now' is easier said than done. My aims in this chapter are to help you to understand what is meant by 'nowness'; to see how nowness helps resolve the distracting sensation of having two heads; and to understand why an instruction to put out of your mind things you have painstakingly learned in fact clears the way for new learning to express itself.

In order to swim, you have to overcome the fear of drowning.
In order to learn, you have to overcome the fear of forgetting.

A TUTORIAL

Me: Chris, it would help if you'd just summarize where we've got to, mainly to reassure me that I'm not taking too much for granted.

Chris: Right. The consultation's a journey. Five checkpoints along the way. Firstly –

Me: Number them off on the fingers of your left hand as you go through them.

Chris: Okay. Firstly, connecting – that's like establishing rapport. You do it by watching and listening for the patient's minimal cues, and matching some of them yourself. Secondly, summarizing – that means finding out the full extent of what the patient is concerned about, and demonstrating to the patient that you've understood. Then you do the clinical bit and work out a management plan, which you have to hand over so that the patient feels happy about it. Fourth, you think ahead and make a safety net, in case the management plan doesn't work, or needs following up. Finally, you do whatever housekeeping it takes to make sure you're fresh and unruffled for the next patient.

Me: Bravo. For present purposes, the two points I'ld stress are, one, making for the checkpoints in that order; and two, the emphasis on watching the patient's minimal cues all the time, because they give you the feedback you need to keep on course.

Chris: I was going to ask you about the order of checkpoints. Do you have to stick rigidly to the order you've described them in?

Me: Nothing's ever rigid; circumstances alter cases, and some consultations are so clear-cut that you needn't bother with the full sequence. But my aim has been to give you a reliable approach which will apply in most cases, and particularly in the more complicated consultations. The order of check-points is logical, it feels comfortable, and gives you the best chance of covering most of the important ground. So yes, try and keep to it as far as possible. That's why we've used the finger mnemonics as a reminder. I think if you change the order for any reason, you ought to know that you're doing it, and why.

Chris: In one of our earlier sessions, 'On Having Two Heads', you talked about how trying to keep too many instructions in your head while consulting set up an internal dialogue, which tended to be distracting. As far as I can see, although your model is simpler than some, it's going to prove just as difficult to work with it during a real-life consultation. I'm afraid I'll still be put off by my second head, the only difference being that now it'll be saying "Connect, summarize," and so on. The script may have changed, but won't the internal dialogue still continue?

Me: I remember you once saying, "It's not that I don't know what to do, it's that I don't do what I know." The internal dialogue is an inner voice nagging away – "do this, do that, do the other." The more complicated the instructions, the louder the voice of your second head tends to be. The 'five checkpoint' model overcomes that problem by giving you, not a long list of things to do, but a short list of positions to get to. And there's a simple reminder literally always on hand – your left hand. So the internal dialogue, checkpoint-style, just reminds you "get to this position next." The methods of getting to each checkpoint are up to you. They're what you've been practising in the various exercises I've suggested. How did you get on with them, by the way? I'm particularly interested in the 'playing card' exercises, when you were practising one technique for one checkpoint per consultation. Did you find that single instruction very distracting?

Chris: Surprisingly, I didn't. Most of the time, when I turned over the instruction card, I thought for a few moments before the patient came in about how I might introduce whatever technique the card said, but then, in the heat of the moment, I wasn't particularly conscious of the instruction until just before I carried it out. Quite often I just seemed to come out with something that satisfied the instruction on the card.

Me: Precisely. A single instruction isn't too intrusive. And then, without your being particularly self-conscious about it, the necessary behaviour just happens. Putting all the components of the Inner Consultation together is going to be just like that. I'll give you some simple instructions to keep in mind, and you'll find that the appropriate behaviour will just happen, without you having to force it. That's what I mean by 'improving by allowing'.

Do you remember when we talked about 'How People Learn', I said there were three stages in the learning of skills? There's the 'Instruction' stage, 'hearing with the ear' the theoretical stage. Then there's the 'Imagination' stage, 'pondering in the heart', where you learn, consciously and unconsciously, but haven't yet put your learning into practice.

The final stage, the 'Expression' stage, 'practising with the body', is where we are at the moment. I think the phrase 'learning on the verge of action' describes it well. You're like one of those supersaturated solutions we used to learn about in chemistry classes at school, where there is such an excess of solute dissolved that the tiniest speck of dust starts the crystallization process off, and pure crystals come tumbling out of solution.

The tiny shift you have to introduce into the consultation at this stage in order to tap your learning resources is something which for want of a better word I can only describe as 'nowness'.

Chris: What the hell's that? It's not in my dictionary.

Me: Maybe not, but it's certainly something you're familiar with. Let me show you what I mean; then I'll explain how nowness is the key to release your consultation skills.

NOWNESS

'Nowness' means an acute awareness of the present moment. 'Present-centredness' could be another term for it; 'immediacy' sounds a bit abstract; 'The Now', capital T, capital N, sounds unnecessarily arcane. 'Nowness' is having so much of your attention concentrated on what's happening this instant, right here, right now, that there's no attention left to spare for the past or the future, for abstract thought or fantasies.

If an old friend were to walk in and interrupt you at this moment and ask, "What are you doing now?", you might say something like, "I'm working at so and so," or, "I'm decorating the bedroom." "No", says your friend, "I don't mean what are you doing nowadays, or this morning, or later on today. I mean what are you doing NOW?" To which you reply, "Nothing,", or, "I'm reading a book called *The Inner Consultation*, which is about –", "No no," your friend insists, "that's what you were doing until I came in. I mean what are you doing right this very instant?" And if you answered this increasingly irritating question it would have to be in terms of your current sensory experience; "I'm sitting down, seeing you, breathing, feeling this or that."

Rather than describe it any further, I'd like you to create for yourself the first-hand experience of nowness. It's an important prelude to make use of the attention-focusing techniques I'll describe in the next chapter. Read the instructions for this short 'thought experiment', then carry it out, right now.

THOUGHT EXPERIMENT

Take any object – this book will do nicely. Hold it in your hand and give it your full attention. See and feel it for the physical object it is, not for what it represents, or means, or what you think about it, or what you could do with it. Move it around. Notice its colours, its shape, its shadows; how it is in focus while the background is not. Feel its weight, its texture. Hear the little sounds as your fingers move over its surface.

Then add to your awareness of the book your awareness of your own body sensations. Notice your breathing; the rise and fall of your chest and abdomen; the sensations around your nostrils. Hear the soft sounds of breath going in and out. Notice also what your proprioceptive sense is telling you; what muscle groups you're aware of; what feelings you have in your skin.

Quite soon a fusion occurs, and you experience simultaneous awareness of book and body and nothing else. Your awareness of time becomes narrowed down to the present 'now', while your awareness of the sensations that occupy that 'now' expands. The boundaries between 'book' sensations and 'you' sensations become blurred; you temporarily lose the distinction between your self and the world 'out there'.

That experiment produces on a small scale an experience which occasionally happens spontaneously on a larger scale. Sometimes the richness of the present moment doesn't just wait to be noticed: it forcibly claims and seizes our total attention. The psychologist Abraham Maslow, whose 'Hierarchy of Needs' I've referred to, studied and researched such moments, which he called 'peak experiences' [1]. At times of physical, artistic or sexual ecstasy, or when we are struck by creative insight, or moved by awe-inspiring natural beauty and grandeur, the present moment is for a short time all we are conscious of. There is nothing else – no self, no 'not self'; no past, no future – only now. For some people nowness comes when concentrating on sporting activity or strenuous exercise. It can be found in music, or mountains, or making love. The English language acknowledges these moments of total attention in phrases like 'losing oneself in ..." and "being completely absorbed."

One December, just after Christmas, I had been ill with a respiratory virus, and had spent two days in bed. The weather was vile; the view from my windows was as dreary as I felt, the barometer and I were equally depressed. Then came the morning when as soon as you wake you know you feel better. Your body feels lighter. Muscles feel indefinably different; eyes feel slightly wide; you move gingerly, but with a feeling of leisured lightness. During the night a cold front had passed and the weather too was different. The wind had dropped; also the temperature. There was a frost, and for the first time in weeks – sunlight. The world glistened with motionless sunlight. The lightness that glowed outdoors I could also feel. My lightness and the world's were each other's. We reflected each other's change, and in that identity there was no longer any each and any other. I spent two or three hours in the timeless presence of the present, doing the normal things one does in a morning, but effortlessly. Then the feeling faded. I and the world resumed our separateness. I felt the same, and the world looked the same; but of the unity only a memory remained, and a search for words which would in describing inevitably betray it.

If we were sitting round swopping stories of our peak experiences, what would be yours?

The odd thing about peak experiences is that, although at the time our awareness is in fact restricted, we nevertheless continue to function quite efficiently, as it were on auto-pilot. We may be disproportionately conscious of only a fraction of all the sensory information available to us, but our performance of skilled tasks while in this state is actually significantly enhanced. People speak of being 'on peak form', or 'in the groove'; they say, "everything just clicked," or, "I got it all together". I don't know whether you have any particular motor skill requiring great co-ordination – a sport perhaps, or playing an instrument, drawing, public speaking – but if you do, you'll know that when you're doing it especially well it no longer feels as if you need to monitor and adjust what you are doing; the action just seems to perform itself. It's as if there was a direct line from ability to performance that doesn't need any help from self-consciousness. In Maslow's phrase, you become 'like a river without dams'[2].

Though peak experiences are relatively infrequent, everday life is full of lesser occasions when we are so absorbed in some activity that we lose the sense of 'watching what we're doing while we're doing it'. Think of something mundane that not everybody can do but which you've managed to become good at, e.g. playing squash, or making pastry, or driving a car. Things done well are often done 'without a second thought'. While you're occupied (and in fact pre-occupied) with the activity, you presumably are noticing and responding to the various cues necessary to carry it out, but you aren't aware of them. Your monitoring processes go on unconsciously. You don't think twice about it; the competence is there, you have the necessary skills, and the situation releases them. Only when there's a problem, or a choice to be made, does conscious awareness reassert itself.

In fact, the first principle of gamesmanship – deliberately spoiling the performance of someone who's 'on a winning streak' – is to make your rival become conscious and critical of what had hitherto been automatic. "You're serving extra well today," you tell your squash opponent when the points are 8–nil against you. "What are you doing different?" Instantly on the shoulders of the skilled Responder who until then had been winning comfortably there appears the second head of the Organizer, asking, "Well, what *are* you doing different? Is it the throw-up, or the follow-through? Or maybe it's the angle of the wrist at impact." And as Organizer and Responder squabble for control, performance flies out of court.

TWO HEADS, ONE MIND

It is just such a squabble between Organizer and Responder that, as we saw in Chapter A4, causes the distracting internal dialogue while we are consulting. Let me restate the paradox of 'improving by trying', and then, drawing together the themes of this chapter, tell you in principle how 'nowness' provides the key to 'improving by allowing' and so resolves the paradox.

The paradox is this. The wish to improve consulting skill leads us to analyse and make models of it. Consciously trying to improve by putting theory into practice produces the distracting sensation of having two heads. The internal dialogue between them is counter-productive, and in fact interferes with the full deployment of whatever skills you have consciously and unconsciously learned.

The resolution of the paradox is this. The two heads can be encouraged to work with one mind by having them each contribute to a common task. Their joint task is to provide the conditions in which your previously-acquired knowledge and skill can be best deployed. The Responder works best when your attention is concentrated in the 'here and now'. So make it the Organizer's job to keep your attention directed to those aspects of the here and now which the Responder finds most useful. (The next chapter will tell you specifically how to do this.) Then there is no conflict of intention between your two heads. The inner dialogue is quietened, and the illusion of having two heads disappears, leaving you functioning at your most effective, with 'trained intuition'.

If you can drive a car you'll know what I mean. Most of the time when you're driving, you don't notice too much about how you manipulate the gears and pedals and steering wheel. Consciously, you confine your attention to the relatively simple task of 'keeping track' – following a particular road, keeping a safe distance from other traffic, watching out for anything unexpected. The technical details take care of themselves (though it would be more accurate to thank your unconscious mind for taking care of them). This is not to say that every consultation can be as easy as a car-ride with a skilled driver, let alone one continuous peak experience. But just as a learner driver gradually learns what to pay attention to and what not, so you can learn to direct your attention in the consultation in the most profitable directions.

It's a matter of common experience that our best performances come when we are totally absorbed in what we're doing. It seems that:

> when we are functioning at our best,
> our awareness is mainly concentrated in the here and now,
> and we find the distracting internal dialogue disappears.

There is nothing immutable about the sequence of those three linked ideas. We don't need to wait for chance or inspiration to strike in order to improve our performance. A different combination is equally true:

> if we concentrate our awareness in the here and now,
> the distracting internal dialogue disappears,
> and we find ourselves functioning at our best.

The 'Inner Consultation' calls for a leap not in knowledge but of trust – your own trust in your own unconscious processes. This trust is the necessary final step to give solid expression to the head's understanding and the heart's good intentions. It takes a good deal of trust to consult as if all you've learned needn't be consciously remembered. But nothing once learned is forgotten; it is merely stored beneath the threshold of conscious awareness. Although you forget the lessons, the learning remains. In order to swim, you have to overcome the fear of drowning. In order to learn, you have to overcome the fear of forgetting.

Chuang Tsu again [3]:

Fishing baskets are employed to catch fish, but when the fish are got, the men forget the baskets; snares are employed to catch hares, but when the hares are got, men forget the snares. Words are employed to convey ideas; but when the ideas are grasped, men forget the words.

C2
The inner consultation

Sitting quietly, doing nothing, Spring comes and the grass grows by
itself.

The Zenrin

During my very first driving lesson, I was overtaken by a milk-
float. I was eighteen inches from the kerb in a deserted back-street,
keeping as little pressure on the gas pedal as I could get away with,
doing a steady four miles an hour in the only gear I knew, first. My
instructor was holding forth about clutches and mirrors and things. I
was silently promising all my goods to the poor if only God would
keep the road empty for the next half-hour. Then with a scream of
machinery this electric milk-float hurtled past, doing every bit of five
miles an hour, and was soon just a vapour trail on the horizon. I like
to think it made the milkman's day; it certainly spoiled my
instructor's.

I found reversing round corners the hard part. You had to line up
the kerb opposite a certain spot on the rear window, and remember
the nose swings out, and keep a look out, and not go as fast as that,
and straighten up not yet, not yet, now, NOW! I needed so much
practice that the neighbours started asking when we were going to
get the car's forward gears fixed.

Emergency stops were another matter. In theory they were no
more nor less complicated than the other manoeuvres: "When I give
the signal, depress the clutch, apply the footbrake, maintain your
steering, handbrake on, select neutral, check the mirror, indicate and
look round before moving off again." But I soon discovered an
important educational principle. When my instructor gave me plenty
of warning, and told me in softly modulated tones that when we were
abreast of the next lamp-post but one he would say "emergency stop"

269

and require me to bring the vehicle to a stop in the shortest possible time, anything could happen. I would try to carry out the sequence with careful attention to every detail. As a result, I might depress the clutch beautifully but forget about the brake, or vice versa. If the footwork was right, I forgot the steering. When all three were correct, in my pride I forgot to select neutral. The car was quite likely to end up stalled broadside across the road. But when the instructor took me by surprise, suddenly convulsing when I least expected it, roaring like Tarzan, and slamming his fist on the dashboard, my emergency stop was a lot better. Without forethought, in automatic response to the violent stimulus coming from the left-hand seat, my hands and feet of their own accord did all the right things perfectly.

Years earlier, when I was five, there were two groups of children in my first-year class at school – those who could tie their own shoelaces and those who couldn't. One day in October our teacher made all the 'couldn'ts' sit on the floor and practise lace-tying. She showed them all about ends and loops and what went over and what went through and what went round and underneath. The 'coulds' sat and smirked while the 'couldn'ts' one by one gave up in tears, defeated. The next day the teacher changed tack. "There are lovely big conkers under the horse chestnut tree in the playground," she told us, dangling a huge glossy specimen tantalizingly on a string. Our eyes widened with what at five passes for lust. "Now get out your outdoor shoes," she continued, "and as soon as you have put them on and tied your laces you can run outside and pick up the biggest conkers you can find." Some of the 'coulds' in their eagerness became all fingers and thumbs, and were overtaken by some of the 'couldn'ts' who, their mind fixed on the alluring prospect, discovered that they 'could' after all. The remaining 'couldn'ts' were still fumbling around in mounting despair. The teacher went up to them and waved a glorious conker in front of each pair of eyes. Thus distracted from the technical problems of knot-tying, every last child found that the task which had proved impossible yesterday came quite naturally today. Before long the conker tree was bare.

HISTORICAL BACKGROUND

The presence of a flaw in the perfection of man's nature – one part of his mind being at odds with another – is an idea that has pervaded every human culture throughout history. The earliest language used to describe this duality was that of religious allegory and myth: Original Sin, the fall from grace in the Garden of Eden, the Olympian heights to which all may aspire and the Underworld which claims so many. Various philosophical traditions, including the Taoist notions of Yin and Yang, have conceived of man's predicament as oscillation between two extreme opposites in his nature. With the development since Freud of our understanding of psychological processes, speculation about the origin of man's imperfection has shifted from the general philosophical plane to the domain of individual human beings, whose problems became explicable in terms of conflict between ego and id, the conscious and unconscious determinants of behaviour and experience.

The distinction between conscious and unconscious processes is now widely accepted in everyday speech. It has become commonplace to distinguish reason from emotion, logic from intuition, intellect from instinct, prose from poetry, science from art, the head's decisions from the promptings of the heart. That these polarities are held to be a source of tension is apparent from the greater value attached in Western cultures to logic, intellect and predictability. Their opposites – intuition, instinct and spontaneity – have frequently been perceived as threats to individual and social stability, and as such, required to be suppressed or kept within bounds.

But the wheel is coming full circle. The virtue of the unconscious mind has found an unlikely defender in neurology. Freud himself wrote:

> I have no inclination to keep the domain of the psychological floating as it were in the air, without any organic foundation ... Let the biologists go as far as they can and let us go as far as we can. Some day the two will meet.

That day has come. Developments in neuroanatomy and neurophysiology now allow us to understand in reassuringly concrete and organic terms the dichotomy which hitherto could only be described in symbols and metaphor. While the exact mapping remains incomplete, we can nevertheless discern the correlates of conscious and unconscious experience in the functional distinctions between left and right halves of the brain, dominant and non-dominant cerebral hemispheres, neocortical and limbic systems. Since the right hemisphere is manifestly as real a physical entity as the left, we can concede that the right brain makes a contribution to our overall mental functioning which we deny to our impoverishment. The last two decades have seen the beginning of the rehabilitation of the more nebulous functions associated with the right hemisphere. Intuition and unconscious learning are no longer aliens to be suppressed, but long-lost allies with whom it is profitable to be reconciled. Our previous suspicion is seen to have been a misunderstanding brought about by poor communication within the brain. It seems that there is an inbuilt paucity of neuronal connections between the evolutionarily new and old parts of the brain, and between left and right hemispheres. This imbalance has been emphasized by our traditional methods of education; its redress has become the goal of people interested in self-fulfilment from California to Katmandu.

The wish to integrate the potential benefits of conscious and unconscious processes is not new. But how is the recovery of wholeness to be achieved? For centuries the only methods were the exhortations of philosophers and the rigours of disciplined religious training. At some periods of history and for some individuals these have been successful. More recently hope has been offered by psychoanalysis and the various psychotherapies it sired – counselling, Gestalt therapy, Transactional Analysis, encounter groups, est, and an assortment of guru-centred cults. But the appeal of these relatively esoteric methods is limited. What has long been lacking is a simple and practical technique for mobilizing the unconscious mind's contribution to the everyday life of work and leisure. We have come some way already in understanding how unconscious learning occurs; this book has used a range of such methods to help you acquire a repertoire of skills appropriate to the task of consulting. But, as we saw in the last chapter, unconsciously learned material is better recalled and applied by 'allowing' than by 'trying'. Again, how?

I first came across the answer in an unexpected quarter. And it's simple –

To release your latent skills, all you have to do is direct your attention to the right part of the here-and-now.

TIMOTHY GALLWEY

In 1974 Timothy Gallwey, a respected American professional tennis player and coach, published a book called *The Inner Game of Tennis* [1]. I don't play tennis, but at that time in my life I was becoming interested both in the psychology of the consultation and in Zen Buddhism, and the word 'inner' in the title caught my attention. In the opening pages of Gallwey's book [2] I read:

> Every game is composed of two parts, an outer game and an inner game. The outer game is played against an external opponent to overcome external obstacles, and to reach an external goal. Mastering this game is the subject of many books offering instructions on how to swing a racket, club or bat, and how to position arms, legs or torso to

achieve the best results. But for some reason most of us find these instructions easier to remember than to execute.

It is the thesis of this book that neither mastery nor satisfaction can be found in the playing of any game without giving some attention to the relatively neglected skills of the inner game. This is the game that takes place in the mind of the player, and it is played against such obstacles as lapses in concentration, nervousness, self-doubt and self-condemnation. In short, it is played to overcome all habits of mind which inhibit excellence in performance ...

... The player of the inner game comes to value the art of relaxed concentration above all other skills; he discovers a true basis for self-confidence; and he learns that the secret to winning any game lies in not trying too hard...

... Reflect on the state of mind of a player who is said to be "hot" or "on his game." Is he thinking about how he should hit each shot? Is he thinking at all? Listen to the phrases commonly used to describe a player at his best: "He's out of his mind"; "He's playing over his head"; "He's unconscious"; "He doesn't know what he's doing." ... Athletes in most sports use similar phrases, and the best of them know that their peak performance never comes when they're thinking about it...

... But can one learn to play "out of his mind" on purpose? How can you be consciously unconscious? It sounds like a contradiction in terms; yet this state can be achieved. Perhaps a better way to describe the player who is "unconscious" is by saying that his mind is so concentrated, so focused, that it is still. It becomes one with what the body is doing, and the unconscious or automatic functions are working without interference from thoughts. The concentrated mind has no room for thinking how well the body is doing, much less of the how-to's of the doing. When the player is in this state of concentration, he is really into the game; he is at one with racket, ball and stroke; he discovers his true potential.

Gallwey's experience as a tennis instructor confirmed that when his pupils were off form they kept up a running commentary on their own performance, often out loud, in which they would scold and criticize themselves, telling themselves what was wrong and what they jolly well ought to do about it. The images which Gallwey used to describe this internal conversation were of 'Self 1' (the conscious nagger) and 'Self 2' (the unconscious automatic doer.) Other observers of the same phenomenon have used different terms: Eric Berne's Transactional Analysis uses Critical Parent and Free Child ego-states; Arthur Koestler speaks of the Robot and the Lotus; I prefer the analogy of having two heads, Organizer and Responder.

Gallwey discovered that the intrusive effects of Self 1 can be reduced by distracting it away from trying to stay in control, and instead giving it the task of noticing as accurately and non-judgementally as possible certain neutral features of Self 2's performance. For instance, the player might be told to say out loud "Bounce" at the exact moment he notices the ball bounce, and "Hit" at the instant his racket strikes the ball. He might be asked to look at nothing other than the seams of the approaching tennis ball; to listen only for the sound made by ball striking strings; to feel only the position of the racket head on the backswing. The player was not required to 'try and correct' any of these aspects of his game, merely to observe them with maximum awareness. Self 1 and Self 2 thereby worked in co-operation: Self 1 provided Self 2 with accurate feedback of what it was doing, and Self 2 was freed to get on with the job of hitting the ball, a task too complex to be adjusted consciously in real time. Gallwey's approach, which he has subsequently extended to other sports such as golf and skiing is based on the discovery that improvement occurs as a result of accurate observation of results, not of effort. Mastering the inner game is a question of directing your attention to the right parts of the here-and-now.

Gallwey's penetrating and practical description of the barriers to playing good tennis, and how to overcome them, suggested obvious parallels with the 'two heads' feeling that can bedevil the consultation. I became intrigued to find out whether his technique of 'distracting' the second head could help in the consulting room. There are some similarities between consulting and playing tennis. Both are complex skills; both require the combination and co-ordination of a wide range of sub-skills; both are best done unselfconsciously; both can be inhibited by too much theorizing. But there are also some important differences. Hitting a moving tennis ball is primarily a motor skill taking only a few seconds and involving predominantly cerebellum and motor cortex. Carrying on a consultation is a much more lengthy business; its tasks are more cognitive than motor; its component skills are a mixture of perceptual, intellectual and linguistic. The basic ingredients of playing tennis – running, swinging, hitting – are familiar to everyone even if they have never actually played the game. It seemed to me that consulting presupposed a repertoire of more sophisticated behaviours which could not be taken for granted and which not everyone found easy to acquire.

I experimented in training sessions with suggesting various distractors that a doctor might focus attention on, such as matching the patient's blink rate, or counting the patient's respirations, but these distractors proved to be just that – distracting. Then I learned about two things. The first was the immense power of the unconscious mind to acquire skills and resources provided the information is presented in the right way; this I learned from studying the clinical and hypnotic strategies of the late Milton Erickson. The second, which I learned in conversation with Timothy Gallwey, was what made for an effective distractor.

THE INNER CONSULTATION

In hindsight, I realized I was being too complicated. During a consultation, the doctor essentially only does three things: he listens, he speaks, and he thinks. Listening, speaking and thinking – these are the basic ingredients of consulting, in the same way as running, swinging and hitting are the basic ingredients of tennis. To be sure, the doctor attends to a great many things while listening, and tries to achieve a great variety of results by what he says, and his thoughts range over a multitude of topics, just as the tennis player puts together a wealth of different strokes. But listening, speaking and thinking remain the doctor's fundamental activities.

Each of these three we often perform unselfconsciously: we can listen attentively, speak effectively and think reliably without at the time being particularly aware of what it is we are doing. But at other times each activity is liable to be interrupted and spoiled by internal dialogue. Periodically, as we have seen, the second head will appear and attempt to muscle in on the act. As a rule, for maximum empathy when we are listening and speaking, we want the Responder to be in charge. Logical thinking, on the other hand, is best performed by the Organizer. So, if we want each of our two heads to be allowed to get on with what it is best at, we need to be able to distract the Organizer if it interferes with the Responder's listening and speaking; and to distract the Responder if it prevents the Organizer from thinking.

To develop the ability to consult with 'trained intuition', two things are necessary. The first is for your resource store to contain an adequate repertoire of knowledge and techniques. This you already possess. You do indeed have the body of theoretical and clinical knowledge without which your thinking processes would be suspect. You know the sequence of five checkpoints which, taken in order, will ensure you achieve the consultation's various goals. Your experience prior to reading this book, and the skill-building programme it contains, will have installed an adequate selection of consulting techniques. (And by practising the various exercises you can further consolidate your repertoire.) So both your Organizer and your Responder are fully equipped to carry out their respective tasks.

The second thing you need is to know how to maintain single-mindedness – how to distract your interfering second head when it gets in the way. You need to know where to direct your attention if internal dialogue impedes your listening, speaking or thinking. While I was researching this book, I met with Timothy Gallwey; and over lunch at a beachside restaurant near Los Angeles we discussed what made an effective distractor. As we talked, a mile or two off-shore in

275

the Pacific Ocean a whale surfaced, and spouted (as far as I could tell) unselfconsciously!

An effective distractor or target of attention:

(1) is something clearly observable in the here-and-now;

(2) provides feedback directly relevant to the performance of the desired task;

and (3) is non-judgemental, i.e. it can be observed with greater or lesser accuracy, but carries no value-laden connotations of success or failure.

In the context of the consultation, effective targets of attention – distractors – are to be found in the **minimal cues** which have been a recurring theme in this book.

Minimal cues, you will recall, are the physical signs of mental states. Here to remind you are some aspects of the consultation to which accurate observation of minimal cues provides the key:

rapport
the patient's mood and emotions
language of self-expression
speech censoring
representational systems
internal search
the acceptance set
incongruities
deletions, distortions and generalizations
frameworks
gift-wrapping
recognizing arrival at the checkpoints
your own signs of stress
   – muscle tension
   – negative thoughts and feelings
   – behaviour rituals

Although in this book I have dealt with minimal cues at some length, and suggested a variety of training exercises to familiarize yourself with them, during an actual consultation there is not enough time to interpret them consciously and systematically. In real life, however you do not even need to attempt to. It is enough just to keep track of them as distractors, as targets for your attention to quieten your internal dialogue. Your unconscious mind will make of them whatever sense is necessary. Minimal cues fulfil the criteria for effective distractors in that they are constantly changing in the here-and-now; they provide feedback which is extremely relevant to the doctor's performance; and, (since sensory information can be 'accurate' or 'inaccurate', 'reliable' or 'unreliable', but not 'successful' or 'unsuccessful',) minimal cues are devoid of value-judgement.

In the next sections I am going to suggest how and when to direct your attention to various minimal cues when internal dialogue intrudes into the consultation. A lot of the time there is no sensation of a second head, and hence no need to distract it; but when there is, you will find it helpful to know how to direct your attention according to whether you are listening, speaking or thinking. Remember: listening and speaking require the ability sometimes to distract the Organizer. Thinking requires the ability to distract the Responder.

When internal dialogue disturbs your **listening** –
> **watch the patient's minimal cues**.

When internal dialogue disturbs your **speaking** –
> **watch where your words are landing**.

When internal dialogue disturbs your **thinking** –
> **notice your own breathing**.

Listening – watch the patient's minimal cues

It is while we are trying to attend to what the patient is saying that we are most prone to the disturbing effects of internal dialogue. Ideally, your attention should be directed outwards, to whatever the patient is communicating verbally and non-verbally. In order to miss as little as possible you need all your senses functioning at peak sensitivity, i.e. the Responder in charge. But the Organizer is ever ready to chip in, diverting some of your attention away from the patient, and starting to analyse, interpret and structure the incoming information. If the Organizer succeeds in taking over, you suddenly become aware, with a start, that you had drifted off into your own thoughts and completely lost track of what the patient was saying. This is the point at which you need to distract the Organizer, leaving the way clear for the Responder.

What you do is this: when you realize that you have lost concentration, consciously redirect your attention so that you keep track of the patient's minimal cues. Don't try to interpret them; just notice as much as you can. Think of yourself as a camera that registers without editing. Follow the patient's facial expressions; her eye movements and gaze; her posture and gestures. Notice her breathing rate, and the places in her body where tension seems to be located. Listen to the pitch of her voice; its volume and pace; its rise and fall. (Turn back to Figure B2.1 (page 123) to remind yourself of the range of minimal cues.)

The effect of intentionally tracking all these minimal cues is to re-establish your attention firmly back onto the patient sitting three or four feet in front of you. So great is the amount of information conveyed by the minimal cues that the Organizer is swamped – it can't possibly analyse and interpret it all. The Organizer gives up in disgust and retreats, leaving the intuitive Responder to sort it out, which it does, quite automatically. Subjectively, what happens is that your super-awareness of all the minimal cues quickly fades, leaving you unselfconsciously concentrating on what the patient is telling you, and picking up enough of the non-verbal cues for your intuition to interpret automatically. Without you consciously knowing how or why, the internal dialogue disappears and you find yourself back 'in the groove'.

EXERCISE

"When you catch your mind wandering, watch the minimal cues like a hawk" – it sounds an easy enough piece of advice. And indeed it is, but it feels risky. Not surprisingly, your Organizer doesn't like it. You are afraid you might miss something 'important' or 'significant'. In other words, you are a little wary of trusting the Responder to manage affairs satisfactorily. Try it. Better still, before you try it during a consultation, try it out in a safe social context. When you are chatting with a friend, periodically think 'minimal cues'. Notice and listen to the non-verbals as intently as you can for a few moments, and let your responses take care of themselves. You will find that not only do you not miss anything important, but also your conversation takes on an intuitive and spontaneous quality which is often witty and perceptive. Without knowing quite why, your companion will detect that there is something special about the quality of your attention, and respond accordingly.

> In order to swim, you have to overcome the fear of drowning.
> In order to listen, you have to overcome the fear of not hearing.

Speaking – watch where your words are landing

Intrusive internal dialogue is not usually such a problem when we are speaking as it is when we are trying to listen. We are all much better talkers than listeners. But sometimes our speech becomes hesitant and awkward. We get tongue-tied, and aren't clear exactly what we are trying to express. We make false starts, or we flit inelegantly from one topic to another. In the 'two heads' analogy, the Responder is the best judge of when to speak, what to say and how to put it – provided the Organizer lets it get on with it. When the Organizer's intentions conflict with the Responder's responses, speech becomes stilted and ineffectual.

When you notice this starting to happen, watch the patient closely and notice where your words seem to be landing. When we use the phrase 'my words had an impact on someone', we usually mean it metaphorically. In this context I mean it literally – watch whereabouts on the patient's face or body your words are making their impact. Is it the patient's eyes that are reacting as you speak, by widening or narrowing, or moving in a particular direction or becoming still? Or are your words landing on her face, causing her brow to furrow, or the lower lip to sag, or the cheek muscles to tense? Or are you having an impact on her posture and gestures? Odd though it sounds, you will soon be able to spot, for example, that one remark landed just above the bridge of her nose, the next at the left angle of the mouth, and a third on the fingers of the right hand. Don't try to make 'sense' out of what you see – the object of the exercise is merely to observe as accurately as you can.

What is the point of this? By giving your Organizer the task of identifying the landing-site of your remarks, you prevent it from interfering in the Responder's natural ability to carry on a spontaneous and appropriate conversation. The minimal cues which are the object of your scrutiny provide the precise subliminal feedback that the Responder needs in order to function effectively.

There is an alternative distractor which some people prefer to use to keep their speech on target. You can keep track of where the *patient's* attention is directed while you are talking. It is quite easy to tell whether the patient's attention is directed towards you, or inwardly (as in internal search), or to some extraneous object, or is flitting about from one thing to another.

Again, your fear may well be that paying such close attention to the effects of what you say might inhibit you. Again – try it; discretely in social company first, if you prefer. Whichever distractor you choose, you will find that in real life you very quickly forget about it; but in the process, your speaking will have reverted to its normal unselfconscious fluency and pertinence.

In order to speak, you have to overcome the fear of not being heard.

Thinking – notice your own breathing

Thinking (at least about the technicalities of a medical consultation) should be a rational, logical and systematic process. You might be wondering what to do next, or deciding what further information you want, or formulating a management plan, or weighing up how best to explain a particular point. These are all things that are best done by the analytical and clear-headed Organizer. If you find yourself having trouble thinking clearly – perhaps apparently irrelevant thoughts keep intruding, or you begin to feel some unpleasant emotion like irritation or bewilderment – try this. Turn your attention determinedly inwards, and target it on the physical sensations of breathing. As I have described in an earlier exercise, notice the rise and fall of your chest and abdomen; the sensations around your lips, nostrils and mouth; the different temperatures of inhaled and exhaled air; the soft sounds your breath makes. Paying attention to these sensations acts this time as a distractor for the Responder. Your awareness becomes rooted in the here-and-now, and by the time you have allowed a few breaths to register you will find your mind has cleared, you feel calmer, and your thought processes are sharper. Try it.

> In order to think you have to overcome the fear of being without thought.

TUTORIAL

Me: How does the Inner Consultation sound to you?

Chris: A bit weird. I mean, we set out trying to make consulting simpler, and what you've said about the checkpoints certainly helps that; and the training exercises have helped as well. I'm just not convinced you need at this stage to introduce any extra complications about redirecting one's attention.

Me: There speaks a true Organizer! Yes, there's a limit to the number of items you can consciously keep in mind at any one moment, and during the consultation most of your attention span is devoted to organizing and assessing the clinical problem you're presented with. I think, Chris, your doubts are the protests of an Organizer whose in-tray is already piled high. The Inner Consultation techniques are intended to be ways of reducing your mental work-load, not adding to it. They allow you to delegate more of the consultation to your underestimated but perfectly competent Responder. All it needs is for you to be willing to trust your own unconscious processes. And why shouldn't you? They've served you well all your life so far.

Look, the 'two heads' are just an analogy, a way of describing the very real experience of having logic and intuition pulling you in different directions. The Inner

Consultation is a method of reducing that tension. It works by reining in your attention when it wanders, and bringing it back to those aspects of the here-and-now which provide you with the information your conscious and unconscious minds need in order to function at maximum efficiency. You still look a bit sceptical.

Chris: Mmm. I guess I just have to try it out, and find out whether it actually works in practice.

Me: Exactly. Let's keep it in proportion: for most of the time you needn't think about the Inner Consultation. As long as things are moving along steadily in a direction you and the patient are happy about – fine! As someone said, 'If it ain't broke, don't fix it'. The Inner Consultation techniques are for you to use when you lose track of where you're going, and the internal dialogue starts to confuse you.

Chris: Could we just think a little bit more about how it works in practice?

Me: All right. Here's the overall strategy.

Item one: Be clear about which checkpoint you're making for next. If you like, use the left hand finger mnemonics to remind you. So you think, for example, 'Okay, first checkpoint – CONNECTING', 'next – SUMMARIZING', and so on.

Item two: Make for that checkpoint, in whatever way you want to, or whatever way comes naturally.

Item three: When you catch your attention wandering, use one of the listening, speaking or thinking distractors to bring your mind back onto track.

I think a couple of diagrams might help you understand what I mean (Figures C2.1 and C2.2).

I think the diagrams are self-explanatory. The area of the graph above the base line represents the amount of attention that's wasted when your concentration lapses. As you see, by using a distractor you bring your attention back on course more quickly, and so waste less time.

Chris: It certainly sounds plausible. Are there any snags to the Inner Consultation, apart from the mental discipline of trying something unfamiliar?

Me: Yes. The first is; because it's unfamiliar, you may simply forget all about it the first few times you mean to try it out. I've found the best way to overcome this is to put a small card

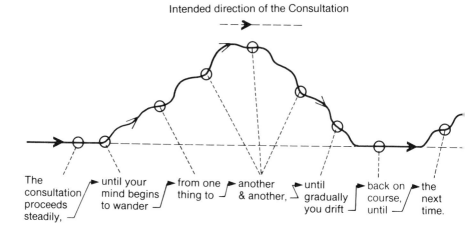

Figure C2.1 Attention wandering during normal consultation

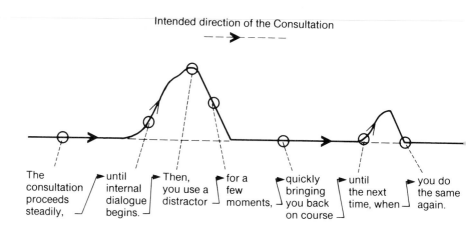

Figure C2.2 Control of attention during the Inner Consultation

saying MINIMAL CUES on the desk, on the periphery of your line of sight to the patient, as an unobtrusive reminder. It also helps to try using the distractors in everyday conversation first, as I've already suggested.

The other drawback can be more serious. Because the Inner Consultation relies heavily on unconscious recall of skills you have previously learned and consigned to the resource store, you can only be as skilled in action as you have previously been in practice. The way I've presented my material helps with this, because it's been designed to be understood both consciously and unconsciously. But you still need to practise the component skills, by doing the various training exercises, so that the skills are there when you need them. It's a good idea periodically to carry out some of the 'playing card' exercises as a refresher. Otherwise you may find you drift back into your old ways – either selfconsciously 'trying' to improve, or consulting in a kind of 'decerebrate reflex' fashion.

Chris: Let's assume I get into the swing of it; are there any 'fringe benefits' to the Inner Consultation?

Me: Apart from well-deserved job satisfaction? Well, for one thing, you'll find that you spend a noticeably greater amount of your surgery time in the here-and-now. You'll discover that that's a less stressful way of working, because most stress is caused by worrying either about the past or the future. You won't be quite so prone to 'if only' thoughts: 'if only' I wasn't seeing this patient; 'if only' they hadn't come about this particular problem; 'if only' I felt different today. Tolerance of the way you are and the way the patient is leads on to greater empathy and compassion. As you get better at 'nowness' – non-judgemental awareness of the present moment – you become gradually more accepting of the way things actually are. Paradoxically, you'll find then that you can intervene and change things with comparative effort-lessness.

Chris: Why do you think some people might find this approach difficult to accept?

Me: Old habits die hard. We are so used in our culture to the belief that you can only improve by putting in a lot of effort. And until recently we've been very unused to the idea of developing our unconscious potential, although that's now changing in many different spheres. As a society, we're over-Organized and under-Responsive. In this respect we have a lot to learn from the cultural traditions of other civilizations, notably some of the Eastern philosophies. If Lao Tsu were alive today, he'ld have no difficulty at all in understanding the truth beneath the paradoxical catechism of this chapter:

In order to swim, you have to overcome the fear of drowning.
In order to learn, you have to overcome the fear of forgetting.
In order to listen you have to overcome the fear of not hearing.
In order to speak, you have to overcome the fear of not being heard.
In order to think, you have to overcome the fear of being without thought.

EXERCISES

Here are several exercises which you can do in order gradually to accustom yourself to the techniques of the Inner Consultation. They are best done in the sequence given. The first three involve you watching a video recording of some consultations, preferably your own, but not very recent ones. They provide you with some safe practice at targeting your attention on the patient's minimal cues.

First video exercise

Turn down the sound on the television. For about two minutes, try to keep constant track of as many of the patient's non-verbal minimal cues as you can. Don't try to interpret what you see, just observe in a neutral non-judgemental frame of mind.

Then, as a variation, turn the sound up and watch the same consultation again. Still do nothing more than keep constant track of the minimal cues (though this time there will be the auditory ones in addition). As reassurance that you don't in fact miss anything important while doing this, ask a third party to test your comprehension by asking you a few apposite questions about the content of the consultation while your attention was on the minimal cues.

Second video exercise

Play another video consultation, with the sound up. This time, watch the patient closely while the doctor on the screen is speaking. Notice what minimal cues appear in response to what he says, i.e. the point of impact of his speech. Again don't try to interpret the responses you see, just allow them to register as completely as possible.

Third video exercise

Watching another consultation, keep track of where the patient's attention is directed while the doctor is speaking. Notice how it shifts between being directed towards the doctor, inwards as during internal search, or ranging around the room.

You might find a noticeable difference in the ease with which you can do the second and third exercises. Your preference can guide you in your choice of a 'speaking' distractor for your own use during live consultations.

Awareness of breathing

You are familiar with the instructions for cultivating the awareness of your own breathing, which I first described as an exercise in 'nowness'. Try it out in real-life consultations. The best time to do it on the first few occasions is when you are carrying out some physical routine, such as preparing to take a blood pressure. This will give you the confidence necessary to centre yourself periodically while you are thinking.

The remaining exercise should only be done when you have tried the use of distractors during actual consultations, and feel you have some familiarity with the idea.

Differential distractors

Most of us have a preference for one or other Representational System (Visual, Auditory or Kinaesthetic). Decide which is yours. Try choosing another, and concentrating on the patient's minimal cues in just that less familiar modality.

C3
Zen and the art of the consultation

It is one of the most beautiful compensations of this life, that no man can sincerely try to help another without helping himself.

Throughout this book, we have been thinking of the consultation as a journey, with checkpoints along the way. The first four checkpoints, from CONNECTING to SAFETY-NETTING, mark out what we might think of as an outer journey through the objective 'real' world. A neutral observer watching on closed-circuit television would be able to estimate at any given moment how much progress had been made along the way – his own eyes and ears would provide the evidence.

With the fifth checkpoint, HOUSEKEEPING, however, the journey takes an inward turn. The path now leads into the private subjective territory of the doctor's inner thoughts and feelings. In the Inner Consultation, you the doctor travel alone. Neither the patient nor the neutral observer has any direct evidence of your experience at this stage. Only indirectly, by your equanimity and perspicacity, is your progress revealed to anyone other than yourself.

Any surprise you might feel at being led in this inward direction would be shared by a number of influential and academically respectable Western scientists. Take physics: as long ago as 1925, the 24-year-old physicist Werner Heisenberg, racked with hay-fever, took himself off to the island of Heligoland and invented quantum mechanics, a set of premises which turned the mechanistic Newtonian tradition on its head. In his famous 'Uncertainty Principle', Heisenberg pointed out a fundamental misconception about our ability to perceive 'reality'. It is possible by experiment to determine the position of an electron, or its momentum. But it is impossible, even in principle, to know both. Measuring either one changes the other. So what you find out about an electron is governed by what you're looking for; that is, by the experimenter's choice. At the subatomic level, observable reality is ultimately and inescapably dependent on the mental state of the observer.

Contemporary physics abounds in mysteries. Einstein with his well-known $E=mc^2$ expressed the astonishing notion that matter is nothing more than energy, enormously concentrated. Space is curved in the vicinity of large masses. Time, it seems, does not move inexorably in one direction: a single mathematical equation describes with equal validity a positron moving from the past to the future, or an electron moving from the future back into the past. Ask a physicist whether light is a wave or a particle phenomenon, and you will be told, "It depends – either one, or neither, or both. "[1,2,3,4]

Paradoxes like these are insoluble to the everyday logical mind. Yet it is science – the distillation of everyday logical mind – which has given birth to them. Such truth as these puzzles contain can only be comprehended by suspending for a time the 'normal' rational processes of everyday thought. The key to their understanding is the transformation of the everyday consciousness of the individual person who confronts them. Science has become in part an inner journey.

The East long ago arrived at a similar position, but from the opposite direction. The ancient cultures of India, China and Japan left no legacy of scientific enquiry to match that bestowed by the Greeks and Romans on Western civilization. But their long traditions of philosophy and introspection have withstood erosion by intellectual sophistication far more successfully, and it is to them that Westerners increasingly turn for guidance in the task of self-transformation.

Every culture tries to explain mankind's dissatisfaction with the human condition. Man and Nature are universally perceived to be at odds in some fundamental way. The Western approach to resolving this malaise has historically been to control and coerce nature into submission. Through rational analysis and scientific endeavour the West has sought the means of achieving mastery over the natural world. But there is an increasing sense of disillusion with this prescription, whose side effects have been industrial sprawl, self-assertive materialism, pollution, war and exploitation. The Eastern diagnosis of Man's predicament has always been different. The origin of, and remedy for, our sense of alienation lies not in the natural world – which just IS the way it is – but rather within the minds of individual human beings. If for no other reasons, this approach to peace of mind commends itself because it comes free, and harms nobody.

HISTORICAL NOTE – THE ORIGINS OF ZEN

Taoism, of which I have already given you a taste, was one of China's established schools of thought four centuries B.C. Its central theme was the intrinsic rightness of the Universe, which is indivisible and ever-changing. Man's nature is best fulfilled by flowing in harmony with the natural order, not by struggling to oppose it. The constant flux of events is seen as arising from the interplay of two extremes, called Yin and Yang. The wise man espouses neither extreme, nor resists their waxing and waning, but aspires to a state of 'non-action' – refraining from activity contrary to nature. By having no wishes that 'go against the grain of things', he lives spontaneously, intuitively, and without undue effort.

Taoist writings are strong on poetical descriptions of the ideal state, but weaker on the practicalities of how to attain it. Here is Lao Tsu putting his creed into language that I find moving [5]:

Something mysterious formed, born before heaven and earth.
In the silence and the void, standing alone and unchanging,
Ever present and in motion.
Perhaps it is the mother of ten thousand things.
I do not know its name. Call it Tao.
For lack of a better word, I call it great.

Being great, it flows. It flows far away.
Having gone far, it returns.

Man follows the earth.
Earth follows Heaven.
Heaven follows the Tao.
Tao follows what is natural

Meanwhile, two hundred years earlier in what is now Nepal, Prince Siddhartha Gautama had forsaken the luxury of his royal birth and submitted himself to years of ascetic discipline in an attempt to understand the cause and cure of suffering. One evening, after several days and nights of meditation seated under a tree by the river Neranjara, he succeeded, and became thereafter 'the enlightened one' – the Buddha.

The Buddha's insight was to realize that human suffering is caused by the fruitless search for something permanent – possessions, beliefs, principles – in a world that is endlessly changing instant by instant. Nothing endures, not even that which we call the 'self'. The idea of a lasting 'I' is an illusion. During meditation – opening up one's awareness to the ever-changing 'now' – the impermanence of the self is discovered not as a theory but as a direct experience. When the sense of self evaporates, nothing stands in the way of seeing the world as it really is. There is no 'I' to want things other than as they are. The Buddha spent the rest of his life as a peripatetic teacher of his method of enlightenment, which he insisted was attainable this side of the grave by anyone who would practise meditation and a simple ethical code.

In the Buddha's time, the social culture was such that after his death his teaching became codified and elaborated into a formal system of dogma that some felt ran counter to his essentially practical message. Such a one was Bodhidharma, an itinerant monk who in 520 A.D. undertook the hazardous journey to China, bringing the Buddha's method of 'enlightenment training' into a culture still predominantly Taoist. According to his pictures, Bodhidharma was an unlikely sage. Fat, bald, cantankerous, with an ear-ring in his right ear, Bodhidharma looked more like a pirate than a saint. He knew that the liberation he himself had attained could not be passed on to others save by their own efforts. Enlightenment must be won afresh by each individual, for the self each man must lose is his alone.

Bodhidharma's meeting with the Chinese Emperor Wu was a stormy confrontation. The Emperor was a staunch lay Buddhist already, and had endowed many monasteries and temples. He asked Bodhidharma how much merit he had acquired by such munificence. "None at all!" Bodhidharma told him. The Emperor, taken aback, enquired, "What, then, is the sacred doctrine's first principle?" "Vast emptiness; there's nothing sacred," came the reply. Emperor Wu, with understandable petulance, demanded, "Who do you think you are to stand before Us?" "I've no idea," said Bodhidharma; whereupon he turned on his heel and left, and meditated nine years in a cave.

The meditation that Bodhidharma taught ('dhyana' in Sanskrit, 'Ch'an' in Chinese) proved to be the teaching technique that brought the wisdom of the Tao within the grasp of the ordinary 'philosopher in the street'. Ch'an rapidly permeated Chinese life, and in the twelfth century was introduced into Japan, where, as 'Zen', it has flourished ever since. Bodhidharma summed up the teaching of Zen in this quatrain:

> A special transmission outside the scriptures;
> No reliance upon words and letters;
> Pointing directly at the human mind;
> Seeing into one's own nature and attaining Buddhahood.

WHAT IS ZEN?

An understandable question: if someone asks it, and another answers, neither of them knows.

A recipe is not a taste, though it tells you how a taste may be created. Talk about Zen is a finger pointing at the moon, not the moon itself. Hints can be given, but no one can tell you how things really are. Zen is a way for you to find out for yourself: beyond that, words betray it. Zen is simple: and nothing is simple that can be put into words.

There are three ingredients in Zen training (and now you will begin to discern why Zen and the art of the consultation are linked):

(1) Meditation (by which is meant systematic practice in 'nowness', non-judgemental awareness of the present moment);

(2) Daily life practice – single-minded attention to the job in hand;

and (3) Carrying thought beyond the limits of the intellect. (In the language I have used in this book, this means using your intuitive Responder as well as the Organizer.)

Zen has its own peculiar way of suppressing the intellect in favour of the intuition – the koan. A koan is a mental exercise or puzzle that defies the power of the intellect to solve it, however hard it tries. Two classic examples are; "What is the sound of one hand clapping?", or, "Show me your original face before you were born." Koans drive the intellect into a logical impasse from which no amount of theorizing can rescue it. Then, in a flash, the intuition bursts in with a response born of the immediate moment – a smile, a shout, silence, the sight of a rain-drop trickling down a window-pane. The answer is to un-ask the question. The problem itself was the creation of the intellect, and had no more validity than the intellect's attempts at a solution. Zen masters are constantly quoted as answering the conceptual questions of their pupils with a remark that jerks them back into the only reality, the present moment. Master Yakusan's trainee once asked him, "What is the truth?" Yakusan pointed up and down, and in turn asked, "Have you got it?" The puzzled pupil said "No." Yakusan added, "Cloud in the blue sky, water in the jar." Then the pupil 'got it'. The truth at that moment was just cloud in the sky and water in a jar; just what was there, nothing special.

In the Inner Consultation, the distractors of minimal cues and awareness of breathing have a similar effect of restoring the right balance of intellect and intuition.

I love this story of nowness, told by the Buddha [6]:

A man travelling across a field encountered a tiger. He fled, the tiger after him. Coming to a precipice, he caught hold of the root of a wild vine and swung himself down over the edge. The tiger sniffed at him from above. Trembling, the man looked down to where, far below, another tiger was waiting to eat him. Only the vine sustained him.

Two mice, one white and one black, little by little started to gnaw away at the vine. The man saw a luscious strawberry near him. Grasping the vine with one hand, he plucked the strawberry with the other. How sweet it tasted!

Although to our Western ears the Zen way sounds quirky, it is very much a practical everyday affair. The Zenist finds the grounds of his realization in the market place and the consulting room, where by doing what comes naturally to him, he may benefit others. The perfection of Zen is to live one's ordinary life to the full.

> The Western intellectual finds mystery at the heart of what at first he took to be reality.
> Zen finds reality at the heart of what at first appears to be mystery.

So the scientist (who is mostly Organizer) and the Zenist (who is largely Responder) are seen to be converging on the same holistic world-view – which is reassuring, since there is only one world to have a view about! But because their cultural backgrounds are different, their approach leads them through different territory on the way. The Western route to understanding emphasizes conceptual thought and rational analysis; the East's way is more holistic and intuitive, rooted in direct experience. The distinction is for the moment important, because it alerts us to the fact that, in analysing and theorizing, something valuable can be lost. A famous Zen Master, Professor Daisetz Suzuki, who died in 1960, was fond of illustrating this point by comparing short verses by two poets, one from each culture.

Do you know what a haiku is? A haiku is a Japanese verse form of three lines, having (in Japanese and in some English translations) five, seven and five syllables in turn. At its best, a haiku captures in a kind of 'action photograph' a single instant in the natural world and the poet's simultaneous experience of it. For example:

> White chrysanthemum –
> In front of such perfection
> Scissors hesitate.

Or,

> Oh stupid scarecrow!
> Under your very stick foot
> Birds are stealing rice!

Or, the best-known haiku of all, by Basho (1644–1694),

Furuike ya	An ancient pond,
kawazu tobikomu	A frog jumps in:
mizu no oto	The splash of water.

Now to Dr Suzuki's juxtaposition of two poets' responses to the unexpected glimpse of a wild flower [7]. First, Basho:

Yoku mireba	When I look carefully,
nazuna hana saku	I see the nazuna blooming
kakine kana.	By the hedge!

'Nazuna' is a rather dowdy and insignificant wild plant. The last two syllables, 'kana', indicate a sudden emotion; in this case, wonder that the petals of so humble a plant can exalt a man's heart and move him to silence.

By comparison, our own Alfred, Lord Tennyson (1809–1892):

Flower in the crannied wall,
I pluck you out of the crannies: –
Hold you here, root and all, in my hand,
Little flower – but if I could understand
What you are, root and all, and all in all
I should know what God and man is.

Tennyson, in his verse, is eager to move his thought on from the flower which he has plucked, and embark upon eloquent speculation as to the nature of the God–Man Relationship. In so doing, he is oblivious to the fact that, in order to satisfy his intellectual curiosity, the uprooted flower has sacrificed its life.

Basho, by not interfering, felt no less intense an experience, yet allowed the nazuna to continue flowering, reproducing and withering in accordance with its natural life cycle. He is in harmony with the Taoist principle of the natural and living worlds in endless cycles of arising, flourishing and declining, while apparent opposites emerge and subside in turn [8].

Under heaven all can see beauty as beauty only because there is ugliness.
All can know good as good only because there is evil.

Therefore having and not having arise together.
Difficult and easy complement each other.
Long and short contrast each other;
High and low rest upon each other;
Voice and sound harmonize each other;
Front and back follow one another.

Therefore the sage goes about doing nothing, teaching no-talking.
The ten thousand things rise and fall without cease,
Creating, yet not possessing, working, yet not taking credit.
Work is done, then forgotten. Therefore it lasts forever.

My reason for underlining the cyclical nature of events is to anticipate a dilemma you may find yourself in. For the greater part of this book, I have been advancing an analysis of the consultation, and proposing a programme of training exercises in order for you to develop your consulting skills for your own and your patients' advantage. And now, I may seem to be implying, analysis is dangerous, and effort unavailing; spontaneity is everything. Confusion?

No; effort and spontaneity co-exist. In the consultation there is a time for analysis and a time for awareness; intellect and intuition alternate. You require both in full measure, at the appropriate times.

Here are some examples, from several contexts, of natural processes that go through three-stage cycles of growth, then development, and finally returning to the origin.

birth ⟶	life ⟶	death
childhood	maturity	senescence
poverty	wealth	renunciation
naïvety	practice	skill
ignorance	analysis	familiarity
novice	apprentice	craftsman
water	steam	condensation
unconsciousness	self-consciousness	un-selfconsciousness
impotence	struggle	effortlessness
silence ⟶	words ⟶	ineffability

In each case, the third state in many ways resembles the first, yet at the same time is different by virtue of what happened in between.

In the pursuit of learning, every day something is acquired.
In the pursuit of Tao, every day something is dropped.

Thirty spokes share the wheel's hub;
It is the centre hole that makes it useful.
Shape clay into a vessel;
It is the space within that makes it useful.
Therefore profit comes from what is there;
Usefulness from what is not there. [9, 10]

The learning programme in this book has been like this. I have tried to lead you through analysis and learning to a state where letting go of them will create for you your own Art of the Consultation. By cultivating intellect *and* insight, Organizer *and* Responder, left *and* right hemispheres, concepts *and* nowness, you allow a balanced state of trained intuition to emerge.

Sometimes in Inner Consultation training sessions I have tried an experiment, which you might like to repeat. Instead of making the usual clinical entry in the notes, capture the important feature of a consultation in haiku form: three lines, five, seven and five syllables. Your perceptiveness will surprise you. Here are two translated examples by Japanese poets, describing moments you will recognize from your clinical experience.

Cherry trees:
Contemplating their beauty,
Strangers are like friends.

Issa [11]

The piercing chill I feel:
My dead wife's comb, in our bedroom,
Under my heel ...

Buson [12]

Here are three more, by contemporary English doctors:

Lady softly sobs –
Tears of a living doormat.
Whose the trampling foot?

Feeling a headache
As I leave to dine with friends –
No sense of outrage.

Young girl needs the pill
Hesitates before leaving.
Not her fault I'm tired.

The closing stages of the Inner Consultation are also the first stages of a further journey, this time one that leads towards the awakening of the doctor's own heart. As you begin to feel more secure with the resources of your unconscious mind, you find that the self-assertive tendency to cling on to control of the consultation begins to slip away, to be replaced by a trusting sense of coming alongside the patient, which is the start of compassion. Or rather, not the *start* of it; for compassion was what prompted you into medicine in the first place. Such a lot has happened, and here we are at the origin again.

The misty rain on Mount Ro and the waves of the Setsu River are famous. Nostalgic after many years' absence, the Zen poet Sotoba at last made the journey, and on his return wrote [13]:

Mount Ro and the misty rain, and the waves in the Setsu river –
Before I had been there my thousand longings never ceased.
Then I went, and came back. Nothing special –
Mount Ro and the misty rain, and the waves in the Setsu river!

Appendix 1
An 'Inner Consultation' training programme

If you are glancing at this chapter before finishing the main text – please read on: I hope you will now see how the effort you put into reading *The Inner Consultation* can bring about lasting and valuable changes in your consulting style, so that you can return to the text with a clearer sense of where it may lead you. If on the other hand you have already read the preceding chapters – congratulations! The hardest work is done.

In Chapter B1 (How People Learn) we distinguished 'conscious' learning from 'unconscious' learning, and roughly equated these processes with the Organizer and Responder respectively. (Turn back to Chapter B1 now, if you need reminding of this.) We also saw how learning occurs in three distinct stages, which I called the INSTRUCTION stage, the IMAGINATION stage, and the EXPRES-SION stage. By reading the text, in particular Sections A and B, you have already accomplished the Instruction stage. Because of the way I have written and structured the text, you have also gone a considerable way towards incorporating the material unconsciously into your own resource store – the Imagination stage. I have tried to make my various points in language comprehensible to your logical left hemisphere; and at the same time I have presented the same ideas indirectly, through analogy, metaphor, humour, literature and anecdotes, to your more intuitive right hemisphere. The final stage of Expression, in which you discover your own way of grafting your new knowledge onto your everyday working style, no book can do for you. Nevertheless, I can make some suggestions as to how you can practise the simple training exercises in order to achieve this integration efficiently and enjoyably.

The exercises I have introduced in the body of the text and at the end of many of the chapters are of three kinds. Some are 'thought experiments', which you can do (and may already have done) while sitting reading the book. Others are designed to sharpen your ability to observe and discriminate the various patterns of behaviour I have been describing; these are the exercises involving watching video-recorded consultations or sitting-in on another doctor's consultations. Finally there are exercises which can only be done during real live consultations. Most of these are of the 'playing card' variety, where you remind yourself to practise a single new skill whilst simultaneously consulting with a patient.

Here are my suggestions for an integrated training programme, extending over about two or three months.

Week 1

Do the 'thought experiment' in Chapter A1 (recapturing the memory of your own successful consultations) a few times.

Make sure you understand the concepts of Internal Dialogue, and of the 'Organizer' and 'Responder', by re-reading the relevant parts of Chapter A4. Then do both exercises in this chapter, the 'Internal Dialogue' and 'captioning the cartoon' ones. Draw your examples from some of your own current consultations.

Finally, make sure you have committed the five checkpoints to memory, and 'imprinted' them on the digits of your left hand, by doing the exercises in Chapters A5 and A6.

Weeks 2-6

For the next five weeks, take the checkpoints in turn, a week each.

Re-read any parts you need to of the relevant chapter in Section B. Then, in one or two sessions during the early part of each week, do the appropriate 'video' or 'sitting-in' exercises, so that you feel confident at discriminating the ideas described. Then do the corresponding 'consulting' exercises, intensively during one surgery session and sporadically during another.

Week 7

Keep your hand in by repeating some of the earlier weeks' exercises if you like. But give more attention to the Inner Consultation exercises in Section C.

Re-read Chapter C2. Do the 'awareness training' exercise in

Chapter C1 several times, until you can slip into an 'awareness' mode with some familiarity. Then practise the 'awareness of breathing' exercise described at the end of Chapter C2, both on your own and in some appropriately quiet moments of real consultations.

Then carry out the video exercises from the end of Chapter C2, to familiarize yourself with the 'minimal cues' distractors for listening and speaking. Without consciously trying, you will now find yourself directing your attention appropriately during real-life consultations.

Weeks 8 and subsequently

Put a 'reminder' about the Inner Consultation somewhere on your desk – perhaps a card on which you have written:

Listening	**– Watch the patient's minimal cues**
Speaking	**– Watch where your words are landing**
Thinking	**– Notice your own breathing**

Periodically (say twice a week) do one of the skill-building exercises from Section B.

Then forget all about the Inner Consultation until you feel in a position to comment on what changes you have noticed in your consulting style. Then, if you like, remember my hope that you might drop me a line to tell me your experience. My correspondence address is:

"Argowan",
Bell Lane,
Bedmond,
Herts WD5 0QS
UK

Appendix 2
Annotated bibliography

CHAPTER A1 – PROBLEM? WHAT PROBLEM?

1. Laing, R.D. (1970). *Knots* (London: Tavistock Publications) Dr Ronald Laing is an innovative and sometimes provocative psychiatrist who in the 1950s and 60s worked extensively on the family dynamics of schizophrenia. One of his best-known books is *The Divided Self* (1959) (London: Tavistock Publications). [Extract from *Knots* reprinted by permission of the author and Tavistock Publications/Pantheon Books.]

2. Transactional Analysis. TA is a model of the structure of the personality and of the interactions between individuals developed by Eric Berne. It describes three 'ego-states' – Parent, Adult and Child. Berne's most popular book is *Games People Play* (1966) (London: Andre Deutsch) A more comprehensive work is *What Do You Say After You Say Hello?* (1974) (London: Andre Deutsch).

3. Balint, M. (1957). *The Doctor, His Patient and The Illness*. (London: Tavistock Publications) Although reputedly difficult to read, this book (and the tradition of case study which it founded) had a seminal influence on the thoughtfulness of general practice which still endures. It is easiest to derive benefit from Balint's work once you have had some personal experience of working with 'difficult' patients.

4. Byrne, P.S. and Long, B.E.L. (1976). *Doctors Talking to Patients*. (London: HMSO) Another carefully researched and pioneering study of doctors' verbal behaviour. See Chapter A3.

5. Working party of the Royal College of General Practitioners (1972). *The Future General Practitioner: Learning and Teaching*. (London: British Medical Association) This is the book that first laid out the educational curriculum of Vocational Training in the United Kingdom. Although placing a great emphasis on behaviourally-defined objectives which time has softened, it remains the bedrock for much formal teaching in general practice.

6. Reed, Henry. Lessons of the War (To Alan Mitchell). I – Naming of Parts. In *A Map of Verona* (1946) (London: Jonathan Cape) [Quoted by permission of the author and publisher.]

CHAPTER A2 – HOW HAVE YOU BEEN TAUGHT PREVIOUSLY?

1. Freeman, J., Roberts, J., Metcalfe, D. and Hillier, V. (1982). *The Influence of Trainers on Trainees in General Practice*. London: Journal of the Royal College of General Practitioners, Occasional Paper 21.

2. Heron, John (1977b). *Behaviour Analysis in Education and Training*. Human Potential Research Project, University of Surrey, England. In his earlier posts as Director of the Human Potential Research Project and at the British Postgraduate Medical Federation, University of London, John Heron developed a system of experiential training methods in the 'humanistic' mould, emphasizing the importance of exploring and respecting the emotional vulnerability of both doctors and patients.

3. Pendleton, D., Schofield, T., Tate, P. and Havelock, P. (1984). *The Consultation: an Approach to Learning and Teaching*. (Oxford: Oxford University Press) [Quoted by permission]. An easy-to-read system of analysing the tasks of the consultation, geared particularly towards the use of video in teaching.

CHAPTER A3 – MODELS OF THE CONSULTATION

1. Illich, I. (1976). *Limits to Medicine. Medical Nemesis: The Expropriation of Health*. (London: Marion Boyars) Judging by the howl of professional outrage that greeted this book, Illich must have touched a sensitive nerve! His central premise – "The medical establishment has become a major threat to health" – is persuasive and chastening.

2. Kennedy, I. (1981). *The Unmasking of Medicine*. (London: George Allen and Unwin) The book of the 1980 BBC Reith Lectures.

3. Cognitive dissonance. A readable account of this and other social influences in illness is given in Totman, R. (1979). *Social Causes of Illness*. (London: Souvenir Press).

4. Working party of the Royal College of General Practitioners (1972). *The Future General Practitioner: Learning and Teaching*. (London: British Medical Association) [Extract used by permission.]

5. Stott, N.C.H. and Davis, R.H. (1979). The exceptional potential in each primary care consultation. *J.R. Coll. Gen. Practrs.*, **29**, 201–5 [Figure used by permission of RCGP.]

6. Byrne and Long, *op.cit.* (reference A1.4) [Quoted by permission]

7. Pendleton *et al.*, *op. cit.* (reference A2.3)

8. Helman, C.G. (1981). Diseases versus illness in general practice. *J.R. Coll. Gen. Practrs.*, **31**, 548–52. [Quoted by permission of RCGP.] The surprisingly rich vein of medical anthropology is further mined in the same author's *Culture, Health and Illness* (1984). (Bristol: Wright).

9. Becker, M.H. and Maiman, L.A. (1975). Sociobehavioural determinants

of compliance with medical care recommendations. *Med. Care*, **13**, 10–24

10. Heron, J. (1975a) *Six Category Intervention Analysis.* Human Potential Research Project, University of Surrey.

11. See reference A1.2 (Transactional Analysis)

12. Bendix, Torben (1982). *The Anxious Patient.* (Edinburgh: Churchill Livingstone)

13. See reference A1.3 (Balint)

14. Winnicott, D.W. (1971). *Playing and Reality.* (Harmondsworth, Middlesex: Penguin Books)

CHAPTER A4 – ON HAVING TWO HEADS

1. Left brain/right brain dissociation. For further reading I suggest the following:

Watzlawick, P. (1978). *The Language of Change.* (New York: Basic Books)
Koestler, A. (1967). *The Ghost in the Machine.* (London: Hutchinson)
Balint, M. (1968). *The Basic Fault.* (London: Tavistock)
Hampden-Turner, C. (1981). *Maps of the Mind.* (London: Mitchell Beazley)

CHAPTER A5 – THE CONSOULTATION AS A JOURNEY

1. Milton H. Erickson, M.D. (1901–1980). In his early adult years, Milton Erickson suffered two attacks of polio which left him physically weak and eventually confined him to a wheelchair. He nevertheless built up a psychiatric practice and established a legendary reputation as an enormously effective hypnotist and psychotherapist. His lack of physical mobility led him to a heightened awareness of the subtleties of language and non-verbal communication. In his work he stressed the creativity and resourcefulness of the unconscious mind. "Each person is an individual", he wrote. "Hence, psychotherapy should be formulated to meet the uniqueness of the individual's needs, rather than tailoring the person to fit the Procrustean bed of a hypothetical theory of human behavior."
Erickson was also a charismatic teacher. The best introduction to his style and methods is to be found in the following works by some of his pupils:
Haley, J. (1973). *Uncommon Therapy: The Psychiatric Techniques of Milton H. Erickson, M.D.* (New York: Norton)
Lankton, S.R. and Lankton, C.H. (1983). *The Answer Within: A Clinical Framework of Ericksonian Hypnotherapy.* (New York: Brunner/Mazel) The overall and chapter structure of 'The Inner Consultation' is derived from the Lanktons' model of 'multiple embedded metaphor'.
Zeig, J.K. (ed.) (1982). *Ericksonian Approaches to Hypnosis and Psychotherapy.* (New York: Brunner/Mazel)
Rosen, S. (1982). *My Voice Will Go With You: The Teaching Tales of Milton H. Erickson.* (New York: Norton)

CHAPTER C3 – ZEN AND THE ART OF THE CONSULTATION

1. Capra, Fritjof (1975). *The Tao of Physics*. (London: Fontana)

2. Capra, Fritjof (1982). *The Turning Point*. (London: Wildwood House)

3. Wilber, K. (ed.) (1984). *Quantum Questions*. (Boulder, Colorado: Shambhala Publications)

4. Dossey, L. (1982). *Space, Time & Medicine*. (Boulder, Colarado: Shambhala Publications)

5. As reference B5.2, chapter 25

6. Quoted in Reps, P. (ed.). *Zen Flesh, Zen Bones*. (Harmondsworth, Middlesex: Penguin Books)

7. Suzuki, D.T. (1960). *Studies in Zen*. (London: Unwin)

8. As reference B5.2, chapter 2

9. *ibid.*, chapter 48

10. *ibid.*, chapter 11

11. Quoted in Holmes, S.W. and Horioka, Chimyo (1973). *Zen Art For Meditation*. (Tokyo: Tuttle)

12. Quoted in Hoover, Thomas (1978). *Zen Culture*. (London: Routledge & Kegan Paul)

13. Quoted in Leggett, T. (trans.) (1960). *A First Zen Reader*. (Tokyo: Tuttle)